Gadamer and the
Transmission of History

Gadamer and the Transmission of History

Jerome Veith

INDIANA UNIVERSITY PRESS

Bloomington & Indianapolis

This book is a publication of

INDIANA UNIVERSITY PRESS
Office of Scholarly Publishing
Herman B Wells Library 350
1320 East 10th Street
Bloomington, Indiana 47405 USA

iupress.indiana.edu

© 2015 by Jerome Veith

♾ The paper used in this publication
meets the minimum requirements of
the American National Standard for
Information Sciences – Permanence of
Paper for Printed Library Materials,
ANSI Z39.48–1992.

Manufactured in the
United States of America

Library of Congress
Cataloging-in-Publication Data

Veith, Jerome, 1981–
    Gadamer and the transmission
of history / Jerome Veith.
    pages cm. – (Studies in
Continental thought)
    Includes bibliographical
references and index.
    ISBN 978-0-253-01598-3 (cl :
alk. paper) – ISBN 978-0-253-
01604-1 (eb) 1. Gadamer, Hans-
Georg, 1900-2002. I. Title.
    B3248.G34V45 2015
    193 – dc23

                              2014049506

1 2 3 4 5   20 19 18 17 16 15

FOR MY PARENTS

Jede Antwort bleibt nur so lange als Antwort
in Kraft, dass die Frage auch bewusst bleibt.

MARTIN HEIDEGGER,
"Der Ursprung des Kunstwerkes"

I project the history of the future.

WALT WHITMAN,
"To a Historian"

Contents

Acknowledgments

IN THE CONSIDERABLE TIME THIS BOOK SPENT COMING TO fruition, many people contributed to its course. I owe my initial fascination with Gadamer's ideas to James Risser, who introduced me to hermeneutics as a student and who remains an ongoing interlocutor in all matters philosophical. The core thoughts presented here took shape in my years at Boston College, during which I gained immensely from conversations with colleagues, friends, and mentors. John Sallis, Bill Richardson, and Susan Shell provided both sustaining encouragement and strengthening criticism. In many Gadamer reading groups over the years, I gleaned insights from Fred Lawrence, John Cleary, Robert Kehoe, William Britt, James Brennan, and Byron George. Through conversations with Vanessa Rumble, Jeffrey Bloechl, and Dennis Shirley, I was able to develop several tacit themes of my project. In their own ways, the following friends aided my thoughts and abetted my writing: Madeline Ashby, Kevin Berry, Paul Birney, Jon Burmeister, Neal and Tanya Deroo, Daniele DeSantis, Shane Ewegen, Emily Johnson, Ariane Kiatibian, Emmaline McCourt, Nicola Mirkovic, Paul Prociv, Erin Stackle, Laura Tomlinson.

I am grateful to the Ernest Fortin Memorial Foundation for a generous summer grant in 2011, and to the Fulbright Scholarship Board for a research grant to Freiburg in 2011–2012, during which I enjoyed a wonderfully rich environment of discussion and insight. I owe special thanks to Günter Figal and Tobias Keiling for helping sustain an atmosphere so conducive to thinking. Finally, I would like to thank the publishers Vittorio Klostermann (Frankfurt am Main) and Mohr Siebeck (Tübingen) for permission to use previously published material for chapters 1 and 2.

List of Abbreviations

WORKS BY HANS-GEORG GADAMER

BP	*The Beginning of Philosophy*
CPA	*Century of Philosophy*
HD	*Hegel's Dialectic*
GW	*Gesammelte Werke*
GW 1	Hermeneutik I: Wahrheit und Methode
GW 2	Hermeneutik II: Wahrheit und Methode, Ergänzungen
GW 3	Neuere Philosophie I: Hegel, Husserl, Heidegger
GW 4	Neuere Philosophie II: Probleme, Gestalten
GW 8	Ästhetik und Poetik I: Kunst als Aussage
GW 10	Hermeneutik im Rückblick
PH	*Philosophical Hermeneutics*
RAS	*Reason in the Age of Science*
TM	*Truth and Method*

WORKS BY G. W. F. HEGEL

IPH   *Introduction to the Philosophy of History*

PR   *Philosophy of Right*

PS   *Phenomenology of Spirit*

RH   *Reason in History*

SL   *Science of Logic*

WORKS BY MARTIN HEIDEGGER

BW   *Basic Writings,* ed. by Krell

GA   *Gesamtausgabe* (volume numbers listed in bibliography)

HR   *The Heidegger Reader,* ed. by Figal

SZ   *Sein und Zeit,* Niemeyer edition

WORKS BY IMMANUEL KANT

CJ   *Critique of Judgment*

CPR   *Critique of Pure Reason*

OTHER FREQUENTLY CITED VOLUMES

DH   *Dimensionen des Hermeneutischen,* ed. by Figal and Gander

GC   *Gadamer's Century,* ed. by Malpas, Arnswald, and Kertscher

HAC *Gadamer's Hermeneutics and the Art of Conversation,* ed. Andrzej Wiercinski

HVO *Hermeneutics and the Voice of the Other,* by Risser

HW *Hermeneutische Wege,* ed. by Figal, Grondin, and Schmidt

KA 27 *Sein und Zeit,* ed. by Rentsch

KA 30 *Wahrheit und Methode,* ed. by Figal

SR *The Specter of Relativism,* ed. by Schmidt

Gadamer and the Transmission of History

Introduction

THE PAST IS FINISHED, SO MUCH IS CLEAR. YET IT IS DIFFICULT to determine exactly what kind of finality it possesses. Certainly it cannot be changed or undone. It stands, remains, and retains significance. Were it the case that this significance remained univocal or stable, one could not speak of multiple interpretations of the past; one could extrapolate from the facts only a bare and unchanging meaning that the past possesses. Yet somehow, while being utterly complete, the past continues to be reactivated in different ways.

In a talk delivered in Boston in 2009,[1] the German jurist and writer Bernhard Schlink discussed several ways in which the heritage of World War II has been received domestically by the various generations since its occurrence: first came an initial resistance against investigating the war's atrocities; then there was a thorough confrontation between younger and older generations; and now more recent generations react with apathy, ennui, even resentment toward remembrance of the war. They have grown weary of a standardized moralistic narrative, of visiting yet another memorial or museum, of being burdened with events that, to them, seem long past.

This latter stance, though perhaps not consciously, is a clear response to the fixed message with which remembrance has been imbued over six decades. By sweepingly dismissing this message, some attempt to liberate themselves from the responsibility and perceived burden of remembering the one sanctioned account. Yet Schlink contends that, while the past indeed cannot be mastered and given a finalized, univocal meaning, it can certainly also never be dismissed completely, as this would itself constitute an impossible finality. Instead, the way that each generation takes up or rejects its past depends on that generation's own reactions, questions, and concerns, and this precisely prevents a dismissal of the past, as it entails that history will simply become present in a different way for them.

Coming to terms with the past, gleaning meaning from it, is an apparently universal human concern. Yet it evidently means something other than ensuring remembrance through the permanent formulation of lessons, or else rejecting memory completely for an ostensible new beginning. Rather, the exercise of memory, the understanding of history, means to leave historical meaning and the significance of the past unconditioned by predetermined expectations or categories, to engage with it openly and by consciously acknowledging its role in one's present concerns. It would be inaccurate to describe this as a move from active preservation to passive acceptance, however; the process of understanding history clearly involves both. Yet to grasp this shift, and to elaborate what an open engagement with history entails, involves nothing less than a complete reconception of how humans participate in and advance history.[2]

Hans-Georg Gadamer, himself a witness to the entire twentieth century's historical developments, provides just such a reconception in his philosophical hermeneutics. His magnum opus *Truth and Method*, with its core assertion of the historicity of understanding, attempts to describe individual interpretive experience, and thereby the movement of history in general, more adequately than philosophies based in epistemological frameworks. Gadamer analyzes our intrinsic ontological involvement with the past and underscores that tradition, or historical transmission, is something that we always stand within and continually pass along. It is a process that, because of its continuity and fluidity (especially also its linguistic register), will always generate understanding in different ways. Importantly, and contrary to many detractors of Gadamer's hermeneutics, this does not relinquish the notion of any meaning in history whatsoever, nor relegate the pursuit of truth to relativized, incommensurable subjects. Instead, it challenges us to inquire into the way that truth occurs within history and the differential space of intersubjectivity, to uncover what makes the continually different understandings of history possible to begin with, and to ask what kind of truth these interpretations amount to. As Gadamer puts it, "the task of hermeneutics, seen philosophically, consists in asking what kind of understanding, what kind of science [*Wissenschaft*] it is, that is itself advanced by historical change."[3]

Two crucial aspects of Gadamer's conception of history immediately show through here. The first is that historical transmission is taken to advance something: it bears a force, has an effect, is effective (*wirksam*). Thus, when Gadamer develops his central concept of *Wirkungsgeschichtliches Bewusstsein*, or consciousness of historical effect (often also translated as historically effected consciousness), the effect here denotes not an effect *in* history – as if it involved tracing an idea's influence over time or some event's causal repercussions like ripple dynamics in a wave chamber – but an effect *of* history, a genitive in which history itself bears the character of an active and transmissive event. To be sure, it may be through the engagement with specific effects in history that we ultimately come to encounter history's effect reflectively (indeed, herein lies the significance of exposure to historical material); but this latter effect is an ongoing "supportive ground of the course of events,"[4] and while there can indeed be an alienating temporal distance between ourselves and particular aspects of the past, we nevertheless always belong to the transmission of events in general (what one should call *Überlieferung* in contrast to the more specific German term *Tradition* or cultural tradition).

To be conscious of this constant transmission and our belongingness to it means to encounter history as an undetermined and ongoing source, rather than as a medium or a sealed container of past occurrences that merely have residual effects because of their erstwhile prominence or force. Thus, the consciousness of historical effect entails a twofold insight concerning historical truth itself: it is a recognition both of one's own participation in the process of transmission and of the kind of meaning that results from this engagement. Yet more is involved in this consciousness than just a metacognition of historicity, and Gadamer's characterization of history as an address lends some clarity to the notion that it is an understanding that arises here. For an address elicits a response, which initiates a dialogue through which understanding can occur.

This leads to the second point, namely that the knowing that Gadamer takes history to advance is a *Wissenschaft,* a science in the broad sense of a human pursuit of truth. It is the object and nature of this science that is at issue in philosophical hermeneutics, and that Gadamer seeks to clarify and contrast with the methodological truth of the natural sciences. While the historical situatedness of understanding pervades all human experience, it is when one reflectively engages in dialogue with the historical effect of this situation that truth arises. Though not possessing the character of objectivity that one expects from natural science, this truth nevertheless has a discursive valence, exemplified paradigmatically in the work of art, but reigning throughout those human sciences where the aim is not primarily a finalization of fact. The aim, instead, is the continual arrival at interpretations; a process that, given the character of historical effect just indicated, requires an openness to historical claims to meaning, a willingness to reside in their questionability and always reapply their significance in light of one's situation.

To show that this interpretive aim is not a purely theoretical concern, Gadamer underscores the similarity between the historical task of application and the moral task of *phronêsis* as outlined in Aristotle's *Nicomachean Ethics.* Crucial to any such practical wisdom, after all, is the ongoing development and deployment of experience, a process that Gadamer believes to lie at the core of the consciousness of historical effect, yet that he laments as one of the still "most obscure" concepts we possess.[5] To Aristotle, it is clear at the very least that the *phronimos* is experienced only if he knows himself in relation to his past, his broader aims, and the demands of his present surroundings; most importantly, he must understand that this knowledge is liable to revision. To Gadamer, the openness demanded in the application of historical meaning has a similar connection to self-understanding and social aims, and thus holds not only in the realm of science, but in all human conduct.

Yet as Schlink's example above and countless others show, neither the recognition of history's effective address nor the open interpretive discourse with its meaning is a guaranteed result of human historical involvement; they remain cultural and philosophical tasks for us. The need for a hermeneutic elaboration of history's effect, and of the truth that it advances, lies precisely in our typical failure to recognize this effect – partly because we stand within it, but largely because we lack an adequate conception of how it occurs. Whether this lack stems from unresolved crises of nineteenth-century historical consciousness, from the remnants of positivist models of truth, or from some other source, remains to be seen. The danger that the privation poses, however, is none other than a complete abnegation of our nature as historical beings, and thereby of our concomitant transmissive responsibilities. Stated at the outset of *Truth and Method*, Gadamer's goal in response to this lack and danger is clear: "to correct false thinking about what they [the human sciences and the conduct of life] are."[6]

This goal's phrasing is doubly significant. On the one hand, it underscores the broad horizon (in fact, the universality) of Gadamer's hermeneutics, one that reaches beyond the confines of mere conceptual clarification to human conduct itself. Indeed, as Gadamer has frequently asserted, his theoretical contribution to the grasp of historical understanding goes hand in hand with a practical philosophy. For while his inquiry could be said to lie in a long tradition of metaphysical questioning about human temporality, what is at stake is not merely a reformulation of the concept of history, a revised philosophy of history in light of recent theoretical upheavals. Gadamer's philosophical corrective strikes not only at an important philosophical issue, but at the root of human cultivation and social life itself. He contends that an adequate grasp of our historical situatedness will engender a transformation of our stance toward history and reveal the ethical task of hearing and responding to history's constant address.[7] Taking on this task, in turn, will ideally give rise to a "critical consciousness"[8] that acknowledges the ways that the past already ensnares us and repeatedly makes claims upon us, that applies this awareness to human scientific and social endeavors, and that develops a cultural memory that avoids sedimentation. It is only through this task, Gadamer believes, that we might disabuse ourselves of the tendency to foist lessons of the past on future generations or, what is perhaps worse, to ignore the historical altogether.

On the other hand, Gadamer focuses his hermeneutic corrective upon the seemingly narrow horizon of the historical human sciences.[9] Inquiring about their "possibility," he intends for them to gain a better self-understanding of the historical effect from which they derive their truth.[10] There is a good reason for this focus on Gadamer's part, and for the fact that he utters it along with general human conduct in one breath. Gadamer is well aware that the task of openness to historical meaning cannot be surmounted once and for all, and that a critical consciousness cannot be delineated formally through a set of norms. Philosophical hermeneutics, after all, is in the business not of setting methodological guidelines for understanding, but of inquiring into its conditions of possibility.[11] Just as the task of openness itself is not posited subjectively or dogmatically, but arises in the very engagement with the past, so an openness to history does not consist in a subjective decision or the mastery of a technique, but must instead be cultivated as an ongoing human practice in the face of historical change.

The humanities, at their core, represent just such practices. Their subject matter is characterized by questionability, the openness of which "consists in the fact that the answer is not settled."[12] By focusing on these sciences, and with his goal of bringing them to a proper and explicit self-understanding of their historicality, Gadamer underscores their deep connection to human historical existence as such: they thematize, question, and learn from the historical ground that always already supports and shapes our understanding.

In drawing this connection to our attention, Gadamer indicates a way that the broader enactment of openness might be practiced, learned, and cultivated. While himself perhaps too reticent to call for this cultivation on a wide institutional scale, Gadamer finds exemplary resources for this hermeneutic training both in Platonic dialectic, the linguistic bearing of which is intimately tied to ethical commitments, and in the German tradition of *Bildung*, whose formative aim lies not in a specific curriculum but in a stance of "keeping oneself open to what is other"[13] and of "acknowledging the past in its otherness, but in such a way that it has something to say to me."[14] This dialogical stance, however, along with the practical insights that it presupposes, can be developed only on the basis of an awareness of the historicity of understanding. This, in turn, is made possible through encounters with actual historical material that serves as a site of questionability, be it an artwork, text, event, place, person, or idea.

The humanities thus occupy a central position at the intersection of historical understanding and social existence. They are not merely a paradigm of historical application, a structural example of how one might go about interpreting the past critically; rather, they actually serve as a middle term of sorts through which one first arrives at anything like a social reason or critical consciousness.[15] Drawing out the full implications of Gadamer's theory, one arrives at the conclusion that the human sciences serve to cultivate, through their reflective enactment of historical experience, a type of human conduct that is adequate to its historical nature. This conduct would be of a kind that is both free and responsive to its situatedness.

The aim of the present work is to elaborate in detail Gadamer's argument leading up to this conclusion regarding the humanities, their historical core, and its ethical significance. In tracing this entailment, the work will delineate the constellation of ideas forming Gadamer's hermeneutic reconception of historical understanding while investigating its ramifications for ethical life. The gravitational center of this constellation lies in the concept of historical effect. My approach will involve an exhaustive analysis of this concept, along with its origins, limits, and *aporiae*.

Yet since Gadamer's account of historical effect is not located in any single work, but is spread across decades of writings and connected to an array of accompanying concepts, a direct exegetical approach to this analysis is unthinkable. I will therefore undertake this analysis simultaneously both from within Gadamer's conceptual framework, elucidating the core principles and their fundamental ambiguities, and by considering these principles in relation to those of other philosophers whose thought concerning historical understanding influenced Gadamer's. This latter approach can certainly be justified methodologically, but it also has quite strong reasons internal to the subject matter. Given the dialogical nature of Gadamer's thought, elaborating any of his concepts *in abstracto* would severely stunt the hermeneutical provenance of his ideas, and would thereby renounce the very principle of historical effect in question. Instead, a better grasp of Gadamer's own situation in discourse with the tradition will help clarify his position with respect to the concept of this tradition's underlying and ongoing transmission. The analysis of this transmission will thus proceed by way of an outward concentric movement, from the core of Gadamer's conceptual framework, to his immediate philosophical environment, to broader and more universal issues in critical-historical thinking. This movement will also coincide with a regression of sorts, from the twentieth century to the eighteenth, from Heidegger's influence on Gadamer through Hegel's substantial modifying force to Kant's lasting effect. It will become clear through this path of inquiry that Gadamer not only formulates conceptually what it means to understand historically, but places this formulation in concrete contexts, and thereby also enacts the very consciousness of historical effect that he describes.[16]

Through this analysis, which takes place in the first four chapters and draws on texts spanning Gadamer's career, I will gradually elaborate how he takes a critical-historical consciousness to operate in, rather than above or beyond, the intertwining or "interplay" of self and tradition. The remaining step, in the final chapter, will be to trace the possible genesis of this critical consciousness – which amounts to the cultivation and application of experience – to the practices of the historical human sciences. What follows is a brief outline of the book's individual chapters.

At the core of Gadamer's universal theory of understanding lies his account of historical effect and the historicity of understanding. Yet since this effect and historicity are not simply forces that act upon us, but constitute both the medium of our activity and our activity as such, they cannot be described as mere qualities attached to some independent or underlying existence. They envelop the totality of our relations with the world, and represent the ongoing interpretive site of our intertwining with time and alterity.[17] Because of this aspect, historical effect and historicity are not adequately studied from fixed or sedimented poles (of either tradition or the subject), but are instead to be investigated in their constant enactment. The opacity of this chiasmic and enacted structure, as well as the difficulty in describing it, has typically led to misunderstandings of Gadamer's position with regard to historical transmission. Rather than investigating the in-between space of interpretation as such, one has taken him to espouse some form of one-sidedness in the relation.

Chapter 1 will untangle and elucidate the finer points of historical effect's intertwining, in order to show its foundational role within Gadamer's theory as a whole, to dispel misreadings of his position on tradition, and to indicate the ethical significance of that position. An initial section will also delineate this stance with regard to those he takes to be inadequate altogether. On a conceptual level, it will be necessary to investigate the operation of prejudice and interpretive horizons, the notion of fusion and application, and the primacy of questioning. By then transposing the discussion of historical meaning into an ethical register, I will begin to uncover the significance of historical effect with regard to alterity and social life. This will prepare the way for more complex comparative analyses in the central chapters.

Chapter 2 clarifies Gadamer's relation to Heidegger on the question of historical belonging. After a thorough account of Heidegger's own development on the subject of history and temporality, I investigate points of proximity between the two thinkers, which prominently include the concepts of facticity and enactment. A further step then describes the distance that separates Gadamer from Heidegger, finding expression in such issues as *Destruktion*, language, and attunement. My overall aim here is to show that, while deeply indebted to many of Heidegger's insights on the theme of historical understanding and situatedness, Gadamer departs from his teacher in two crucial respects: First, he sustains the inquiry into conditions of human freedom and cultivation that Heidegger fails to pursue to their full extent even in *Being and Time*, and completely neglects afterward; second, Gadamer refuses to follow Heidegger with respect to the notion of a forgottenness of Being and his theories concerning retrieval through the overcoming of metaphysics. Pervading Gadamer's relation to Heidegger, I wish to argue, is a separation that amounts to an "ethical turn."[18] In this turn, it is the social dimension of historical understanding that comes to the fore.

In separating from Heidegger on this point, Gadamer looks to Hegel for inspiration. Chapter 3 will accordingly outline how Hegel's theories regarding mediation and development enter into Gadamer's thoughts on historicity. Each of these thinkers, in his own dialectic, strives to situate understanding within an intersubjective space that accords principles their own movement and force. Yet while Gadamer recognizes Hegel's elevation of self-consciousness above the immediate subjective realm as a praiseworthy "shattering [of] the predominance of subjectivism,"[19] Gadamer worries about attributing this elevation to a reflective activity of just another form of consciousness, in this case the historical self-consciousness of *Geist*. The mediation at work in experience is, for Gadamer, something that ultimately always happens to us, not something of which we are in complete control – whether as individuals or as a rational, political, and *geistig* community. Gadamer thus stresses the need to admit an experience that "exceeds the omnipotence of reflection."[20] Such an experience is entailed precisely in the factical limits of historical effect, which circumscribe reflective consciousness both at its present situated root and in its open futural development. This concession to what Hegel calls "bad infinity" ultimately involves an opacity at the heart of historical situatedness that must always be played out in an infinite dialogue, rather than eventually being subsumed in thought. In this way, Gadamer can be said to open Hegel's system.

Another thinker to whom Gadamer bears such an ambivalent relation is Kant, whose notion of reflection maintains a strong hold on hermeneutic practice while also bearing the brunt of Gadamer's criticism. Contrary to continued accusations of romanticism, Gadamer takes the consciousness of historical effect to indeed amount to a form of reflective social reason, but he also turns Kant's own warning about reason overstepping its bounds back toward Enlightenment aspirations themselves, deeming them illusory. Reflection, Gadamer holds, will always remain situated. Chapter 4 traces the more recent forgetfulness concerning this situatedness back to Kant's *Critique of Judgment*, which, due to its bridging function between Enlightenment and humanism, remains "a lasting challenge to our thinking."[21] Gadamer elucidates this challenge by delimiting the dual reduction of the hermeneutic, applied core of *praxis* in the third *Critique*: taste is limited there to the realm of aesthetics, "out of the center of philosophy,"[22] and furthermore has value only as a formal feeling, meaning that its normativity is severely stunted.[23] By retrieving a self-sufficiency of art that avoids reductive subjectivization, Gadamer connects the aesthetic back to historical human self-understanding. Gadamer's wager is that the "moral relevance of the artwork steers us towards the idea of art's ability to 'enable man to encounter himself in [...] the human, historical world.'"[24]

Taking up the analyses from chapters 1–4, chapter 5 presents the potential impact of historical effect, through the humanities, on human conduct as such. The stance of the consciousness of historical effect amounts to a form of social reflection that, in its attentive openness, bears resemblance to Aristotle's ethical ideal of practical wisdom, and involves a similar primacy over methodical technique. The humanities play a central role in bringing our historical situation to light, and thus in cultivating an adequate stance with regard to tradition and its transmission. Indeed, if the humanities fail to identify and align with their historical and experiential core, they risk pursuing paths that are alien to their nature. By uncovering the historically effected nature of understanding and tracing its universality, Gadamer can elucidate the significance of the humanities and begin to outline their transformative capacity with regard to human conduct. By encompassing everything from texts to human relations, the engagement with historical material in the humanities ultimately represents a formation of freedom and a concomitant development of communal praxis.

This broad relation of the humanities to social existence might be considered an external application of Gadamer's thought, one of the many ways in which hermeneutics is currently being taken up by other disciplines.[25] Yet since historical effect, on Gadamer's conception, is a universal characteristic of human hermeneutic situatedness, it is present wherever we engage in or draw on experience. Moreover, Gadamer himself stressed the expansion of hermeneutics beyond the sphere of philosophy and the humanities into issues of social reason and political discourse, such that these applications are actually endemic to hermeneutic practice itself. In this respect, the present work aims to make explicit some of the core theoretical commitments of Gadamer's thought, to synthesize strains that weave throughout his corpus, and to underscore their practical ramifications. It ultimately treats historicity as an effect that pervades human conduct and that accordingly poses to everyone a reflective and ethical task.

ONE

From Structure to Task

HISTORICAL EFFECT

Until the early twentieth century, hermeneutics, the study of understanding and interpretation, had tended to identify itself as a practice in search of the right methods, by means of which it hoped to become something akin to a science. Taking issue with this alignment toward modern scientific methodology, and critiquing the subjectivistic limitations it entails for any nonmethodical truth, Gadamer formulates his philosophical hermeneutics as a description not of the proper technique of understanding – how it *should* proceed – but of the general ways in which it *does* proceed. Briefly put, he intends to go "beyond modern science's concept of method and to think, in fundamental universality, what *always* occurs."[1] This goal, which Gadamer expands beyond mere textual situations and explicitly associates with Kant's transcendental project, amounts to an account of the a priori conditions of all understanding.[2]

Gadamer ultimately concludes that these conditions are limited by the finitude inherent in our historicity and linguisticality. Situated within these conditions, we are subject to their constraining structures as if by "suprasubjective powers,"[3] and cannot reach a position in isolation from them. Understanding, considered hermeneutically, is thus always situated. Yet this situation does not amount to a privation of possibility; instead, it is paradoxically precisely within these limitations that all of our potential insights and developments are located. As historical beings, we may not be able to raise ourselves above history to ascertain its course, necessity, or overall purpose, but we have the capacity to understand our history from within, and to always do so differently. In this way, we are also generative of the very history that conditions us. This process takes place in the "speculative" medium of language, named so because it mirrors reality in a way that first makes the latter accessible to us, such that we can never reach an initial basis or a final formulation that would exist eternally apart from experience. Our thrownness into language actually frees us from the constraining illusion of univocal meanings and permanent formulations, and frees us up for a discourse that is infinitely iterable.

This discursive-linguistic aspect of Gadamer's hermeneutics has drawn much attention, not least for its significance in the philosophy of language, but also in its relation to poststructural/deconstructive philosophy, social philosophy, poetics, and the philosophy of art. Gadamer's own emphasis tends to fall on this aspect of his philosophy, as it represents an intuitive point of access for anyone engaged in communication.[4] Yet while language may be construed as the basis of Gadamer's hermeneutic ontology, it is at most a condition equiprimordial with historicity, one structural moment of the same phenomenon without primacy over the other. This equiprimordiality makes it just as difficult to shift in the other direction and view historicity as the more fundamental layer of understanding; one might instead describe historicity as the motor at the core of our experience that always finds "its enactment in the realm of language."[5] Gadamer conceives of this historicity under the heading of historical effect (*Wirkungsgeschichte*), and while the latter could be said to serve as the main principle of his hermeneutics from which all others can be derived,[6] it does not stand apart from, nor logically prior to, our involvement in language. Taking over an insight from Heidegger, Gadamer deems it more appropriate to speak of "historicity" or "historicality" (*Geschichtlichkeit*) than "temporality" (*Zeitlichkeit*), since human experience bears the character of occurrence (*Geschehen*), and this is a codeterminant of, rather than simply a temporal container or condition for, linguistic expression.[7]

However, even this core principle of historicity contains ambiguities that are not immediately resolvable and that render opaque not only the nature of language, but also the role of the subject situated in history. In fact, it is due to this lack of clarity that historical effect, and thus Gadamer's position as a whole, has frequently been misconstrued. One of these misreadings is that, since he stresses our historical boundedness, Gadamer has been taken to espouse either a form of traditionalism or perspectival relativism. However, this conforms neither to Gadamer's self-understanding nor to the conceptual foundation of his philosophy. His formulation of an "interplay"[8] (*Ineinanderspiel*) in historicity is intended to eschew several inimical conceptions of history and human historicality, as they all make pernicious assumptions concerning our relation to history, selfhood, and alterity.

The present chapter will begin with a brief outline of these positions. The subsequent analysis of historicity will show how Gadamer responds to and supersedes these stances. The aim is to elucidate the ambiguities at the heart of historical effect, revealing its structure as a situated, intertwined relation and performative enactment, its disclosure of finitude as the "fundamental insight"[9] of philosophical hermeneutics, and, by virtue of this insight, its consequences for the broader philosophical issues of social life and ethics. After all, although Gadamer viewed his project as a largely descriptive endeavor, his concepts are not without their intended philosophical repercussions.[10] Though these are not normative in a strict sense, telling us the steps by which we are supposed to understand, they nevertheless act as a corrective to improper ways of conceiving human historicality, and thus the universal conditions of our understanding. Hermeneutic concepts correct and refine "the way in which constantly exercised understanding understands itself,"[11] and thus play a role in cultivating something like social reason. In line with this role, the oneness of horizons that Gadamer takes to underlie historicity turns out to be neither a relativist indifference to strangeness nor an essentialist demand for complete familiarity. Based on its finite and dialogical character, the oneness can instead be considered a form of freedom, operative throughout the present enactment of our inherently historical situation. Yet for the same dialogical reasons, oneness remains an interpretive task, a social and ethical achievement that requires attention and cultivation.

SITUATING HISTORICAL EFFECT

Gadamer's concept of historical effect did not arise in a vacuum, nor can it be considered independently of the positions to which it responds. As philosophical hermeneutics in general develops out of a long tradition of dealing with interpretive and epistemological issues, Gadamer's own core concepts are part of the development of historical consciousness from the eighteenth century to the present, and his entire thought bears the mark of intense dialogue with this evolution. One might even say that Gadamer's elaboration of historical effect is performative and reflexive, precipitated by the very conditions it describes. Philosophical hermeneutics thus stands deeply indebted to a discourse that it nevertheless intends to correct and supplant. To present this discourse in its entirety is obviously beyond the scope of this work.[12] However, the theme of Gadamer's philosophical origins remains a fertile ground for debating the place and importance of his thought, and the present work as a whole aspires to contribute to this debate, however slightly.[13] While I will return below to the social dimension of this discourse, and while subsequent chapters will elaborate this theme, I will here merely identify four prevalent conceptions of historicality that Gadamer takes to be problematic on the basis of two general presuppositions: (1) the elevation to a perspective beyond human historicity and (2) the pretension to immediacy in historical experience. While one pair of historical conceptions is guilty of only the latter assumption, another pair, which Gadamer identifies as historicist, makes both. I will turn to this latter group first.

Detached Historicism

What Gadamer calls historical consciousness or historicism had arisen as a philosophical view of history during the nineteenth century, through respective pushing and pulling factors.[14] It can be described as a response to the collapse of teleological-metaphysical explanations of history, be they eschatological or speculative. Thinkers no longer accepted accounts of the goal-directedness of history, but struggled with great difficulty to elaborate an alternative theory. This lack of foundations impelled philosophy to seek its stability elsewhere, to find more plausible descriptions of historical development and knowledge, and thus to account somehow for philosophy's continued relevance. A great attractor in this pursuit was the burgeoning dominance of natural scientific method, which, with its mechanical-positivist aspirations toward general laws, promised philosophy a similarly grounded study of the past, no less than a vindication of its own scientific status. In adopting the naturalist viewpoint that sees time, in spatial terms, as the uniform and infinite container for historical events, historicism was able to treat all points in history as essentially equal, and to survey these points as if from above. Two distinct approaches took shape at this suprahistorical level.

One, a historically objective approach or "theoretical historicism," took history to be largely immobile and continuous.[15] In the terms of the dominant Neo-Kantian school within this approach, one desired to discover and justify the knowledge-claims contained in history. One thus engaged in a Kantian critique of history, separating contingent facts from historical truths by tracing law-like patterns of meaning. This focus on formal-logical patterns gave rise to a history of problematics (*Problemgeschichte*), which treated the past as the arena of recurring problems (and which Gadamer labels "a bastard of historicism"[16]).

In a programmatic 1910 essay, Nicolai Hartmann proposed a historiography of philosophy founded on *Problemgeschichte*, a conception of the history of philosophy that is centered around the self-unfolding of perennial philosophical problems over time.[17] This approach allows one to treat philosophy as an historical process, yet to also join various insights together across time into a broader corpus possessing scientific objectivity. This presupposes, of course, some access to the perennial problems. Hartmann himself acknowledges this: "we must already possess the problems in order to conduct a history of problems."[18] To explain this possession and the conditions making this approach possible, Hartmann cites the capacity – indeed the necessity – of abstracting both from the concrete factual basis of philosophical insights and from the specific lives of individual thinkers. What remains are "problem-lines" of which particular people and eras are merely intersections.[19] The problems that *Problemgeschichte* treats thus function as formal-transcendental categories that allow one to establish "historical continuity," and any variability in the philosophical content thus attaches not to the problem, but merely to its historical instantiation.[20] From this angle, then, the history of philosophy is a gathering process that collects knowledge from across history in a precise and cumulative procedure.

The philosophical import of history, then, was that humans sought to answer perennial questions, and past attempts to address these could be aligned with, and serve as material for, present research. One had to admit, of course, that questions undergo variations in their formulation, and even that present concerns were not always in direct correlation to those of the past. Yet the thinker of problematic history, so the Neo-Kantians imagined, could surmount these obstacles by normalizing the terms and conceptual structure under which past questions were raised – in short, by producing a transcendental logic of history. In this way, one could identify the transhistorical topics (or "values," to use Rickert's term[21]) of historical reason, fusing them into one discourse. As a detached surveyor of this whole, the historical objectivist could take his or her own position as a sign of the scientific nature and scope of historical reflection.

A divergent, discontinuous approach arose as a reaction to this unifying stance. This approach, while maintaining a quasi-scientific overview of history, stressed the limitations of comparing various times to each other. Rather than emphasizing the continuity between philosophical questions and concerns across time, one relativized the views of each age to its historical environment. This plurality and discontinuity demanded that historical research be mobile: that it place itself within the age under consideration and assess the latter's concerns on their own terms.

Gadamer's critique of these two approaches hinges on what unites them as historicist stances. First, both try to rise above history in such a way as to ignore the researcher's embeddedness within it, and render his or her own standpoint insignificant. This naive leap constitutes a neglect of what Gadamer describes under the term of historical effect, and thus amounts to a misunderstanding of our historicity. The danger here, echoing Nietzsche's second *Untimely Meditation,* is that this account of history weakens one's values, that in elevating ourselves we risk extinguishing ourselves and becoming mere capstones with no concerns or sources of our own from which to draw inspiration.[22]

As an initial step toward addressing this danger, Gadamer bluntly describes our situation as presenting limits that are finite and insurmountable: As historical beings, we belong to history more than it belongs to us.[23] The present is characterized by its own questions and concerns, and any reflection on history, as for example the historical objectivist's search for law-like patterns, is actually rooted in these current concerns. Thus, the problem of *Problemgeschichte* is that it fails to recognize the retrospective projection of its own peculiar questions as presently motivated concerns – not to mention its failure to capture the way in which genuine questions arise to begin with. In taking problems to remain the same across time, it imposes an artificial framework of sameness upon historical effect, normalizing language in the process and creating an insidious demand for identity – what amounts to a confirmation bias.[24]

The relativist position fares no better under this charge, for even though it does not standardize the structure of its approach, it nevertheless believes that it can study past ages without having an intrinsic and generative standpoint of its own. Correlated to historicism's detachment from history, then, is Gadamer's second point of critique: the claim to immediacy. Once one has assumed an overview of history, one takes the objects within history to lie within immediate grasp. To cross from the present to the past and enter into the views of another age is, for the historical relativist, perhaps a difficult endeavor, but ultimately merely a matter of information and method. With the right approach, there is even the possibility of understanding past views better than they grasped themselves.

The historical objectivist espouses a similar dedication to method: he or she traces formal themes that purportedly remain the same across time, and leaps over great distances to connect them. One could view this, conversely, as the retrieval of past objects out of their original context into a present logical framework. Yet the logic of this framework makes the transmission of history appear to be immediate and automatic.[25] A further step toward alleviating historicism's danger, in Gadamer's view, is therefore to recognize the mediating capacity of finitude: to begin from the actual differences between our situation and the one we intend to grasp. We cannot assume that past concerns were exactly the same as ours, even if similar terms are used in both instances. There is no immediate way to know, for example, whether the problem of freedom was of the same concern in antiquity as it is now; our emphasis on this problem could stem from our own current historical occupation with it.[26] This is not to say that questions across history cannot prove themselves to be similar and of comparable significance; however, the identity or difference of horizons – and thus of questions as well – emerges only *in* the encounter between horizons and their possible fusion. In other words, one must pose the questions as questions rather than prefigure them in advance. The identity of history cannot, as in *Problemgeschichte*'s notion of continual problem-lines, be presupposed from the outset.[27]

The first of Gadamer's concerns with historicism can be resolved by formulating a philosophy that affirms human situatedness in history and that treats historical knowledge from within this situation. The observer of history, as Gadamer reminds us, is herself located in history. There still remains, however, the issue of immediacy, and it looms large even among positions that directly account for our historical situation. To fully resolve it, therefore, Gadamer must distance himself from two positions that seemingly lie on either side of his own philosophical stance, adumbrating it and rendering it indistinct.

Immersive Historicism

On one side lies the position of traditionalism. Here, as with historical objectivism, the emphasis is on continuity over time. The traditionalist takes history to stay identical to itself, repeating itself forward without undergoing any substantive change. As there is no perspective upon history from the outside, as it were, history becomes just another name for the views that come to dominate, the canons that agglomerate, and the lineages that hold power. To practice historical reflection, then, is a matter of finding essential significance, of appropriating meanings to an account that remains univocal over time, or at least tends toward univocity. Moreover, as confined to and conditioned by this tendency, the historical subject cannot acquire any distance from its purported authority (nor, perhaps, even see the need to).

Quite correctly, the traditionalist position has been criticized for its hegemonic-fatalist narrative and engulfing appropriation. Yet if, by contrast, one merely negates traditionalism and asserts a discontinuous history, one is left with a conception of various disjointed and incommensurable perspectives that echo the historical relativism treated above. With the added qualification that one is now situated within history, tied to one's age and culture, this stance lacks the capacity to simply transfer out of one perspective and into another. One may recognize that there are many histories and ways of life, but the only standard of choice one knows is that by which one is already conditioned. This perspectivism, in turn, weakens the force of any claim one might make in one's contemporary situation.[28]

To many readers of Gadamer, this latter perspectivism seems to ring close to his own position. Indeed, his denial of the existence of objective historical truth, coupled with the insistence on being situated within history, seems to place him squarely in this category by default. Yet there have also been those who take Gadamer to espouse a form of traditionalism, given his emphasis on our belonging to tradition.[29] It is clear, however, that he cannot stand for both, and indeed he stands apart from either of them.[30] Even to say that he falls somewhere in between might be incorrect. Gadamer's avoidance of these stances rests upon his account of a mediated situation within history, but the success of this avoidance has not been widely recognized, for this requires a synthetic grasp of Gadamer's position not just concerning historical interpretation, the history of ideas, or the philosophy of history, but regarding the historicity of human understanding as such.[31] It is a universal and ontological project. After all, Gadamer does not simply reply with an alternative to theoretical historicism's failed method or with a critical technique by which to emancipate oneself out of a given tradition or perspective.[32] His aim is neither to perfect formal knowledge of history along Neo-Kantian lines nor to justify the accounts of a life completely enclosed by history (a justification that would remain in place if he simply sought a way to navigate out of a given situation of containment). Instead, he gives the ontological reasons why such perfection or enclosure is impossible to begin with, and it is to these reasons that I will turn in the next section.

In clarifying what Gadamer means, on the one hand, by our situated belonging to historical transmission and, on the other hand, by the mediating enactment of this transmission, I will show what kind of relation to the past he in fact espouses (a crossing-over of questions, a fusion within "one great horizon"[33]), and what kind of truth he thinks can arise within human history (the productivity of distance and continued openness). Just as the positions elaborated above are not merely historical but also social-ethical stances, our clarification of Gadamer's position will ultimately reveal his philosophy to be not just a critique of theories of history, but an elaboration of an ethical social discourse.

BELONGING AND ENACTMENT

Situation

Due to the opacity of the subject matter, the description of Gadamer's concept of historical effect cannot proceed in a direct, definitional fashion. Our analysis will instead need to account for the many layers of human historicity, and also take great care in sorting out the terminology available to describe this phenomenon. To begin elucidating the situation in which we are said to belong to tradition, let us first address the elements of prejudice and horizon that fundamentally constitute this situation.

What Gadamer means by prejudice is not the negative denotation of a fixed false judgment or belief, but instead the enabling fore-understanding that we have in our approach to anything. He underscores that "all understanding inevitably involves some prejudice,"[34] noting that we always peer out from our present situation with some concern, intention, impression, or judgment. Put simply, we do not gaze upon reality from a position of neutral observation. In this sense a prejudice is everything but false, in that it frames something precisely as we take it to be. Further, our perspective is not attached to any one position. Prejudice is not static and engrained as commonly conceived, but undergoes constant revision as new experiences and stances inform our views.

This may not yet be controversial in itself, for one could still retain a sense of one's own masterful centrality amidst varying experiences and positions. If one had full control of one's fore-understanding, one could determine which prejudices to admit and which to exclude. However, Gadamer stresses that the origin and arrangement of prejudices is not strictly autonomous or rational. Against the Enlightenment notion that we might free ourselves of all unwanted influences (*"sapere aude!"*) and thereby make a clean incision between past and present, foreign and familiar, Gadamer contends that our conceptions, rational or otherwise, are not derived solely from our activity as subjects, and are thus not at our free disposal.[35] Instead, they can be traced to our psychological experiences, our familial and social environment, our education and cultural tradition.[36]

We can never expect to begin an endeavor from scratch, as it were. Any behavior of our own takes place in a situation already configured by prior commitments, and even these are responses to factors beyond our control (and often beyond our awareness). Yet this should also not deceive us into thinking that prejudices stem entirely from external, causal forces. Indeed, prejudices are precisely not arbitrary and unidirectional influences. They are not forces at another's whim that cover over or supplant one's own agency, but are instead operative within all subjective acts, and constitute the very medium of our biography.[37] Even if we are not aware of them as such, prejudices are the threads of our agency, woven together into an overall sense of reality that amounts to the scope and depth of one's understanding. It is this fabric of prejudices that Gadamer has in mind when he speaks of one's horizon.

As woven together from prejudices, from the specific expectations of a given position, a horizon is by definition limited. However, given what we have already said about prejudices and the kind of subjectivity that goes along with them, this limitation must itself be characterized appropriately. Rather than being the limitations of a fixed entity existing in itself, horizons are limits that can move, expanding and contracting as positions shift and new understanding takes place. In this way, they are as ungrounded, flexible, and revisable as the prejudices that constitute them. Similarly, horizons are also not one's own in the sense that one is in control of their scope; they arise in response to the world, and constitute only a provisional familiarity. One can certainly become more conscious of one's horizon – a point I will develop in more detail below – but if one were to attempt an inventory of one's understanding, one would find much that is foreign. Indeed, one can never trace out the perimeter of what is enclosed by one's horizon, as its origin lies in a past beyond retrieval and in sources that are most certainly unfamiliar.

Yet as we saw in the case of prejudice, this strangeness is also not utterly foreign and imposed from outside. The incomplete familiarity of one's horizon, as well as the inability to delimit it, lead Gadamer to call this perimeter "open," and this extends to any horizon by definition.[38] If, accordingly, no horizon is bounded completely within and for itself, an encounter with something beyond our horizon is not an experience of utter alterity or strangeness. This other horizon does not exist across a chasm that must first be bridged through transposition into what is foreign (as in the case of reconstructionist worldview-philosophy) or appropriation into the sphere of sameness (as with theoretical historicism or traditionalism). Nor, along perspectivist-incommensurabilist lines, is the other horizon sealed off from any understanding whatsoever. Rather, there is always some connection of horizons through which we understand what is beyond our own, and Gadamer attributes this connection to "one great horizon."

An ancient civilization may have engaged in practices that we consider revolting or immoral, and lived a daily existence that bears virtually no resemblance to our own. Yet there are aspects of life, perhaps not easily indicated, that this ancient culture shares with the present: concerns for shelter and survival, recognition of authority, and expression of meaning. Even more fundamentally, there is the basic historicity and linguisticality of these common concerns: they once took place, and continue to reverberate, in human time and language. The life of this culture need not have influenced the present in any direct fashion for these shared aspects to arise. The elements of shared life stem, rather, from a horizon broader than either the past or the present.[39]

This broad horizon is, then, properly conceived as a condition (or medium) of all understanding.[40] Any partial horizons that come into contact with one another are ultimately connected by the "higher universality" that pervades them both.[41] After all, if every horizon is fundamentally open and ungrounded, it does not stand on its own apart from history, but is a part of this larger whole. Thus, when Gadamer speaks of the "fusion" of horizons, it is not the meeting and amalgamation of two separate and preexisting entities, a confluence that would assimilate one side to the sameness of the other. Instead, "understanding is always the fusion of the horizons *supposedly* existing by themselves,"[42] and in fact both the difference between the horizons and their unity emerge only in the understanding encounter itself. This is not to diminish difference, but to emphasize that it is something that occurs, and that takes shape differently in each occurrence. What enables these events of difference is the overall horizon of history. It is crucial to note once more, however, that this is the lived, experienced history of shared human life, and not the formal-transcendental history of Neo-Kantian *Problemgeschichte*.

Our analysis remains imprecise, however, if we simply account for the movement of difference, the event-character of understanding, on the subjective side of historicity, as if it occurred against a permanent backdrop or from out of a stable unity. Even if it is clear that we are dealing with history as an ontological experience rather than a transcendental category, we must avoid reducing self and other to mere epiphenomena of one underlying and fixed totality. To achieve this, one has to pay close attention to Gadamer's description of the whole of history. On the one hand, it is not a structural or formal condition for the occurrence of understanding. The oneness of horizons means more than the simple temporal provision of possibility for encounter. Accordingly, history is more than a container – real or imagined – for shared life; it actively contributes to the emergence of prejudice and the formation of horizons, and does so not just once, but constantly. As I will elaborate shortly, this has decisive consequences for the conception of history's effect.

On the other hand, when Gadamer develops his concept of the oneness of horizon(s), he takes caution not to define its content too precisely. To be sure, this lack of articulation leaves much room for interpretation, and has led to many a misunderstanding of Gadamer's position. Yet this vagueness is precisely intended to eschew any association with a traditionalism that would imbue shared life with a specific content. The ambiguity also helps Gadamer in avoiding such pitfalls as the Kantian notion of an infinite task of reason, the Neo-Kantian formulation of permanent problems, the Hegelian teleology that grasps history absolutely, and the Heideggerian uncovering of a fundamental question that subsumes all subjectivity. Against these conceptions, Gadamer asserts the unity of history to consist not in any definite progression, but in an open, fluid movement that articulates itself "from within."[43] The one horizon of tradition ultimately has as little fixity as the horizons it gives rise to. Just as no partial horizon within history is complete, so the horizon of time itself is still open and unfolding.[44]

It should therefore be clear why, given the nature of our historical situatedness, we must revise prior conceptions of historicality, including their assumptions of immediacy. We neither stand detached from nor are we completely subsumed by our historical situation, so we are never in a state of pure agency or pure submission to external factors. In fact, we are identical to the situation itself, inasmuch as our understanding at any point is partial, but not constrained to fixed limits. Our position is constantly generated anew in the occurrence of encounter, and this event is itself part of a movement unlike any linear causality that would have a traceable beginning. The situation, then, "is an event and not a process."[45] The overall horizon of tradition in which we are situated does not possess the stability of a ground, only the unity of (a) movement. Gadamer refers to this movement as the occurrence of transmission.

Transmission

The analyses of prejudice and horizon have shown that we are situated in a structure that exceeds our individual rational powers. We are both thrown into historicity and carried along by it in such a way that our doing is never entirely our own; it belongs to the greater horizon of the movement of tradition. Yet while I have emphasized that this belonging does not amount to an external determination of our agency, this assertion remains to be substantiated through Gadamer's own concepts; it remains to be elaborated what exactly history's effect amounts to. Whereas we have seen that we do not occur without history, it bears exhibiting how history also does not occur without us.

We need not look far for a sense of this reversal. The term Gadamer selects for the transmission of tradition, *Überlieferung*, denotes a delivering-over from the past to the present and concisely indicates an intertwined connection. Gadamer has already dismissed the notion of our autonomy over history, so the subject cannot serve as the sole agent of historical transmission. In ruling out, further, that this process could occur automatically, Gadamer avoids the lawful naturalism of theoretical historicism and the assimilative grasp of traditionalism. Finally, and perhaps most crucially for his determination of historical effect, he also denies that the agency of transmission lies in history itself as if in some higher force, ruling out eschatological-teleological explanation and the notion of a quasi-Heideggerian "destiny of Being" (*Seinsgeschick*). This leaves a chiasmic structure of reciprocal effect as the only alternative.[46]

As "the reality of history within understanding,"[47] transmission indeed brings about one's stance in history, but not as a metaphysical or naturalistic *archê*. The causality involved is instead one of ongoing effect (*Wirkung*).[48] Gadamer found inspiration for this historical causality in Aristotle's conception of *energeia* as a being-at-work, and the latter also informs the concept of "play" in Gadamer's aesthetic analyses.[49] This constant being-in-effect intertwines both past and present, the effecting and the affected. Gadamer speaks of an interplay between "the movement of tradition and the movement of the interpreter,"[50] which, given the analysis above, amounts to the fusion of the individual horizon with the horizon of historical transmission itself. Yet this interplay must be something other than an exchange between two distinct entities.[51] We have already seen that the split between purportedly stable subjects and objects is senseless. Not only are the two involved dialectically – the past shapes my horizon just as I recognize the past and understand it anew – but this involvement takes place on an ontological rather than methodical level. The involvement is itself the "one great horizon" of an ongoing movement. Our belonging to historical effect is thus not so much a situation we are in, an a priori condition we are exposed to, as much as it is a process that we are and enact. If tradition is an ongoing event, and understanding a crucial perpetuation of this, then "understanding itself is a historical event."[52]

This bespeaks far more generative participation than the term "'belonging" would initially imply. We may belong to historical transmission more than we possess ourselves, but tradition also belongs to us more than it rests on its own apart from us. If tradition is not a brute force like nature that operates without our action, we must somehow be involved in its continuation.[53] Indeed, what arises in history never does so without the mediation of those who take part in it. Tradition, the transmission of history, is actually more aptly conceived as the mediation itself, as opposed to the sedimented past that is merely carried forward (by either its own or some other's impetus).[54] In this way it is far clearer how we ourselves play a role in perpetuating and preserving tradition. Our historicity (*Geschichtlichkeit*) is not simply conditioned by a permanent effect (*Wirkung*), but itself bears upon transmission as a historicity of effect (*Wirkungs-Geschichtlichkeit*). In the reciprocity that thus obtains between past and present, there is a "unity of effect".[55] To speak of tradition is to announce the continual preservation of the past. Put differently, the enactment of history's effect constitutes our very being.

To exhibit this more clearly, one need only think of how tradition is in fact delivered over to and through the present. Without human effort, no idea, object, or event retains its significance, and by embracing some things rather than others, we alter the substance of history. Thus, everything we find with us today has in some way been preserved through an act of mediation, and it needs this mediation if it is to perdure. Yet this ongoing transmission need not occur explicitly as a conscious, subjective act. Gadamer underscores that "preservation is an act of reason, though an inconspicuous one."[56] It already occurs when we take over the historical horizon we are given, and continues in our everyday social concerns and aspirations. However future-oriented we may be, and however vehemently we might rebel against what preceded us, our participation in transmission will always persist. As an example, Gadamer takes what we consider the "classical" to embody this mode of historical existence that continues through our involvement, but not necessarily on the basis of a conscious decision, and certainly not due to preformulated standards. It persists, rather, on the basis of its ability to speak to us and to compel our continued affirmation.[57]

Through this exemplar, we can fully uncover and summarize the intertwined structure of transmission. In one respect, tradition cannot persist without the engagement of humans who value and cultivate some things over others; without our concerns and commitments, enduring preservation would cease. Our attempts to understand the world inherently draw on and converse with, but also revise, transform, and subvert the precedents and prejudices we inherit. In another respect, however, there are limits to this transformation. First, it is impossible to start completely anew, to eradicate all connection to the past. As always engaged in the transmission of the past, we perform its preservation whether we actively choose to do so or not. Second, it is equally impossible to ever complete this mediation, to establish once and for all what is worth preserving, or to know definitively what can be brought forth to endure from history. We can never fully know history, nor our place in it.

Since history is itself an incomplete whole, a moving horizon and not a totality, it retreats from our final grasp at the same time as it lies open to our ongoing engagement and interpretation from within. Tradition both gives itself over to our understanding and withdraws from it. This ambiguous nature of tradition, for Gadamer, contributes to the seemingly paradoxical character of our finite historicity: Our existence is an infinite possibility of meaning within a bounded situatedness of limited understanding.[58]

Yet while we tend to have a blind spot for our own historicity, this finitude need not remain inconspicuous.[59] One might wonder, in fact, whether a form of awareness could alleviate the typical opacity of our involvement in transmission. Gadamer's own analyses appear to answer this in the affirmative. After all, his philosophical hermeneutics serve as a higher reflection on our finitude, as a conscious and theoretical description of what occurs in all pretheoretical situatedness. In this respect, we seem to be capable of rising above our finitude, but it remains to be seen how far this elevation takes us.

REFLECTION, FINITUDE, AND OPENNESS

When Gadamer introduces the notion of a consciousness of historical effect (*wirkungsgeschichtliches Bewusstsein*), one might be tempted to view this as a step beyond the intertwined nature of transmission to a rational subsumption that enables the proper adjudication of prejudices. The desire for this movement is, philosophically and hermeneutically speaking, quite understandable. Indeed, were Gadamer to assert the opposite, that no awareness of our finitude is possible, he would succumb to the accusation of incommensurable perspectivism, in which a specific cultural tradition absolutely, prerationally, and irrevocably determines our consciousness.

Contrary to both of these stances, however, the consciousness introduced here amounts neither to a reflective critical distance nor to a realization of perspectival determinism. Rather, this additional step on Gadamer's part serves only to extend the ambiguity and paradoxical finitude already at work in historical effect itself. If historical effect encapsulates both our belonging to tradition and our enactment of it, then the consciousness of this situation, by nature of its double genitive, entails another layering *within* historical effect rather than beyond it. This is evident in Gadamer's term itself, which is frequently also rendered in English as "historically effected consciousness." As a consciousness "of" historical effect, "it is used to mean at once the consciousness effected in the course of history and determined by history, and the very consciousness of being thus effected and determined."[60] This extension of the chiasmic structure of historical effect, while ultimately quite revealing of Gadamer's theory as a whole, is an element that has evoked many misunderstandings of his position. By elaborating in more detail how consciousness relates to historical effect, I aim to correct these errors while accounting for the immense importance that Gadamer attributes to the consciousness of historical effect.

One might be tempted to conceive of this consciousness as "that which is involved in historical effect." Regardless of this involvement's character of occurrence, then, from this point of view it remains an object of detached interest, or that which was analyzed under the heading of historicity and finitude in the previous section. The term "consciousness," then, merely refers to the situated character of any human's existence whatsoever. This third-person perspective, one might say, does not rob the particular consciousness of its individuality; the fact that consciousness has a blind spot for its situatedness, that the latter always retreats from view, does not diminish the specifically conscious nature of historical life, which philosophy in turn can investigate. As already indicated, one need not be aware of historical transmission in order to take part in it, and just because this transmission takes place inconspicuously does not amount to any sort of unconsciousness on the part of the historical human.

If, however, the consciousness that is typically involved inconspicuously in historical effect has become an object of hermeneutical investigation, then the results of this analysis constitute another, less detached meaning of the consciousness of historical effect. In conducting its analyses, our consciousness – which is no less historical than the kind being analyzed – has indeed shown that "it can rise above that of which it is conscious," the latter being the hermeneutic situation as described earlier.[61] Yet since we are that very situation, this consciousness of historical effect amounts to a kind of self-reflection, and the preposition "above" loses its seemingly detached objectivity.

Given the claims regarding historicity and finitude that are made at this level of reflection, more needs to be said concerning the status of this purportedly elevated consciousness. Gadamer, in fact, denies that this higher-order consciousness can reach a level of atemporal universality, that it can regard history and human existence in a logically scientific manner.[62] Instead he insists that, like situated historicity, even higher-level consciousness "is so radically finite that our whole being, effected in the totality of our destiny, inevitably transcends its knowledge of itself."[63] This, Gadamer contends, is a "fundamental insight which is not to be limited to any specific historical situation."[64]

With this, Gadamer underscores that all reflection upon history, regardless of the elevation it indeed attains, still belongs to the effect of transmission. If the consciousness of this historical effect cannot subsume historicity, then, but instead remains under the universal sway of it, then consciousness cannot detach itself from tradition, nor can it seek unchanging knowledge of historical laws. It cannot make metaphysical claims concerning history's substance or *telos,* nor can it become the sort of critical reflection typically pursued since the nineteenth century's discovery of historical consciousness. In short, it does not possess the status or aims of a technical skill, an a priori account of values, or a natural science. This, for Gadamer, actually liberates the concept of reflection from the narrow confines of methodical and teleological procedure, from abstruse academic debates and their concomitant inscrutable systems. Instead, it underlines that the consciousness of historical effect remains an inherent and constant possibility for any participant in history. Such reflection is not confined to the philosopher's theoretical analysis but pervades all interpretive tasks of social life and human conduct.[65]

Yet this is not to flatten historical reflection to the point that it becomes indistinct from any other human action. The relinquishment of technical prowess and scientific method is not to deny that historically effected consciousness pursues its reflection "in a regulated way,"[66] nor that there are criteria for its successful operation. Indeed, by showing that the consciousness of historical effect "is at work in all hermeneutical activity,"[67] Gadamer can trace historical reflection to the element of application that is intrinsic to such activity, and by elaborating on what such application entails, also elucidate reflection itself. This avoids the pernicious adversary to scientism in nineteenth- and early-twentieth-century debates on historicism, the relativistic agglomeration of *Weltanschauungen*.

Some of Gadamer's most popular and poignant examples of hermeneutical activity include the interpretations performed by judges, theologians, literary critics, and historians. While varying in their degree of technicality and precision, these interpretations share in common the employment of historical understanding in the grasping of their objects. That is to say, the general object under consideration is never a delimited universal in itself that is subsequently applied, ready-made, to a current situation. Nor, conversely, is that object subsumed as a particular under universal laws of judgment. Instead, the general object – be it law, sacred text, literary object, or historical event – is first understood in and through the conscious formulation of its relevance to the present. The changing demands of the present thus affect the understanding and application of the object. The demanding nature of application therefore lies in the fact that it never consists in mere adherence to fixed standards or rules of interpretation, as if one's situation (or that which is applied to it) were a stable entity. Since "the movement of reflection has its place within the context of a beginningless and endless tradition," there is no such stability.[68] Rather, given the fluid mobility of our horizons and of transmission as such, application remains an ongoing activity.

Gadamer, once again drawing on Aristotle, finds a further exemplar and conceptual analogue for the ongoing nature of application in the concept of practical wisdom or *phronêsis*. This central insight of the *Nicomachean Ethics* reveals that ethical action involves a continual exchange between one's moral ideals and the given situation one finds oneself in. It requires having an attentive openness to the demands of one's circumstances, while at the same time considering what response to the situation best preserves one's broader commitments.[69] Transposing this ethical structure into the hermeneutical,[70] Gadamer thereby underscores that "the relation between the universal and the particular is not that of logical subsumption, but rather of co-determination."[71] Taking this circular exchange to underlie all interpretive engagement between selfhood and alterity, Gadamer can clarify the task of application – and thus of historical reflection – as an openness to ongoing, mutual determination.

Yet just as one might ask how the *phronimos* enters into the stance of circumspective openness, one can wonder how the consciousness of historical effect comes to acknowledge the need for, and engage in the practice of, continual historical application. On the one hand, this question could be taken to misunderstand the character of historical reflection, as if the latter were a resolute decision on the part of the subject. A far better conception would be one that takes application to lie among the individual's constant interpretive possibilities. Yet the question of the genesis of application, on the other hand, pertains to the real aspect of application as a task. After all, even though it is always a possibility for us, this reflective exchange arises only if application becomes actualized or necessary for one reason or another. Just as a student of Aristotle's will concern himself only with the ethical potential of his situation if his upbringing has taught him to attend to it – that is, if he is experienced or self-aware enough to apply ethical knowledge[72] – so our (reflective) concern with our finite situation will arise only out of some form of experience.

To become conscious of historical effect, historicity thus apparently needs teachers of its own, or at least an experiential path to reflection. Yet what sort of experience could generate this movement? Gadamer has already ruled out an internal origin, in which application would stem merely from the subject's own resolve to reflect upon her prejudices. Such a conception of experience is entirely too voluntaristic. Our prejudices may be our own, and weave together to constitute our reality, but they belong to a movement that is not entirely within our control, and become visible to us only through engagement with something that provokes them.[73] It bears noting, however, that application does not simply arise on the basis of external influence, either. It is only by putting our prejudices at risk that we experience – and potentially broaden – our horizon. Put differently, it is the experience of negativity, or "genuine experience," that "teaches us to acknowledge the real."[74]

Entering into the activity of application, then, involves the same experience as that of continually engaging in application itself: putting one's position at risk over against something foreign, and allowing each to codetermine the other. The reflection involved in the consciousness of historical effect, therefore, entails hearing "tradition's claim to validity, not in the sense of simply acknowledging the past in its otherness, but in such a way that it has something to say to me."[75] Crucially for Gadamer, and for everything that follows in our analysis here, this means that the oneness of horizons described above is more than a mere background condition of experience; it is also an achievement on the part of the individual.[76] The experience that brings forth reflection, while not strictly subjective, is still connected to an individual's activity, and this activity permits of gradations; it can be performed well or poorly. It is by this evaluative standard of engagement that the application of historical reflection can be assessed.

Here, Gadamer's notion of truth apart from method becomes more apparent. As "a genuine form of experience [*Erfahrung*]," historically effected consciousness shares the structure of experience as such, and Gadamer conceives of both in decided opposition to the scientific notions of induction, repeatability, and positivity.[77] Rather than seeking the closure of established fact and treating experience "in terms of its result," Gadamer contends that genuine experience "is a process" and knows itself to be contingent.[78] Similarly to the way in which the reflective aspect of historically effected consciousness exceeds "the limitations of reflective philosophy"[79] and has no beginning or end, experience has a completely different sense of completion (*Vollendung*) here than it does in scientific methodology.[80] Drawing on the notion of negativity in Hegel to develop this conception of experience (a concept that Gadamer takes to be "one of the most obscure we have"[81]), Gadamer concludes that "[t]he dialectic of experience has its proper fulfillment not in definitive knowledge but in the openness to experience that is made possible by experience itself."[82]

As the result of a dialectic, this openness does not stem from a decision on the subject's part, nor does it constitute a relinquishment of subjectivity in the face of overwhelming experience; it is not an accession to foreign impositions, as some have misunderstood it to be. Instead, this openness can be viewed as an extension of, and now a conscious engagement with, the ontological chiasm that was shown to reside at the basis of historicity. There, at the root of our familiarity with the world, lay a fundamental openness of our individual horizon onto the broader horizon of transmission itself. The two could ultimately not be delimited as subject and object. Now, at the level of consciousness, the same intertwining persists. Even when we retrieve our horizon into reflection, we can never fully envelop our effectedness. The reversibility between self and tradition is thus not a closed circle, but remains open.[83]

This constitutes Gadamer's fundamental insight concerning the pervasiveness of finitude, and it has significant repercussions for any conception of historical reflection. The fact that the consciousness of historical effect repeats the chiasmic structure of that effect means that they are not two distinct operations. The conscious reflection merely echoes the historical structure of our existence; it is an experience of experience, an understanding of understanding, and to this extent can be called reflective. Yet since we cannot reflect ourselves out of our situation, this reflection does not stand above history or historical life; neither is it confined, however, within the prejudices of one's time and place, or within a univocal boundary of a specific tradition. To be sure, the openness of historically effected consciousness amounts to a form of humility before the ongoing movement of tradition, but this tradition is not the transmitted endowment of a given culture, nor is it fixed to a given meaning. The meaning of history is, rather, infinitely revisable, and this revision is a continual task. However, such a task cannot become just another Rickertian transcendental value; it arises only once the openness toward historicity has become necessary, and this depends on the experience of negativity or ruptures. To underscore an earlier point, history cannot be presumed in advance to be "about" any particular meaning or project; its questionability precludes any formulation of perennial problems. Accordingly, historically effected consciousness is far more a decentered stance or attitude of lived questionability than a critical-logical thought process; it is "more 'being' [*Sein*] than consciousness [*Bewusstsein*]."[84]

CONSCIOUSNESS OF HISTORICAL EFFECT

Despite the limitations that Gadamer extends to the consciousness of historical effect, he nevertheless takes this consciousness to reside in a crucial position apart from traditionalism or perspectivism. Gadamer takes the significance of this position – indeed, the dire need for it – to lie in several connected hermeneutic aspects, namely the cognitive, reproductive, and normative. Emilio Betti had initially distinguished these categories in his *General Theory of Interpretation*, but Gadamer takes issue with this distinction and asserts that "all three constitute one unitary phenomenon."[85] In the following pages, I will draw out these aspects and demonstrate their unity, thereby arriving at one of the central premises of the present work, namely that the consciousness of historical effect is significant not only for the narrowly theoretical and interpretive application of historical reflection, but – as a universal characteristic of understanding – for social existence as such.

On the opening page of *Truth and Method,* Gadamer asks "what kind of knowledge and what kind of truth" arise in the understanding of tradition.[86] As we have seen, he takes previous accounts of historical knowledge to be inadequate, and presents his own account of historically effected consciousness as a response to this question. The answer boils down to the claim that historically effected consciousness contributes to scientific knowledge. In a passage that encapsulates many of his core assertions, Gadamer notes that "[o]ur need to become conscious of effective history is urgent because it is necessary for scientific consciousness [*wissenschaftliche Bewusstsein*]."[87]

Of course, it should be clear from our previous analyses that Gadamer does not have the narrow, methodical standpoint of natural science in mind here, but instead the broad scope of any inquiry into truth. In stating the necessity of reflection so strongly, he is underlining the universal claim of his insight into historicity. After all, the "genuine" or dialectical experience that he proposed as underlying historical reflection should not be viewed as a devolved form of rigorous induction, as something inadequate to the high standards of science and relegated to the arts as the antechamber of science. Instead, dialectical experience constitutes the very origin of any insight and principle whatsoever.[88] Furthermore, just as Gadamer shows this origin to lie in a movement of negativity, so too the fulfillment of experience consists only in openness to further experience. Thus, the whole conception of science here is one of ongoing investigation and revision, of movement within an indeterminate whole. Given the limits that Gadamer has indicated, a historically reflective scientific consciousness would therefore proceed along the same path as before, but with the recognition that any absolute fulfillment is precluded.[89] Gadamer's assertion of finitude, then, amounts not to a denial of progress, but to a reconception of it.[90]

Gadamer is aware that his reconceptions in general, and this one in particular, ask "something unusual of the self-understanding of modern science."[91] Indeed, he asks nothing less than an overhaul of this very self-understanding. The intensity and breadth of Gadamer's demand derives from the fact that our entire engagement with the world tends to be conceived from the side of modern science. The urgency "that we should understand ourselves better" thus arises from the "actual deformation of knowledge" that can occur through this skewed scientistic emphasis.[92] The cognitive significance of historically effected consciousness, then, lies in its delimitation of what human knowledge is and can be, and in its discovery of a truth beyond method. This consciousness therefore figures equally as importantly in the self-understanding of science as it does in human self-understanding in general.

This self-understanding, of course, cannot be equated here with self-consciousness, with absolute self-reflection, or with any rational interiority of modern proportions.[93] This is because, as we have seen, no subject exists in complete isolation from its other, so that "[u]nderstanding is understanding of the self and the other *at the same time*."[94] Further, it is not simply subjects who advance science, but historically transmitted change itself.[95] Thus, the sort of self-understanding that historically effected consciousness grants is an insight into the shifting nature of one's horizon and the movement of tradition. It is the point at which understanding "knows itself" as an effect.[96] Yet this sort of adequate understanding of one's situation, and indeed any reflective engagement with alterity, can occur only if one takes account of one's prejudices.[97] I have already indicated that, since so much of one's horizon is shaped historically (one need only think of tacit cultural and metaphysical assumptions), the awareness of these prejudices can arise only when they are challenged. A true understanding of oneself depends on the experience of negativity, and this includes acknowledgment of something beyond oneself. Ultimately, then, the recognition of the revisability of knowledge depends on a fundamental openness.

This openness and the decentering, dialectical experience that undergirds it contribute to what I have called the reproductive and normative significance of the consciousness of historical effect. The reproductive, or as Gadamer would rephrase it, productive aspect of this consciousness is that it recognizes both the forward movement in all understanding and the contribution that distance makes to this progress.[98] Taking the nature of transmission to heart, one knows that no outright retrieval of the past is possible: first, it does not exist as a distinct and self-enclosed entity, but belongs to a movement of which we are a part as well; second, any understanding of the past is a conjunction or fusion of this past with one's lived present, and will always carry with it the task and residue of application. This has the scientific consequence that a detached reconstruction like the history of problematics becomes impossible.[99] Yet it also carries with it an implication for any involvement with history, namely that the past cannot simply be appropriated into complete familiarity or kept in place as dogmatic authority. It must be reproduced through a continued conversation.

In this necessity lies the normative character of historically effected consciousness. As Gadamer underscored with his assertion of the unity of this consciousness, the normative dimension is not a notion appended to the hermeneutical situation, as if it were the philosopher's demand of what reflection should someday become. Rather, Gadamer's aim is to account for what is given in the structure of human existence itself, and he draws his conclusions strictly from these conditions.[100] In this way, the task of historical reflection that I described in the previous section is not a distinct stage added to the structure of historical consciousness, but arises from an adequate understanding of this very consciousness. Our historicity already involves an inconspicuous dialogue with the past, and historical reflection merely raises the ontological factors of this dialogue to awareness. Precisely because this awareness cannot reach the subsumptive and exhaustive perspective of a Hegelian absolute knowledge, the dialogue with tradition bears its own continual, intrinsic hermeneutic demands.[101]

First of all, the awareness entails seeing that the past is not a silent screen for our projections; it makes its own claims, and these inevitably confront our own prejudices. To actually engage with the past means to put these prejudices at risk and allow them to become questionable.[102] In this acceptance of indeterminacy, what was previously called the fusion of horizons here takes the shape of a crossing-over or intermingling of questions.[103] There are not only the questions that we pose to the past, but also the questions to which the claims of the past are themselves answers. To understand these latter questions means to pose them genuinely for ourselves.[104] A further demand, then, is an openness of listening as opposed to a reconstruction of fixed meaning.[105] Crucially, however, this listening and posing of questions does not entail agreement with whatever claims arise. The recognition of a question, after all, does not amount to an embrace of its traditional answer(s). Instead, the recognition requires a form of freedom: the ability to maintain enough distance to even hear the question, the openness of allowing something to become questionable to begin with.[106] Any acknowledgment of authority that occurs in the crossing-over of questions, then, stems not from a blind deferral to the past,[107] but from an act of preservation based on resonance with the questions, a recognition of standards beyond one's historical present.[108] The past may pose its questions to us, and transmission intrinsically involves us in this dialogue, but it is we who, in understanding and living the questions, decide whether or not to keep asking them, thereby indicating – often only performatively – what constitutes a satisfactory answer.

It is no coincidence that historically effected consciousness comes to evince a fundamentally conversational character. Even though this character arose here only through the analysis of the normative aspect of historical reflection, it is not difficult to see that it pervades the aspects of productivity and cognition as well. The various hermeneutic dimensions of historically effected consciousness thus appear to find their unity in a transmission that is historical as well as linguistic. This is hardly surprising since, as I mentioned at the outset of the chapter, the equiprimordial counterpart to the universality of historicity is that of linguisticality. Put differently, the transmission of tradition is nothing other than the ever-changing shape and texture of human community and communication.[109]

The significance of this unity cannot be overstated. It reveals, on the one hand, that language cannot be separated from the historical core of

Gadamer's theory as a realm where his hermeneutical insights merely find application (as if the final third of *Truth and Method* were separable from the rest). On the other hand, it makes clear that historicity is not involved only with the historical or historiographical. Even a dismissive response to a given tradition or aspect thereof is a form of engagement that preserves transmission as such.[110] All meaningful social involvement, furthermore, has an historical dimension, even if it does not engage with tradition as such or with a specific traditional content. This is a point that Gadamer himself lamented as remaining underdeveloped in the central sections of *Truth and Method*. Given his emphasis there on textual encounter in the historical human sciences, it appeared that the general issues of distance and alterity lay beyond his purview, or in another area of hermeneutics.[111] However, it is precisely this social and ethical dimension in which Gadamer takes the ultimate significance of historical effect to lie, and to which he subsequently dedicated more attention.[112]

THE ETHICAL REGISTER

Since my aim in the present work is to establish this significance, it will be necessary in the coming chapters to extend the analysis of historical effect to the structures and strata of social existence. I will conclude this chapter by transposing the discussion of historical positions from earlier sections into social categories. There, I noted that Gadamer's position on historicality has been associated with traditionalism on the one hand, and on the other with a relativist perspectivism that asserts an incommensurability among historical epochs. Having analyzed Gadamer's concept of historical effect, we are in a better position to see both how he navigates away from these positions, and how this shifts his philosophy into a social register.

Traditionalism, when viewed from a social perspective, amounts to a denial of alterity. It may admit that the other at first seems distant and foreign, but supposes that some process – be it the psychologism of romantic hermeneutics or the subsumption of Hegelian absolute mediation – is capable of fully uniting self and other. Since nothing and no one, therefore, is outside the reach of one's appropriation, everything is at least potentially familiar. To the incommensurabilist, the opposite is the case. The relativism of views is based on the assumption that there is no common experience, actual or potential, that could unite self and other. The two are separated by an insurmountable strangeness, which is held at bay either through a tolerance of the other's position or through an elevation of the other to a position above the self.[113]

While proponents of each of these positions frequently accuse Gadamer of espousing the other, he in fact inhabits a position that eschews both.[114] His is not exactly a mean position between the two, but some sort of middle stance is suggested by his assertion that "[t]he true locus of hermeneutics is [the] in-between" of strangeness and familiarity.[115] We saw this in-between in the intertwining of self and tradition, and can translate that here into a recognition of difference without utter division. The fusion of horizons entails a thorough mutual determination of self and other, such that neither exists completely in itself. The introduction of one great horizon is a way of formulating this relation negatively ("There are no closed horizons"[116]), and does not involve a thorough appropriation on the part of the subject, as some have claimed.[117] Gadamer certainly makes no effort to hide his indebtedness to romantic hermeneutics and Hegelian dialectic, but his defense of finitude supersedes their conclusions. While the ongoing movement of transmission involves mediation, our limitations, as well as the factual ruptures of history, preclude this from ever becoming absolute or complete.

If Gadamer thus avoids the danger of totalizing essentialism, the openness that he identifies in historical effect does not, in turn, amount to a social indifference. To claim that human lives are incommensurable through and through would be, as Gadamer puts it, "a kind of Robinson Crusoe dream" that encloses each in his or her own selfhood.[118] The supposed asymmetry between individuals is negated by our belonging to a shared life, however minimally that may be determined. That this life is perpetuated through the constant movement of transmission and the infinite iterations of dialogue only serves to strengthen the normative characterization of historical effect as an ongoing conversation possessing intrinsic demands. It should now be clear that these demands are not expressible as moral codes or social techniques (nor as any methodology in general), but lie rather in the responsive structure of historicity and linguisticality themselves. One of the deepest demands, then, according to the openness and iterability of these structures, is the acknowledgement of an abyssal freedom, of the fact "that we live in a world that is greater than that which we can determine or control."[119]

While his overarching social stance may yet remain opaque, we can perhaps already see, in profile, how Gadamer conceives of the historical subject's place in society. To be sure, it is a nonfoundational role that eschews the critical-theoretical ambitions of either side of historicist debates, but it also intends to avoid the "disappearance of the subject" in the overwhelming movement of historical epochs.[120] It is, ultimately, a consciousness that recognizes both its boundness to tradition and the fact that "in tradition there is always an element of freedom."[121] This chapter has given a glimpse of how Gadamer takes transmission to embody this freedom, in that it is at once a structural inheritance and a constant task, "both a presupposition and an achievement" of openness.[122] In subsequent chapters, I will amplify the analysis of this ambivalence, and develop further the theme of freedom within tradition.

TWO

Historical Belonging as Finite Freedom

ENACTMENT AND INFLUENCE

As I began to develop in the previous chapter, the openness of the transmission of tradition entails a form of freedom for Gadamer, and this freedom undergirds transmission both as a structure and as an ongoing task. Structurally, it finds expression in the infinite iterability of language, and in the capacity of history to always be interpreted anew. This capacity, when considered from the side of our situatedness in history, brings out the nature of freedom as a task, for it is our inescapable engagement with tradition that evokes the constant necessity of retrieving the past – which is to say, the task of interpreting, applying, and understanding differently.

While few studies have dedicated themselves specifically to Gadamer's indebtedness to Martin Heidegger in this aspect of his hermeneutics,[1] it is well known that Gadamer draws from his erstwhile teacher many crucial insights regarding historicity, the structure of historical effect, and the achievement of the past's retrieval. Many commentators point to Heidegger's *Being and Time* as the main locus of this influence, and this indeed seems confirmed by an extensive passage in *Truth and Method*.[2] Yet Gadamer evinces a far more complex and pervasive relation to Heidegger's thought, making a sustained effort to grapple with his teacher's entire corpus, not just with those ideas gleaned during his "philosophical apprenticeship." In fact, Gadamer compiled a whole series of essays into a volume on Heidegger (*Heidegger's Wege*), now making up part of volume 3 of Gadamer's collected works.[3] What is more, this occupation with Heidegger's thinking is far from a direct amalgamation of his ideas. As I hope to show in the present chapter, Gadamer certainly owes an important conceptual impetus to his teacher, and shares with him similar structural accounts and descriptive concerns, yet he also deals with the issue of history differently than his teacher. He not only differs from Heidegger in his fundamental stance toward historical occurrence, but also draws from this difference alternate conclusions concerning our possibilities of engagement with tradition.

Indeed, if on Gadamer's account the transmission of tradition requires a certain kind of freedom – a freedom that will turn out to be both a 'distance from' and an 'openness toward' – then Gadamer himself exemplifies this freedom in his complex relation to Heidegger, and reveals firsthand what it means "to belong to the historical effect of a significant thinker."[4] Extending this effect to any historical effect whatsoever, one can see that Gadamer not only formulates his conception of historical understanding as a theoretical position that bears a Heideggerian influence, but that he enacts the process of historical understanding – i.e., fulfills the task of belonging to tradition – in his very account of it. It is ultimately in the confluence of both the performance and conception of this belonging to tradition that Gadamer evinces the greatest distance from Heidegger.

As incidental as it might seem, Gadamer's rich layering of the performative dimension on top of the theoretical elaboration of historicity cannot be considered a mere stylistic aspect of his thought, as a feature extraneous to the subject matter itself.[5] Rather, it underscores a crucial point already made in the previous chapter, namely that reflection upon historical effect does not elevate one above tradition, but maintains and indeed extends the intertwined relation at work in historical effect itself. Gadamer's stance with respect to other thinkers (especially Heidegger) thereby ranks as exemplary evidence for the universal conditions of understanding that he aims to elucidate, and counts as an essential rather than a superficial feature of philosophical hermeneutics. After all, the great hermeneutic turn that both Heidegger and Gadamer undertake is to view understanding no longer as a strictly epistemological or methodical technique, as a rational process that takes place outside or beyond the realm of situated and prejudicial involvement, but instead as an ontological factor in our being, as "the originary form of Dasein's enactment."[6] When Gadamer formulates the historical dimensions of this understanding, he does so not simply from the standpoint of a theorist, but from within the experience of constant historical occurrence and effect. His work at understanding Heidegger, then, is as much an involvement with specific theories as it is an enactment of hermeneutics as such.

Accordingly, what I intend in this chapter (and, indeed, in the subsequent chapters on Hegel and Kant) is not a mere tracing of influence from one thinker to another, a comparison and contrasting of ideas, but an elucidation of historical effect in both its conceptual and enacted forms. In order to grasp both of these layers in Gadamer's complex relation to Heidegger, I will need to compare their engagement with tradition both as an object of philosophical scrutiny and as an ontological condition of thoughtful inquiry. An initial investigation of these aspects in Heidegger's thought will prepare a subsequent delineation of his proximity to and distance from Gadamer.[7] Ultimately, this delineation will reveal how Gadamer avoids what he takes to be pernicious elements of Heidegger's thought, highlight the practical philosophical underpinnings at work in philosophical hermeneutics, and thereby help in characterizing Gadamer's historical concepts as possessing an inherently social dimension.

HISTORICITY AND FREEDOM IN HEIDEGGER

Two misconceptions typically plague the approach to Heidegger's thoughts on history. The first concerns the breadth or scale of his thinking. Although it is often broadly labeled as an attempt to elaborate the "history of Being" (*Seinsgeschichte*), neither Heidegger's original approach nor his ultimate stance on the issue is as monolithic, objectivistic, or univocal as this phrasing might suggest. His involvement with and conception of history arises from an oblique philosophical angle, develops over the course of his career, and in this process undergoes many shifts. There is thus little sense in speaking of a "philosophy of history" in the traditional sense for Heidegger. Nevertheless, there is an inner logic to his development, and as much as the "turn" (*Kehre*) of the 1930s can be viewed as a reversal from a prior position, it can also be seen as a deepening pursuit of a series of questions concerning the past.[8] These questions pertain both to the sense of tradition as a historical human phenomenon and to the conceptual content of a specific tradition, namely that of Western civilization and its philosophical underpinnings. Heidegger's quest is, therefore, not for a universal definition, explanation, or overall meaning of history – which he would deride as an impossible "metaphysical" grounding of the temporal – but instead for the character of meaning's occurrence within history, including its peculiarities and the broader ontology of its movement. Heidegger thus poses himself the challenge of thinking at once about the structure and source of historical occurrence as well as about its basis and effect in significant human attitudes, thoughts, and decisions.

The second major misunderstanding of Heidegger's historical thought is related to the first, and pertains to his stance over against his own tradition. This approach takes Heidegger's position to be so enveloping of the Western tradition as to place him in a category completely apart from both his predecessors and his contemporaries, and it makes his work out to be more independent – and, perhaps to some readers, more unfounded – than it actually is.[9] To be sure, Heidegger stood out from debates on historical crisis at the outset of the twentieth century. He was no mere Spenglerian prophet of cultural decline, with which German society was replete at the time; Heidegger himself cultivated a certain critical detachment in stressing the radicality of his thought – indeed, his last published work contains the lecture titled "The End of Philosophy and the Task of Thinking" – and a superficial reading of his works might compel one to conclude that he really deals only in the great ideas of the West in order to refute, dismiss, or completely undermine them. A problem-historical approach that views Heidegger largely as a critic of the Western tradition, especially of specific historical thinkers like Plato or Hegel, only risks exacerbating this angle.

Another reason for the nebulous nature of Heidegger's stance is the indirect path of its provenance. Heidegger's beginnings as a thinker of history are, certainly, situated in the atmosphere of the debates concerning historical meaning that were kindled in the eighteenth century, were fanned in the nineteenth, and exploded at the outset of the twentieth. This discourse, some basic standpoints of which I outlined in the previous chapter, concerned the role of historicity in human knowing, and the possibility of finding systematic stability or logical objectivity in the study of the past. Heidegger aptly perceives this discourse to issue in a fundamental crisis in general human self-understanding and philosophy in particular, and he succeeds in pushing the debate far beyond its Neo-Kantian or Husserlian contributions.[10] Yet it is precisely the way in which Heidegger approaches and appropriates these matters that lends itself to misconstruals of his distance. After all, while he engaged in this discourse in a direct fashion in his lectures, he actually arrived at the thematic far more obliquely, from the side of theology.[11] To understand the development of Heidegger's thoughts on historicity and tradition, on both the structure and task of historical enactment, one must therefore begin very early in his career, and follow his steps into the formulation of *Being and Time*.[12] It is beyond the scope of the present work to uncover all of the sources that feed into these steps, and indeed the various angles of this early work need not be fully accounted for here; it will suffice to indicate that the approach taken in that magnum opus of 1927 already represents a culmination of sorts of over a decade of intense engagement with historicist issues. Only with this preparation will it make sense to turn to what Heidegger eventually presents under the label "history of Being" (*Seinsgeschichte*).

From Verflüssigung to Destruktion

While the entirety of Heidegger's thought could be said to be occupied with tradition in one form or another,[13] the role of tradition in his early writings is perhaps most notable for its relatively unquestioned provenance and gradual thematic scrutiny. Heidegger's earliest published essay, on the problem of reality in modern philosophy (1912), represents a staunch defense of Catholic doctrines – more specifically, of Aristotelian-Scholastic realism – against the influence of modern philosophies and attitudes.[14] Taking over the Neo-Thomist conviction that "no historical modification could touch the core of human reality and its fundamental truths," Heidegger here defends what he calls "critical realism" as just such a core path from which both empiricism and Kantianism deviate.[15] Contending that our experience of meaning involves neither psychologically associated sense-data nor categorially constituted sensation, but instead meaningful objects as such, Heidegger wants to clear a way to deal with transsubjective reality as we encounter it, and as the "unanimity" of the realist tradition has conceived of it.

If the realism-essay intends to show how the tradition of realist thought remains valid throughout time, then the dissertation of 1913, on the doctrine of judgment in psychologism, proceeds closer to a thematization of time itself.[16] Here Heidegger elaborates the problem of thinking the relation of logic – which is static, general, and timeless – to reality – which is genetic, particular, and temporal. The way out of this impasse, Heidegger asserts, is to locate the ideality of meaning not in either the mental act of judging or the object judged, but in the conjunction of judgment and its real situation.

Heidegger continues to pursue this line of investigation in his *Habilitationsschrift* of 1915. In this work on Duns Scotus's doctrine of categories and meaning,[17] Heidegger aims at a "making-fluid" (*Flüssigmachung*) of Scholastic ideas in order to underscore the relevance of Catholic thought for modern philosophy.[18] This relevance lies in medieval philosophy's ability to account for logical essences, which Scotus takes to be a priori ideal meanings entirely separate from history, yet which in his conception do also not exhaust the particularity of reality. Heidegger sees in this account a prefiguration of Husserl's concept of intentionality, which elaborates our connection to real objects while at the same time grasping what is ideal in the act of intending.

Scholasticism and phenomenology together, then, allow philosophy to move beyond epistemology to an account of the unity between meaning and the acts that express it. Further, since intentionality resides in a "living spirit," a being that is itself real, particular, and temporal, it is the meaning-expressive act of this being by which universally valid meaning is formulated.[19] One can distinguish between the history of expressive acts (the real constitution of meaning) and the philosophy of the truth of these expressions (their ideal validity).[20] There thus hypothetically exists, according to Heidegger, the possibility of tracing the history of truth, the complete and systematic account of which would involve seeing truth as if from a timeless perspective. Even with this pure possibility of systematization, however, Heidegger insists that the truth will not be found by attending to univocal terms in history, or by tracing law-like patterns.[21] One must rather attend to "living speech" (*lebendige Rede*) in "the peculiar mobility of its meaning."[22]

In the process of making past ideas "fluid," Heidegger thus gradually deals not only with tradition as a content on which he draws, but with this tradition's own inherent structure, movement, and truth. In what amounts to the initial reflective turn of historical consciousness, he recognizes what makes his own "liquidation" (*Verflüssigung*) and application of history possible to begin with: the reality underlying our concepts is itself flowing and inexhaustible, and there is no univocal basis on which meaningful expression rests. To encounter truth, one must turn to life in its enactment (*Vollzug*), not to the terminological sedimentations of (perhaps poorly) inherited traditions.[23] Heidegger is here taking his first steps toward an embrace and elaboration of historical life, and away from the transcendental value system of his Neo-Kantian teacher, Heinrich Rickert.

Such systems, in Heidegger's view, broadly include the dogmatic assertions of Church truths, and it is not long before Heidegger's philosophical development affects his belief in Catholicism. In 1919 Heidegger writes that his "epistemological insights, extending to the theory of historical knowing, have made [...] the *system* of Catholicism problematic."[24] As his course on the *Phenomenology of Religious Life* indicates, he continues to struggle philosophically with the lived character of Christian consciousness, but his adherence to the institution has foundered.[25] This shaking of foundations was of course not unique to Heidegger at the time, nor was it the only area of his life affected by historical insights. Combined with the broad cultural and scientific disenchantment that took hold in Europe after World War I, Heidegger in fact wishes to distance himself from any systematized truths, including those of his philosophical contemporaries.

In his "Annotations to Karl Jaspers' *Psychology of Worldviews*," a highly critical and proto-programmatic piece written between 1919 and 1921, Heidegger underscores his desire to distance himself from various schools of thought and to think through philosophical matters directly. He seeks liberation from pursuits that are too theoretical and distant from life, and wishes to elaborate the "original motives" (*Ursprungsmotiven*) from which the truth-ideals of philosophy were derived.[26] To his student Hannah Arendt, this seemed at the time like a rending of the continuity of tradition, "an absolutely contemporary problematic" that could nevertheless precisely focus on the "cultural treasures of the past" and make them "speak again."[27] This turn to historical truth also signified a turn toward human life in its historical dimension.[28] In accepting the radically historical character of human life, Heidegger stresses that neither these human concerns, nor those thinkers presently engaged with them, are stable entities. The self that forms intelligible meaning is not itself a fixed being or a formal structure (contra Rickert and Husserl), but an enacted subjectivity involved in particular situations. Life itself, furthermore, is an "historically enacted phenomenon [*vollzugsgeschichtliches Phänomen*]" and its historical dimension is "not a correlate of an objectively historical, theoretical observation [*objektgeschichtlichen theoretischen Betrachtens*]," an aspect that is gleaned by simply looking to the past through its universally interpretable accretions (contra Dilthey).[29]

Already convinced of the significance of the past for present philosophical progress, Heidegger adds that this past will make philosophical sense only if viewed accurately in its structure of enactment. Yet Heidegger is not after a definitive theoretical position from which to view history as an object, however fluid this object is taken to be. The historical is not of purely objective interest, but of what Heidegger here labels responsible concern or "conscience" (*Gewissen*), and by which he means to invoke an historical mode of self-experience.[30] After all, any stance we inhabit is itself enacted in the stream of history, and requires a recognition of the same fluidity on our part that Heidegger has sought to uncover in the turn to tradition.[31] As if to emphasize the conjunction of these aspects, he notes that the historical is "what we ourselves are, that which we bear."[32] It is worth underscoring, in this phrasing, the inceptive connection between the structure of historical enactment and the task of carrying it forward.

One basic characterization of this connection is that, since life is constantly being enacted, it must also always be reinterpreted anew. Any rigidly systematic philosophy that neglects, eschews, or prevents this ongoing interpretation is, in Heidegger's eyes, fundamentally misguided. Further, since the tradition of such systematic philosophy, which includes a large part of the history of the West and which offers a "false continuity and accessibility,"[33] can thus be a hindrance to the proper self-understanding (and enactment) of the present, Heidegger concludes in his notes on Jaspers that a "dismantling" (*Destruktion*) of this tradition is necessary, especially of traditional modes of interpreting the self and its experience.[34]

Heidegger's first dedicated formulation and extensive explication of this dismantling approach occurs in the 1922 Natorp-report, a programmatic essay composed hastily in application for a position at the University of Marburg. As a prefatory clarification of his newly developing approach to Aristotle, and thus as a demonstration of what an adequate approach to historical sources might look like, Heidegger here elaborates a methodological framework for any historical research in philosophy. However, this seemingly narrow focus is quickly broadened to include a "hermeneutics of facticity," which amounts to a reflective interpretation of human existence *by* human existence.[35] Such an initial approach is necessary, Heidegger insists, due to the philosophically pernicious tendency to neglect our own historical movement in researching the past. He has already lamented that, in systematically objectifying history, we distort the objects under investigation, and risk taking over blindly what has accrued in the development of tradition. Yet we also, as he now explains, objectify and lose track of our own enacted being by interpreting ourselves in light of traditional conceptual objectifications and involvements with things. Any adequate philosophical research, therefore, must begin with an elucidation of ourselves and of our present situation as interpreters of historical being. The official title of the Natorp-report embodies this intention; it is to serve as an "Indication of the Hermeneutical Situation."[36]

If Heidegger's approach until now has fallen under the general rubric of "making fluid," he is now adding to this the task of making "transparent" (*durchsichtig*), of reducing the opacity in which the present finds itself, and applying the resulting transparency to an interpretation of history and its sedimented concepts (in this case, the ontology and logic of the ancient Greeks).[37] While taking aim at the presuppositions and perspectival determinations of the present, this transparency nevertheless does not involve their elimination from philosophical research. Instead, the goal is to elaborate the way in which we live our situations through these (often unconsciously inherited) factors, and to thereby gain an explicit yet proximate understanding of the enactment-structure of human life. For Heidegger, this is precisely the meaning of entering the historical realm, and it explains his assertion that philosophical activity is itself merely an extension of the fundamental movement of human life.[38]

By operating in and through the present in this way, Heidegger hopes that his analyses might affect both our general attitude toward the past and our specific dealings with concepts in the history of philosophy: "History itself, the past that is appropriated in understanding, grows in its comprehensibility with the primordiality of the decisive choice and the development of the hermeneutical situation."[39] The pointed purpose of his clarification is to show that philosophical research cannot be borrowed wholesale or transmitted purely from one age to another, and that such research can also not deign to take away from future ages their own need and responsibility of radically questioning their concepts. The fluid movement characterizing our present (and indeed all transmission of history) erodes the fixity of philosophical concepts as past "results" that are merely handed down, and reveals a "primordiality of questioning [*Frageursprünglichkeit*]"[40] that can (and indeed should) always be made present again through an act of retrieval or "primordial repetition."[41]

It is precisely such a repetition that Heidegger seeks through the formulation of his *Destruktion*-approach to history. He notes that it is a normal tendency for humans to make things easy for themselves and to cover over the difficulties of life (a process he calls "falling"). Preferring curiosity to wonder and habit to upheaval, we are typically quite unhistorical in our engagement with our traditions, in the sense that we do not acknowledge the past as what it is: "as the other and as a recoil against the present."[42] Instead, one tends to take over the past "undecidedly," without an awareness of this appropriation or of its role in the present. Since philosophy is just an extension of factical life, this tendency reaches all the way to philosophical concepts and paves over their questionability. Yet just as factical life, by reacting against its fallenness, can gain an awareness of its underlying and enacted existence (*Existenz*), so an approach of "radical understanding" can lead one to recognize the past as constitutive for the present. This entails retrieving past concerns as issues not just for the past, but for the present as well.

Thus, Heidegger contends that the history of thought is "objectively present for philosophical research in a relevant sense if and only if it provides not diverse curiosities, but radically simple *things worthy of thought* [Denkwürdigkeiten]" that "force the present back upon itself in order to increase questionability."[43] To reach these *Denkwürdigkeiten* and develop this forcefulness, it is necessary to "loosen up the handed-down and dominating interpretedness in its hidden motives, unexpressed tendencies, and ways of interpreting; and to push forward by way of a *dismantling return* toward the primordial motive sources of explanation."[44] The demand, in other words, is to stand within the tradition differently, to finally "rootedly" (*wurzelhaft*) possess what we have not yet taken over explicitly.[45]

Destruktion in the Natorp-report, then, is the present's path to its own fundamental and hidden movements. Through this approach, history comes to confront the present with the constant question concerning the extent to which the present is worried (*bekümmert*) about its "appropriation of radical possibilities of fundamental experiences [*Grunderfahrungsmöglichkeiten*] and their interpretations."[46] This radical self-possession with regard to history echoes the authenticity that Heidegger describes as a possibility for factical life's overcoming of its fallenness, and this parallel represents more than a structural similarity. Heidegger in fact asserts the identity between the object of *Destruktion* (the traditional concept of human nature, now termed "factical life") and the conditions of *Destruktion's* possibility (its rootedness in factical life). Through this identification, the character of philosophical research is bound inherently to the (self-)interrogation of human life: to clarify any part of life requires a movement through prior history, and to retrieve any part of the history of thought is to participate in the retrieval of one's own Being. What is more, the necessity of *Destruktion* – and therefore the need of philosophy in the present – is thereby intensified, for to neglect the primordial interpretation of factical life means consequently to renounce the possession of oneself, to neglect existence.[47] Given the weight of these points, and the critical tone with which Heidegger treats "the averageness of the *general public* [Öffentlichkeit],"[48] one cannot help but glean that the task of *Destruktion* is a radically individual one, rather than that of a community.

This focus on individual human existence formulates *in nuce* what will become the core issue of the existential analytic of *Being and Time*. There, among other developments, Heidegger will expand the investigation of life's historical involvement under the rubric of Dasein's historicity, analyzing in detail the possibility of "choosing one's fate" over against the tradition. However, in this major work that constitutes a veritable leap in Heidegger's career, new aspects of the problem of history emerge. If the Natorp-report is mostly about the conditions under which we are to engage with certain texts in the history of philosophy, *Being and Time* deals with the possibility of historical being as such. Yet just as the Natorp-report fixes the involvement with tradition upon lived human experience, so *Being and Time*, while broadening onto its expansive ontological theme, also restricts the frame of questioning from the multitude of pursuits in the history of philosophy to the question of the meaning of Being as this meaning is lived in Dasein. In the following section, I will account for this development of the historical thematic with regard to both its overall ontological purview and its narrower description of Dasein's historicity. I will focus on the introductory sections of the work, as well as on the later sections concerning temporality and historicity.

Dasein's Finite Freedom

What is immediately apparent about *Being and Time* is its advancement beyond the rather narrow programmatic scope of the Natorp-report, and indeed beyond any of Heidegger's previous works. Rather than taking aim at an interpretation of specific texts or concepts, Heidegger is here concerned, from the outset, to raise the question of Being in all of its profundity and perplexity. This is certainly related to his prior intentions to make the structure of life transparent, to "increase questionability" in the present, and to pay heed to a "venerable tradition."[49] Yet the move is nevertheless novel and surprising in its scope. This novelty may derive in part from the fact that we tend to take Being to be the most general, indefinable, and self-evident of concepts, having little to do with the concreteness of human existence. Heidegger takes this reaction itself to reveal a lack of perplexity on our part regarding the meaning of Being. Without this perplexity, the present also lacks any explicit question concerning Being, and since "[t]his question has today been forgotten," Heidegger sees the need to revive it.[50] It will become clear as we proceed that this need is more than a philosophical project, in Heidegger's eyes.

This revival of a question – one that Heidegger takes to have been first posed by the ancient Greeks – takes the same general form of repetition that Heidegger outlined in the Natorp-report. Just as the aim announced in that text was to describe present life more adequately by means of a dismantling return through a conceptually formative history, so here the task is to uncover the question of Being by way of a *Destruktion* of the intervening and forgetful tradition:

> If the question of Being is to have its own history made transparent, then this hardened tradition must be loosened up, and the concealments which it has brought about must be dissolved. We understand this task as one in which by taking *the question of Being as our clue,* we are to destroy the traditional content of ancient ontology until we arrive at those primordial experiences in which we achieved our first ways of determining the nature of Being – the ways which have guided us ever since.[51]

Thus, Heidegger is still engaged in the project of *Destruktion,* though on different terms than before. While *Being and Time* might indeed appear as a mere broadening of the approach, its aim is actually more focused than that of the Natorp-report. This focus has three concentric aspects.

First, as the passage above shows, Heidegger seeks to uncover a singular meaning of Being, a concept that actually possesses far more definition than the vague "possibilities of fundamental experiences" mentioned in 1922. Instead of dealing with many possible primordial questions and the concepts to which they gave rise, Heidegger now centers on just one question and its experiential ground. In addition to being targeted, it is also foundational and necessary, for the meaning of Being is what guides the production of the categories and logic of countless regional ontologies. In a telling example concerning one such region, the study of history, Heidegger underlines that "what is philosophically primary is neither a theory of the concept-formation of historiography nor the theory of historiographical knowledge, nor yet the theory of history as the object of historiography; what is primary is rather the interpretation of authentically historical entities as regards their historicity [*Geschichtlichkeit*]."[52] That is to say, it is the being-historical of entities, their belonging to the transmission of history, that most fundamentally discloses and determines their meaning within the positive investigations of historiography; the subsequent delineation of methods and accumulation of knowledge merely builds on the disclosure of this primordial belonging. The example is telling, because it hints at the thesis of the entire work: that the meaning of Being is time, that Being itself is temporal. I will elaborate what this means in more detail below, and the explanation will in fact take us, as it took Heidegger, far beyond *Being and Time*.

In the meantime, this example concerning historicity invokes a second point of focus of the work and takes us to a narrower thematic concern, namely Heidegger's increasing determinacy in the characterization of history. Whereas his 1922 text designates history as the realm of diverse original questions through which we access what might be called the "transcendental" structure of life, *Being and Time* defines the philosophical history of the West fairly directly and narrowly as the forgetting of the question of Being. This diagnosis rests on the more fundamental conclusion that temporality, which undergirds our historicity and thus gives rise to conceptions of history, has been misconstrued and indeed covered over by the Western tradition. This concealment has therefore also hidden our ontological (self) understanding.[53] To recognize and uncover the structure of temporality, then, requires more than an investigation of a conceptual development. It is the history of Western thought itself – its unquestioned conceptuality and not just a concept within it – that is in need of *Destruktion*.

To reach this conclusion regarding tradition and temporality, however, requires a long analysis, and it is this analysis that forms the third, innermost point of focus, and the actual substance of *Being and Time*. This perspective no longer sets its sights upon factical life as the general enactment-structure of human existence, or as the historical concept of this structure's movement, but upon Dasein as the "being which we ourselves are and which has questioning as one of its possibilities of Being."[54] While maintaining many themes from the Natorp-report,

Heidegger nevertheless moves from a concept (factical life) in need of present "hermeneutics" to the so-called fundamental ontology of a concrete being (Dasein) whose everyday activity will disclose and clarify the meaning or temporality of Being. It is as if the identification of method and object previously formulated in 1922 were now simply pushed deeper to the level of Being. Since Dasein, in its Being, already bears itself concernfully and understandingly toward its own Being, to raise the question of Being is precisely to radicalize Dasein's own Being.[55]

It is through the detailed investigation of the everyday, average activity of Dasein that Heidegger wishes to discover not only the temporal meaning of Being, but the reasons for the inevitable forgetting of the question of Being, and the possibility of this question's retrieval. I argue that this possibility, which as we have seen constitutes the broadest aim of the work, lies latent in Dasein's historicity: the condition of its capacity to "have" a history to begin with, and of its ability to authentically appropriate its past (to "choose its own fate"). Accordingly, I will turn to §74 in the second-to-last chapter of *Being and Time* to see how Heidegger analyzes this historicity.

First, however, some background is necessary. Prior to this chapter, Heidegger has already established that Dasein has temporality at the root of its everydayness; temporality is the meaning of the Being of Dasein.[56] That is to say, the whole of Dasein, contrary to past substantializations of subjectivity, has been determined as an ecstatical temporal movement with an incomplete character that is nevertheless complete in that it is "*ineluctably* becoming."[57] The incompleteness stems, first, from our facticity or constant prior determination of who we are (on both our part and others'). Secondly, it arises from the fact that our possibilities are always limited, circumscribed by the situation we are in. Finally, and most definitively, it is rooted in the continual awareness of mortality. It is only on the basis of temporality that we are exposed and present to the world, be it in the inauthentic variant of everyday absorption in things or in the authentic (*eigentlich*) variant of anticipatory resoluteness.[58] The latter is the capacity to accept one's limited conditions, and amounts to the ability on Dasein's part both to choose its actions as its own (*eigen*) and to gain a constancy for its Being.

This being-a-whole of Dasein is thus to be viewed as a connected "occurrence" (*Geschehen*) that "*stretches along between* birth and death," rather than as a substantive entity or focal point in the present that runs along time in a distinct sequence of nows.[59] Heidegger notes the need to examine the historical structure of this occurrence in more detail, for as the ground of all historical meaning, it represents the true "*locus* of the problem of history" over against such secondary phenomena as historiography or its historical objects.[60] The key issues to resolve in §74, then, are how historicity is grounded in the more general structure of temporality, and how historicity factors into historical Dasein's constitution (or authentic life). These could be rephrased, respectively, as the questions of historicity's ontological structure and that of its ontical task, or the ability to "choose one's fate" and the *actual* resolute decision of doing so.[61] ✳

Regarding the first issue, Heidegger underscores that anticipatory resoluteness does not merely guide Dasein's existence in a futural direction (as a being-toward-death), but that it turns Dasein back upon its situation, upon its factical thrownness. Put differently, Dasein's futural self-understanding in terms of its own possibilities (resolute being-toward-death) entails at the same time a return to its own fact *that* it exists, for it is from this facticity that Dasein's possibilities arise to begin with. These aspects are combined in Heidegger's description of Dasein as a "*thrown projection*" (geworfener Entwurf).[62] Through this broad description of temporality, then, we arrive at the central role of "having-been" (*Gewesenheit*) in historicity, for while mortality might disclose one's ownmost and inevitable possibility, the factical (present) possibilities one chooses in resoluteness "are not to be gathered from death" but stem from the "alreadiness" of one's thrown situation.[63]

If "having-been" or "alreadiness" is the ontological condition that "makes possible our existentiel [factical] histories, both individual and social,"[64] then the source of the concrete possibilities of existence lies in the world into which one is thrown. Heidegger calls these possibilities one's "heritage" (*Erbe*), noting that it is both something received and something to be taken over.[65] This heritage is the always-already configured realm of disclosure that shapes and limits Dasein's possibilities. Heidegger considers these limited options under the labels of individual "fate" (*Schicksal*) or of collective "destiny" (*Geschick*), in order to emphasize the ineluctable character of being thrown into them. Yet this emphasis also risks misconstruing Dasein's relation to its heritage. It is not as if fate and destiny exist apart from Dasein as a mere medium in which it passively resides; one of the crucial culminating insights of *Being and Time* is rather that we *are* our fate and destiny, and have the option of *being* them in various ways.[66] The whole development of the book has in fact prepared the distinction between authenticity and inauthenticity for this purpose, making clear that it is up to us how we take up our ontological structure, how adequately we fulfill the task of being what we are. We thus turn to the second main issue of §74.

Following the distinction of falling and authenticity, Heidegger notes Dasein's capacity to take over its heritage either inexplicitly or explicitly, unconsciously or consciously. The course of explicit inheritance involves several interrelated aspects. First, it entails a resolute acceptance not only of one's mortality but of one's finite place in time, meaning that one inhabits the present in such a way that it becomes a "situation" or open space of possibilities. It means to regard one's present not as strictly determined by the heritage, but as open to being chosen authentically. To thus "be" one's fate entails having "a clear vision for the accidents of the situation," and to thereby sort out what is actually open for choice beyond these contingencies.[67]

This discernment of what is open for authentic choice introduces and makes possible a second aspect, which is the "freeing-up" (*Überlieferung*) of the heritage for one's own lived possibilities. In more conventional translations of the term (it would commonly be rendered merely as "tradition"), one could say that it is a "handing-down" or "taking-over" of the heritage, and there is indeed a necessary continuity between the heritage and one's choice; however, these renderings risk characterizing the heritage as something that is adopted uncritically or wholesale, and thus miss the fundamentally liberating aspect of authentic historicity, for the crucial element is precisely Dasein's resolute decision to choose at all.[68] It is, as Heidegger puts it, an exercise of "finite freedom."[69]

This freedom is further borne out in a third aspect, namely the transformative appropriation that Heidegger, in silent homage to Kierkegaard, calls "repetition" (*Wiederholung*).[70] It is here that Dasein "explicitly exists as fate"[71] and becomes its history, for it gathers its possibilities precisely as having been already given, and delivers them over to itself as a ground for resolute decision. As much as it is an explicit decision, however, repetition does not amount to a selective cognitive process; it does not require any actual knowledge of the origin of Dasein's possibilities, and is thus not an archaeological step. Heidegger therefore considers it a retrieval not because anything is actually brought back from the past into the present, nor because one crosses over to the past from the present, but because Dasein must respond "to a given possibility of already-open existence."[72] In further allusion to Kierkegaard, Heidegger insists that this response always occurs in a present "moment of insight," underscoring that repetition does not have a *telos* outside itself: It "neither abandons itself to what is past nor aims at some sort of progress."[73] It is, in its momentary choice, both free *from* these concerns and free *for* its own chosen possibilities. The freedom of retrieval is thus "an enactment of meaning that disrupts continuity."[74]

A question arises here as to what shape this repetition is to take over a human lifetime. On the one hand, it would seem coherent with Heidegger's position to conclude that authentic Dasein must make these momentary decisions as continually as possible, so as to limit the risk of ever taking anything over blindly. This would then be the meaning of resoluteness (*Entschlossenheit*).[75] On the other hand, while certainly espousing a protreptic approach here and in later works, Heidegger rarely describes or instructs about such moment-by-moment detail of authentic existence. This stems, on the one hand, from the difficulty of providing such instruction; after all, given Heidegger's distinction of the existential and existentiel, no such prior knowledge is possible, as the problems of existence only get worked out through existing. On the other hand, it might also remain unaddressed because of the many contextual particulars that would need to be clarified.

Until now, after all, we have only considered Dasein's historical freedom in its fate and individuality. Yet Heidegger has also indicated that authentic Dasein, in being its collective "destiny," is social or communal. Here, then, we should find the account as to how the individual life of momentary free decisions sustains itself as part of a larger whole. However, Heidegger's indication is notoriously difficult to follow, both since he does not spell out its content here (or ever) in much detail, and because, prefiguring on some level his later involvement in National Socialism, it is intertwined with political issues far beyond the scope of my analyses here. Nevertheless, given the theme of social existence that I wish to develop in this chapter and in the present work as a whole, it is worth inspecting what Heidegger has in mind with "destiny."

It may initially appear that authentic Dasein would stand in conflict with any collective existence, both based on Heidegger's descriptions of publicness and the "they" (*das Man*), and because anticipatory resoluteness depends so crucially on Dasein's facing up to its ownmost personal mortality. However, this apparent conflict relies on a conception of collectivity and its destiny as an amalgamation of individual fates, a conception that Heidegger explicitly rejects.[76] Instead, he asserts that Dasein is equiprimordially a being-with (*Mitsein*), such that the involvement with this dimension of life cannot take away from Dasein's individuality, but rather constitutes a broader region of Dasein's own existence.[77]

In terms of history and destiny, this region is that of a people or *Volk*, and it directs fate by shaping the space of possibility of heritage. This influence, according to Heidegger, occurs through two basic events: communication (*Mitteilung*) and struggle (*Kampf*). The former is the articulation of the existential possibilities contained in the given present situation, while the latter denotes the tensions involved in interpreting this situation according to its (hidden) possibilities. The authentic "occurrence" of Dasein, then, amounts to both a resolute personal choice *and* a choice that aligns with one's "generation."[78]

While it is extremely difficult to comprehend how Heidegger conceives of social life and the interaction between fate and destiny,[79] it is even more difficult to conclude that Heidegger favors any sort of radical individualism in *Being and Time*. In a much later lecture course of 1951–52, he in fact criticizes the narrow individual conception of freedom in Western modernity:

> The whole West no longer possesses those instincts out of which institutions grow, out of which a future grows: nothing else, perhaps, goes so much against the grain of its "modern spirit." Men live for the day, men live very fast – men live

very irresponsibly: precisely this is called "freedom." The thing that makes an institution an institution is despised, hated, rejected: men fear they are in danger of a new slavery the moment the word "authority" is even mentioned.[80]

I will have occasion to return to the matter of freedom and authority in more detail below when relating Heidegger to Gadamer. For now, it suffices to see that Heidegger's elaboration of the structure of historicity and the task of enacting it point to two crucial conclusions: first, that authentic history can no longer be conceived in terms of a past or "pastness" that binds and determines the present; and second, that freedom in relation to history does nevertheless not entail a new beginning or expulsion of one's heritage. Instead, only those who dwell in the finite freedom of situated retrieval – finding the "moment" to perceive and interpret anew – are capable of resolutely choosing and thus authentically enacting history. This authenticity of existence, individual and collective, becomes the measure of the adequate appropriation of history.

The significance of these conclusions, and the reason for our detour into §74, should be clearer now. On the one hand, these conclusions help justify Heidegger's stance in the work as a whole. From a methodological perspective, the entire possibility of *Destruktion*, of "leaping into the circle" of present understanding in order to further explicate Being and potentially retrieve its questionability, turns out to be grounded in Dasein's ability to free up its tradition and authentically grasp its having-been. The freeing-up of heritage indeed resembles quite clearly the "liquidation" and "loosening" of the tradition that Heidegger has sought since his earliest essays. The need for articulation and the struggle of freeing up an adequate interpretation of the situation that Heidegger elaborates in his analysis of Dasein, therefore, is itself a parallel to his own approach to the tradition, to his attempt to speak with and to his generation, and to his desire to wrest free the question of Being from its forgottenness.

On the other hand, and on the basis of this reflexive-performative significance, the analysis of Dasein, beyond its methodological significance, also serves to advance the actual freeing-up of the question of Being, and thus plays a crucial role in Heidegger's broader philosophical development. After all, the involvement with tradition that he has described in §74 is not limited to historical or theoretical projects, but belongs to the Being of human beings. If Being remains forgotten or unquestioned, however, then our historical nature remains unfulfilled, our freedom stifled. The issue of freedom, therefore, is not confined to the ontical realm or to regional ontologies, but informs the possibility of retrieving the question of Being itself in all of its ontological profundity.[81] Repetition is thus the name not for a strictly philosophical task, but for the task of authentic existence that everyone faces.

The Dasein-analysis culminates in the conclusion that, since Dasein's Being (which is occurrence) is rooted in temporality, and the understanding of Being thus also occurs temporally, then the horizon for the meaning of Being is time. As noted above, given the radicality of this conclusion, its elaboration necessitates a repetition and reconception of Western ontology on an entirely new basis, which amounts to a retrieval of an "unthought" possibility buried within the tradition.[82] It was this effort that was to constitute the unpublished remainder of *Being and Time*, with a third division of Part One that would work through the history of ontology, and an entire Part Two that would conceive of Being within the horizon of time. Yet Heidegger struggled with his attempt to formulate these ambitious sections, not for merely terminological reasons, but because he lacked the language, the "grammar of Being," that would adequately describe the inner possibility of the tradition without making this dimension out to be a grounding ideal structure, another temporal being, or a mere alternate historical option, a path not factually taken in history.[83]

The difficulty in finding the proper language is that "Temporality [*Temporalität*] 'is' not an *entity* at all. It is not, but it temporalizes [*zeitigt*] itself."[84] Thus, Heidegger needs to find a way to describe the fact, givenness, or occurrence of temporality without objectifying it and thereby either turning it into a being, a subjective or objective process, or an ultimate causal ground for Being or beings. The transcendental terminology and Dasein-centeredness of *Being and Time*, according to Heidegger, remains too close to this metaphysical danger. He now wants to investigate, "along a more historical path,"[85] the "primordial 'fact'" (*Urfaktum*) of temporality, and how this fact might have its own "primordial history" (*Urgeschichte*).[86] This involves inquiring how this primordial history (equatable perhaps to *Being and Time*'s "Temporality") is the "most originary temporalizing of temporality,"[87] or put differently, how time "swings itself [...] into Being [*erschwingt ... sich selbst*]."[88] The (question of the) formulation of the temporalizing of temporality thus includes a nascent demand that we conceive of the question of the meaning of Being differently, which also entails that we reconsider the role that Dasein bears in the posing of the question and, indeed, in its forgetting. Heidegger's revision of his ontology therefore requires a virtual *Destruktion* of *Being and Time* itself, almost as if it were an already-sedimented text of the tradition.

Beyond Dasein: Seinsgeschichte and Ereignis

This line of inquiry already begins for Heidegger as soon as *Being and Time* is published, and continues in some form or another for the remainder of his career. Perhaps the most condensed and thorough version of this development takes place in Heidegger's second major work next to *Being and Time*, the *Contributions to Philosophy*.[89] The latter, written in 1936–38 but never published in Heidegger's lifetime, is a central text in the period of what he called his "turn" or *Kehre*, which amounts to a kind of switchback in his thought.[90] Just as, when ascending a steep slope, one doubles back in order to proceed, so Heidegger now "doubles" the question of the meaning of Being, for it is not just Being in its temporality that has become (or always remains) questionable, but the very eventful character of this temporality. Thus, while the prior developments – both in Heidegger's thought and in the history of philosophy in general – remain important steps in philosophy (they constitute the "guiding question" of Being), it is not sufficient to merely state that Being is understood by reference to time, and is done so historically by entities that we ourselves are. Indeed, the ongoing nature of such understanding, the very persistence of the tradition in the form of the guiding question (a persistence that Heidegger now calls the "history of Being" (*Seinsgeschichte*), turns out to be what spurs Heidegger into his doubling of the question. The ongoing nature of this history of Being itself – including the history of philosophy "within" it and the obliviousness concerning its grounding – needs to become thematic and questionable in order for a transition to occur from the "first beginning" of the guiding question to "another beginning." This other beginning is to inquire into what allows for both historical understanding and the forgottenness of Being to begin with, thereby asking the more fundamental question as to the occurrence or "holding-sway" (*Wesung*) of the history of Being.[91]

In an attempt to navigate out of metaphysical language, Heidegger now archaically labels the ground of the history of Being as "Beyng" (*Seyn*) in order to highlight an originary dimension that is both "beneath" historical occurrence and distinct from Being as understood by the Western tradition. The thought that investigates this Beyng is accordingly called beyng-historical (*seynsgeschichtlich*), and bears its own peculiar traits.[92] In a shift from Heidegger's prior engagement with history, this stance does not aim at dismantling the tradition for the sake of uncovering something else in history, be it an origin of experiential or conceptual character. Put differently, it seeks to grasp not the historical transition from one conception of Being to another, but the unity of both of these – the jointure (*Fügung*) of the history of Being – in a greater event. In brief, the aim is now to see the past, along with the present, as belonging to Beyng.

This all-enveloping, seemingly transsubjective dimension does not entail leaving human agency behind, however. Despite common misreadings to this effect, it is not as if history is now simply conceived as issuing from a higher power or a metaphysical source. Indeed, Heidegger takes seriously the nihilistic challenge that Nietzsche poses to the tradition: the task to engage in a "serious struggle with that 'event' [*Ereignis*]: 'God is dead.'"[93] Beyng is thus not an actual ground of history in terms of an origin, but neither is it just the absence of a source. It is not an event in time, but neither is it an ideal, atemporal entity. Most of all, it cannot be a uniform, undifferentiated event. From what we already know of temporality from *Being and Time,* its occurrence involves all particularity in its momentary detail. Heidegger's attempt to think Beyng is therefore not concerned with a mere erasure of such metaphysical terms as "presence" and "cause," nor with establishing a past or future *telos*. Stating that the *Contributions* are "neither a theory of history nor a philosophy of history,"[94] Heidegger focuses instead on describing the "attunements" that might bring about and make up this beyng-historical form of thinking.[95]

Heidegger's text, of course, aims at far more than mere description. Intensifying such questions as those that open *Being and Time,* his philosophy has shifted quite drastically from being grounded in hermeneutic and phenomenological endeavors, to the point of taking on a decidedly protreptic style and occasionally polemical tone. The aim of Heidegger's *Kehre* is more than conceptual revision; while it certainly is focused on concepts and their history, it ultimately seeks to show that an adequate conceptualization of Being requires that we also transform ourselves. However, just as *Being and Time* remains on a descriptively general level, the *Contributions* do not spell out the exact steps of this transformation or displacement (*Verrückung*).[96] After all, philosophy for Heidegger can only indicate and never directly effect change, and accordingly the fundamental attunement of the "other beginning" is "intimation" (*Ahnung*). Heidegger nevertheless provides a glimpse of what he now takes the role of the present historical subject to be.

Beyng-historical thinking is conceived as a reticent stance that deals with Beyng as an "appropriative event" (*Er-eignis*). In recognizing its belonging to this event, thought "occurs in the enactment of its own passage."[97] While this perhaps carries the connotation of a reflective position, it is actually the circulating movement of a double genitive: both a thinking "of" the event as if of an object (and thus still remaining to some degree historical), as well as a thinking "from" the event as if it were brought about by the latter (and thereby relinquishing all historical determinations).[98] Such thinking therefore bears the paradoxical task of dwelling so intimately with the event that prior historical determinations – unified here under the concept of the "history of Being" – lose their force, yet nevertheless seeking this belonging-to-the-event as a current historical position. It is a way of loosening, and ultimately of freeing, the conditions of understanding history from the broader historical process itself.

One of the key lectures of Heidegger's later career elaborates on these problematics, and extends his critique of a concept of temporal continuity that would rest solely on intrahistorical development. In "Time and Being," delivered in 1962, he takes yet another major step in revising his ontological focus from *Being and Time,* redefining the history of Being from that of a univocal forgetting of Being to an array of different ways that Being has been conceived in the Western tradition. This "abundance of transformations"[99] of the notion of presence, he now concludes, does not entail that Being has one meaning that was covered over at a certain point in time, nor that it is one concept with a linear timeline of mutually exclusive perspectives on it. Such univocity of the history of Being would prevent any discourse from assessing the actual questionability of ontology and from discovering unthought possibilities in history. Instead, then, based on the minimal phenomenological observation that "there is Being and there is time [*es gibt Sein und es gibt Zeit*]"[100] – a linguistic attempt in German to avoid both a definite grammatical subject as well as the use of the verb "to be" – Heidegger speaks of Being having been "given" or "sent" in different ways, and notes that these ways overlap, affect, and obscure each other in history.[101] This heterogeneity is intended to guard against an ontologization of history and to secure the stance that Heidegger had long been seeking, namely a position by which to speak of, and ideally free up and access, past possibilities in the present.

Heidegger believes to have captured this heterogeneity by treating history in terms of "epochs," though not in the usual sense of the term. Since the history of Being (*Seinsgeschichte*) is here conceived as a history of sending (*Schickung*), Heidegger also speaks of a "destiny of Being" (*Seins-Geschick*) in the sense that it is the sending itself that determines ("destines") the various historical conceptions of Being, instead of the latter stemming from any individual and contingent historical occurrences. The character of each sending, as a whole, includes both what manifests itself in history and what remains unmanifest, namely the process and origin of sending itself. Since, with each different manifestation of Being, there is accordingly also a distinct form of "holding-back" (Gk.: *epochê*) in each case, each concealed sending constitutes an "epoch" in the destiny of Being.[102]

As they are not themselves temporal divisions, these epochs are also not traceable to necessary causes. However, neither is the source of the sending of Being simply accidental or haphazard. Rather, the epochs of the history of Being evince a "belonging-together" (*Zusammengehören*) that can still be uncovered through a process of *Destruktion* – though this is no longer the same procedure as Heidegger had pursued in *Being and Time*.[103] It is, however, still conceived phenomenologically, attending now to the manifestation and withdrawal of the meanings of Being.

The new result is that Heidegger uncovers a unity beneath all sendings of Being: the unity of presencing (*Anwesen*) that allows for the past, the now, and the future all to be present in their own way.[104]

This unity can certainly not be characterized as temporal in the sense of "in time," for it does not arise or disappear within time. Yet it is also not atemporal, in the sense of existing eternally in the same way. Thus, it would be "inadmissible to say that future, past, and present are before us 'at the same time,'" as if presencing were an ideal object.[105] Heidegger therefore construes the unity of presencing as an opening-up (or clearing) (*lichten*) of "time-space," underscoring that time is not a product, and that we as humans are also not products of time.[106] In a further step toward explaining this opening (*Lichtung*) and our place in it, Heidegger defines it as the delivering-over (*übereignen*) of Being and time to each other, employing with even greater force the concept of the appropriative event (*Ereignis*) that he had developed earlier.

With the appropriative event as that to which all Being and time belong, it is also the ultimate yet abyssal ground to which we as humans belong – or, as Heidegger also puts it, are "assimilated" (*vereignet*).[107] For this reason, we can never step out of its occurrence and treat it as something over against us. Yet this circumstance poses a dire challenge to any philosophy that seeks to think about or describe it. In fact, such an account cannot rest satisfied with a propositional description. The language by which one speaks of the event would need to adapt to its withdrawing manifestation, and somehow think and speak from within the appropriation itself.[108]

Even if Heidegger never took himself to have achieved this stance, he nevertheless conceived of its possibility, and combined with what he already stated in "Time and Being," this possibility lends some definition to what would constitute a philosophically adequate interaction with history – that is, the fulfillment of our task as historical beings. In a seminar following the "Time and Being" lecture, he conceives of "thinking *in* the event" as a potential end to the history of Being: "Thinking then stands in and before that which has sent the various forms of epochal Being. [. . .] Metaphysics is the history of the formations of Being, that is – viewed from the appropriative event – of the history of the self-withdrawal of what is sending in favor of the destinies given in sending [....] The entry of thinking into the appropriative event is thus equivalent to the end of this withdrawal's history."[109] In belonging to the appropriative event, the thinking that Heidegger describes here takes on a phenomenological rather than ontologically dismantling stance. In its uniquely rarefied view of history, it permits and adheres to the diversity of phenomena, allowing them to appear from out of a fundamental withdrawal. Rather than treating epochs as historically determined, it treats them as "matters of thinking" (*Sachen des Denkens*) whose meaning bears upon thought regardless of historical situation.

Despite superficial appearances, however, this seemingly extrahistorical stance is in fact nothing like the Neo-Kantian survey of problematics that we encountered in the previous chapter. Far from seeking objective distance from history, the thinker "of" the event (recalling the crucial double genitive from the *Contributions*) acknowledges her continual belonging to time, yet recognizes this character of all other historical entities and positions as well. This recognition puts an "end" to metaphysics and the history of Being only to the extent that it precludes any definitive closure of the question of Being.[110] While perhaps "later" in a vulgar sense of time, its interpretation of history is not a subsequent application of something already extant and waiting to be grasped; rather, thinking in the clearing of the event first discloses what is there to be grasped at all. It takes a momentary leap or new beginning on our part to achieve this thinking; it has to reach the very questionability of Being, remain there, leave undecided the meaning of the matters of thinking, and thereby necessitate a continual return to these matters.

This stance "in" the event, which Heidegger distinguishes from philosophical inquiry and – here we again glimpse the broader protreptic impulse – labels the "task for thinking[,] is that of freeing itself and keeping itself free for what is to be thought in order to receive its determination from that."[111] It is conceived as a freedom both *for* the phenomena that show themselves in and as history and *from* the philosophically laden modes of perception that plague even such phenomenologists as Hegel and Husserl.[112] Heidegger thus intends to stave off the temptation to speak of historical progress or of human self-overcoming, as if either of these processes had a determinate *telos* and were even conceivable from within time. For Heidegger, the inherent finitude of human historicity prevents any talk of such absolutes, and therefore also eliminates the idea of condemning the history of Being as a decline or deviation. Thought cannot stand outside of history and judge it, and the recognition of the sent character of history does not imply such a stance; rather, this recognition stands at the cusp of prior history and reveals the as-yet unthought space of the clearing.

The finite freedom that thought is to inhabit – and that in its phenomenological stance has revealed itself as the root of disclosure[113] – can at the same time be equated with the open clearing of the event itself. However, as this openness is not a static container for history, but a continual source, so any thought that engages this openness should come to realize that our destiny "has not yet been decided."[114] The task that Heidegger outlines for thinking is therefore not just a shift in philosophical perspective *upon* history, but a transformed way of belonging *to* history.

One might say that, despite his conceptual shifts, Heidegger was after an elucidation and invocation of this transformed belonging over the course of his entire career. Though not usually phrased as such, one of his ongoing concerns is that of defining the freedom of thought within history, whether this takes the form of a responsible retrieval of tradition, an authentic choice of one's fate, or the leap beyond the history of Being with the attendant reticence of dwelling in the event. Throughout these conceptions, there is a strong sense that the transformed belonging remains an individual's task rather than a collective endeavor. Heidegger appears to underscore this when, in the seminar on "Time and Being," he denies his ability to mediate or bring about *Ereignis*-thinking, and states that his aim in the lecture was instead to merely prepare listeners "for their own experience" of the appropriative event.[115]

Yet apart from such seeming relinquishment of collective agency, Heidegger nevertheless frequently speaks of the transformative task in the first person plural. He speaks of our need to transform our relation to language, of our potential escape from technologized existence, and of changing the way we live among everyday things. Though frequently read in light of Heidegger's own failed political activity and his nostalgia for *Heimat*, these urgings on his part stand independent of any specific political identity or agenda, making it very difficult to ascertain their intended effect.[116] Rather than contradicting the individual focus we highlighted above, however, these calls to collective agency seem to presuppose – and indeed require – the more personal struggle of an initial freeing up of tradition. This can also be conceived as a temporary estrangement from history. It is only on the basis of this leaping and dismantling departure, Heidegger believes, that one can return and belong more rootedly to history.

GADAMER AT THE END OF PHILOSOPHY

As we already saw in chapter 1, Gadamer too conceives of our relation to tradition as one of belonging. Yet despite Heidegger's influence on Gadamer, this conception of belonging cannot be considered a mere appropriation of Heidegger's notion. For one, Gadamer directly studied under Heidegger only as the latter was beginning to formulate the hermeneutics of ontology and *Destruktion,* and even here developed his own interpretation of Heidegger's ideas. One thus cannot speak of an inheritance even of the same problematic. Secondly, while Gadamer certainly followed closely the development of his teacher's thought, and incorporated many of Heidegger's insights into his own work, his incorporation bears the complexity appropriate to such a relation. On the one hand, Gadamer's hermeneutics – in what is often problematically labeled a stunting, moderation, or "urbanization" of Heidegger's position[117] – certainly entail a deviation from Heidegger's longstanding focus on Being. On the other hand, Gadamer is equally concerned to draw out and bolster ontological and social aspects of historical understanding that remain disappointingly underdeveloped in Heidegger. One might say that Gadamer achieves a Heideggerian repetition of tradition that Heidegger himself, focused intently on the singular question of Being, did not pursue.

It is extremely difficult to interpret this failure or decision on Heidegger's part, and a full analysis is beyond the scope of this investigation. Here, I only wish to show that, while Gadamer's approach to tradition might align with Heidegger's in its broadest assertions of finitude, there are considerable differences in how Gadamer conceives of historical situatedness and the ongoing task of historical understanding. In the remainder of this chapter, after presenting some of the commonalities, I will therefore investigate how differences in conceptuality, tonality, and performativity inform Gadamer's distance from Heidegger. I will also note why this distance demands a turn to Hegel on Gadamer's part, a theme that will form the subject matter of the subsequent chapter.

Phronetic Historicity

Gadamer and Heidegger share a common rooting in Aristotelian concepts, particularly those of the *Nicomachean Ethics*. Gadamer's first encounter with Heidegger, in fact, took place in a 1923 Freiburg seminar on Book 6 of the *Ethics*, through which Gadamer came to recognize the importance of *phronêsis*.[118] While differences soon arise as to how each thinker interprets this importance, there can be little doubt as to its centrality in both *Being and Time* as well as *Truth and Method*. For the early Heidegger *phronêsis*, as a practical form of knowing, accounts for the true movements of factical life, movements that remain hidden to *sophia* or *epistêmê*. It therefore plays a central role from the hermeneutics of facticity onward into his fundamental ontology. The description of Dasein's circumspective concern (*Umsicht*), for instance, is a tacit account of the perception involved in *phronêsis*. For Gadamer, as already noted in the previous chapter, Aristotle's concept of practical knowing amounts to "the fundamental form of experience," the true locus of human finitude.[119] This is because, as situationally determined and characterized by application, it envelops cognitive as well as affective and practical dimensions.

   Heidegger's "Indication of the Hermeneutical Situation" helped Gadamer in recognizing this universal character of *phronêsis*. By sheer coincidence, Gadamer was able to read the Natorp-report at the time it was submitted to the Marburg faculty, and Gadamer recalls the text striking him "like an electric shock."[120] Heidegger's stated aim in that text, to make everyday human existence transparent to itself, to philosophically grasp one's possibilities despite being conditioned and finite, was a welcome reprieve to Gadamer from the abstraction and distance of Neo-Kantian debates on epistemology.[121] Since Heidegger – here and in his subsequent development of a hermeneutics of facticity – first draws attention to the fact that we are typically blind to our own activity, and since this insight aligns with the importance of reflection upon historical effect that we saw in chapter 1, Gadamer rightly sees in this text the seeds and strains of his own hermeneutics.

Gadamer's years in Marburg in general confirmed for him the importance of history and historicity. Heidegger's *Destruktion*-approach, after all, sought a thorough investigation of how and what we take over from tradition, and this provided Gadamer a strong ally in his eventual fight against detached historical methods that seek theoretical stability, as well as against historicist positions of incommensurability. With Heidegger's emphasis on facticity and enactment, one could include all human activity in the investigation of meaning, including art, play, and religion. Taking enactment to heart as a constitutive basis of meaning, the approach of *Destruktion*, furthermore, entailed treating the past not as mere historical sediment, but as an ongoing potential source of contribution to the present. Philosophy thus becomes characterized as a repetition of questioning and questionability, amounting to a constant self-interrogation of life. The interpretations borne out by philosophy are thus not subsequent practical applications of something that is first grasped separately and theoretically, but an incipient disclosure of what is graspable (and practically livable) at all. This reflexive conception of philosophical activity – which embodies and intensifies the role of *phronêsis* – greatly influences Gadamer's later elaboration of application as central to the consciousness of historical effect.[122]

Having had this early and thorough exposure to Heidegger's ideas, Gadamer was able to comprehend why "Heidegger's project of fundamental ontology had to place the problem of history in the foreground."[123] Heidegger, after all, not only sought distance from prior epistemological and methical paradigms, from historicist conceptions of time and subjectivity; rather than presenting an alternate stance within modern presuppositions, Heidegger was revising the very framework within which modernity and its concepts could be taken to arise in the first place. He subverts the notion of a fixed grounding of meaning in selfhood, emphasizing instead the temporal occurrence of meaning, the character of Being as time.

In undertaking this ontological rather than epistemological description of truth and subjectivity, Heidegger takes himself to have to uncovered an aspect of existence that had been forgotten throughout the Western tradition, namely understanding, "the original form of the realization of Dasein."[124] In the fundamental and pervasive enactment of understanding, Heidegger has identified something characteristic of life itself, not a mere process beneath our idealities or a methodical structure of our theoretical knowledge. In contrast to theoretical historicism, which takes understanding to be the methodically secured perspective from which we view and grasp life, Heidegger now shows that life *is* understanding, and that it is fluid in its temporality.

This identity and fluidity have the effect of joining understanding to its source: In its historicity, knowledge arises out of the fore-structure of understanding (its "having-been"), such that the knowing and the known belong together. However, this jointure of belonging does not imply a sameness of the two as if they were identical objects. Both Dasein and its world are historical, are thus not objects at all, and can therefore not be equated as one would objects.[125] What is more, while sharing the same historicity, Dasein can never encompass or subsume its world. "Belonging" is thus another term for the fundamental historical finitude of Dasein; as Heidegger puts it, we are *thrown* projection, and far from being a barrier to historical knowledge, this mode of existence is our very means of access to it.

These insights have such a profound effect on Gadamer that he later undertakes an investigation of their significance beyond the purview of Heidegger's thought. Indeed, *Truth and Method* is largely dedicated to the task of drawing out the consequences of Heidegger's insights for the human sciences – which entails investigating how the historicity of understanding actually plays out concretely. In the course of this investigation, Gadamer aims to assess "whether Heidegger's ontological radicalization can contribute to the construction of a historical hermeneutics."[126] Gadamer affirms this possibility, citing the transcendental-ontological interpretation of understanding that Heidegger has outlined in *Being and Time*. This interpretation allows for a properly universal conception of hermeneutics, which can then be "concretized in historical understanding" where tradition has its effect.[127] Another way of phrasing this is that historicity, in its phronetic character, can be raised to the position of a universal hermeneutic principle.

In taking over Heidegger's premises concerning understanding, finitude, and enactment, and seeking to concretize these concepts in the human sciences, Gadamer tasks his own hermeneutics with demonstrating the belonging of the interpreter to his or her object. He does this with such culturally rich examples as art, history, and language, but also demonstrates it performatively through his own works. While remaining in close conceptual proximity to Heidegger, Gadamer's aim and execution could thus nevertheless be viewed as a departure from his teacher's position, inasmuch as the latter never sought any "particular historical ideal of existence," and Gadamer conversely wishes to speak of precisely such particular content in his account of belonging, and to rehabilitate historical authority.[128] Toward this end, moreover, Gadamer is comfortable retrieving concepts from the tradition that Heidegger insistently eschews as metaphysical. As it turns out, however, Gadamer locates the possibility and medium of this retrieval partly in Heidegger's own concepts.

Gadamer underscores that it is not just Heidegger's early thought that influences his hermeneutics, but instead that Heidegger's progression into the *Kehre*, as well as what comes after, greatly affected Gadamer's own development of the concept of the consciousness of historical effect: "That which then led Heidegger, in his thinking, to the *Kehre*, I for my part attempted to describe as a liminal experience of our self-understanding, as the consciousness of historical effect that is more Being [*Sein*] than consciousess [*Bewusstsein*]."[129] The connection lies in the fact that in both accounts of historicity, it is deemed impossible for subjectivity to comprehend exhaustively the basis of its own thinking.[130] It is a matter of incorporating a more pervasive finitude than that expressed in *Being and Time*.

Through the great switchback of the *Kehre*, Heidegger comes to temper both his own transcendental ambitions and his conception of what kind of retrieval is possible on Dasein's part. He comes a long way from his early goal of making-transparent (*Durchsichtigmachen*), recognizing "that an ultimate opacity makes up the actual essence of history and of human destiny."[131] This opacity is that of the appropriative event, which in its abyssal character cannot be traced to any permanent or metaphysically stable origin. In a certain sense, this aspect of finitude had already played a central part in Heidegger's thought from the outset. The challenge then, as we saw, was to find the proper attitude and vantage point from which to describe it. Yet finitude now comes to infuse and infect the very possibility of speaking philosophically about it, for language itself bears the marks of the tradition's quest for fixity and transparency. The event, to recall, is neither temporal nor atemporal – it exceeds our available categories. The phenomenon, as it were, retreats as one tries to describe it.[132] Rather than simply treating finitude as a phenomenon to describe and account for, then, Heidegger locates finitude in language itself.

This localization represents a common stance for Heidegger and Gadamer, as they both emphasize the linguistic situatedness of all understanding. Language is where, for Heidegger, "Being and not-being open themselves," where everything receives its meaningful determination for us.[133] For Gadamer, similarly, language is the middle that all human discourse traverses, and is indeed the center that first unites us and makes any dialogue possible. Yet because of this primordial position, as a projection of sorts that has always already occurred, language is also extremely difficult to articulate – impossible to merely point to, as one can never step out of it – and each thinker develops his own way of dealing with this problem.[134]

As we have seen, Heidegger attributes our envelopment in a certain kind of language to the sustained historical sway of the forgetting of Being (*Seinsvergessenheit*), "the unacknowledged failure of philosophy's attempt to render Being intelligible by analyzing entities from within and through what he calls the 'language of metaphysics.'"[135] To acknowledge our failure and obliviousness would be the first, preparatory step out of this forgetfulness, but Heidegger's critical aim is set higher than mere awareness. There remains, as always, a transformative element in his thought. He famously turns to the poets, and especially Hölderlin, in search of a different language and approach that would, if not entirely eschew the metaphysical baggage of Western philosophical concepts, at least "remain sensitive not only to Being as it manifests itself but to Being's withdrawal, that is, to its radical finitude."[136] He comes to find, enacted in poetry, an originary relation to language that is attuned to the *Ereignis* and that seems to promise another beginning for thought.[137] It would be a beginning that, through a leaping *Verwindung* with tradition, has freed itself of metaphysical structures and returned to the eventful – that is, always ongoing – source of language.

The Ethical Turn

It is in this leap and its necessitating beyng-historical context that Gadamer ceases to follow Heidegger's lead. While Gadamer's concern for an adequate account of language aligns with his teacher's, and even though he shares Heidegger's astonishment at the eventful exemplarity of the poetic word, he takes issue with the way in which Heidegger characterizes our relation to the conditional structures of linguisticality and historicity.[138] It is not that Gadamer wishes to diminish the power with which Heidegger felt his "dire need about language" (*Sprachnot*),[139] nor that he seeks to temper a position that he takes to be too radical on Heidegger's part, but rather that, within the structures of language and history, one can shift one's emphasis in various directions, and Gadamer

seeks to uphold this plurivocity.[140] At the core of language and history lie the tasks of repetition and retrieval, and the historical situation in general is one in which Gadamer chooses to underscore the possibility of openness over the apparent destiny of forgetfulness and the concomitant necessity of dismantling the metaphysical tradition. Some read this critique as a basic assertion of hermeneutic continuity over against Heideggerian rupture.[141] Yet that does not seem to capture the relation. If anything, it is in treating the forgetfulness of Being as an eschatological force that Heidegger lends the past a seemingly stable continuity of meaning that, while it eschews the language of Hegelian teleology, nevertheless makes a similarly pervasive claim. For Gadamer, such a claim to transparency concerning history is impossible; history has no goal, regardless of whether it is defined as progress or nihilistic decline. Instead, the hermeneutic stance is a matter of performing the transmission of history within and through our situation, not leaping or twisting free of a forgetfulness.

For Heidegger the *Destruktion*-approach, which originally sought an underlying diversity of questions, gradually turns into a pursuit of *the* fundamental question (first concerning Being, then its more originary formulation "Beyng"). It eventually becomes the search for the source of questionability itself, the pursuit of an *archê* – however abyssal it may be. Gadamer likens this approach to a logical construction of necessity – not a teleological one, as in Hegel's case, but one deriving "from the beginning [*vom Anfang her*]."[142] Though not entailing, as some have maintained, a "longing for the primeval,"[143] this singular focus on the inception of the forgetfulness of Being still inherently tasks itself with a futural questioning distance from the tradition, and even when formulated as a present phenomenological engagement or *Verwindung* with epochal "matters of thinking," nevertheless seems overly determined and risks becoming a "formal framework."[144] As Heidegger's distance from the particulars of tradition grew, in other words, it was bound to turn into a diagnostic approach that leveled thinkers or texts down to a single statement or idea.[145]

Gadamer does not fault Heidegger for his focus on the question of Being, but rather responds to this direction by underscoring instead the ongoing historical conversation, the "one great horizon" to which we belong.[146] He does not believe that a dismantling distance from tradition is actually necessary or possible – he in fact asserts the "unreality" of any purported forgetfulness of Being – and instead advocates a dialogical approach to tradition's transmission.[147] If the past continually addresses us, after all, our task is to respond, and there is no predetermined way to do so. Against Heidegger, Gadamer denies that metaphysics is tied to a specific grammar or language, noting that ongoing dialogue excludes the need for a new language or a debilitating *Sprachnot*.[148] In pointing to the "living virtuality of language" – an openness exemplified in, but not limited to, genuine conversation – Gadamer conceives of an ontological openness that is akin to an ongoing dialectic.[149]

Heidegger would certainly respond that the notion of dialectical progression is a metaphysical one, but Gadamer claims that, by labeling certain ideas as metaphysical from the outset, Heidegger predetermines the possibilities of present understanding.[150] Indeed, the notion of a monolithic language of metaphysics seems to violate Heidegger's own earlier ideas that there is a "living speech"[151] in history and that all moments of history carry within them a "primordiality of questioning [*Frageursprünglichkeit*]."[152] Even the later Heidegger concedes that an

eventual remembering of Being would not constitute a different historical story from that of forgetfulness. In "Time and Being" he appears to
recognize the ongoing conversation in tradition, seeking to lead a contemporary audience *toward* an open dialogue with this.[153]

Not denying the validity of this futural outlook, but also not at-
tempting a mere reversal into historical remembering, Gadamer turns
his attention toward our inherent *already*-belonging to the ongoing conversation: "I did not attempt what the later Heidegger was after: forcibly
recasting language, so to speak. This is not language anymore, I said to
myself. True, one always searches for the right word in language. Yet it is
not the word which is decisive, but the whole process of communication
[....] I told Heidegger that language is not the powerful word; language
is reply."[154] Gadamer takes Heidegger to reveal the idea, but not pursue
it, that language could be the infinite possibility of making-oneself-at-
home in the world.[155] By eschewing Heidegger's concept of authenticity, Gadamer insists on the impossibility of preparing a "real living on
earth" with a new, nonmetaphysical language.[156] Rather than outright
dismissing dialectic – or any concept in the Western tradition, for that
matter – Gadamer "attempts to recuperate it as the non-metaphysical
center of his own phenomenological project."[157] His position is that, if
we not only engage with it dialogically, but conceive of it as inherently
dialogical in its structure, so-called metaphysical language can "decon-
struct itself" and gain the fluidity that Heidegger once sought – and
demonstrated to be possible – in his earliest hermeneutic ventures.[158]
Gadamer thus contends that "no conceptual language [...] represents
an unbreakable constraint upon thought"; there is no such thing as a
language of metaphysics, only of dialogue and transmission.[159] He thus
continues "Heidegger's project of overcoming metaphysics [...] in the
dynamics of language, not of metaphysics, but 'which we speak with others and to others.'"[160] Twisting free of metaphysics, or becoming twisted
up in it, is thus not something we can decide to do all at once, but must
rather happen in an ongoing dialogue that attempts to hear what tradition already has to say. It is, in this regard, a social and ethical as much
as an ontological task.

Here one can witness the greatest difference emerging between Heidegger and Gadamer with regard to historical belonging and our free-

dom within it. If the past contains the resources for its present retrieval and productive continuation – indeed, if it is a conversation to which we always already belong – then there is no need of a patient waiting for a new epoch's arrival, no need of a drastic transformation of the human into a reticent being that may some day authentically belong (or listen, or co-respond) to the unspeakable appropriative event. Gadamer certainly takes Heidegger's notions of "waiting" and "arrival" to express something true about how we are to approach the future, but understanding is not "primarily futural" for Gadamer; it is inherently bound up with the past and our present situation, and it is in our carrying that situation forward that history transforms itself.[161] Gadamer stays true to Heidegger's insights in that he "refuses to engage in metaphysical speculation out of recognition of the fragmentation of language and of the tradition," and yet it is precisely from this Heideggerian stance that Gadamer embraces "the plurality of dispersed forms."[162] In refusing to treat history as an abyss of forgetting, Gadamer's hermeneutic openness eschews the necessity of a leap beyond our present circumstances, of a disavowing distance from the past that would prepare a new beginning. Rather than locating freedom in such a decisive disavowal – a location that Heidegger arguably undertook in §74 of *Being and Time* – Gadamer finds freedom at work in the ongoing self-transformation of tradition. Freedom arises when one risks one's having-been in the intertwined interrogative of tradition – being questioned by it, but also uncovering its utter questionability.

While Heidegger certainly deserves credit for introducing the problem of freedom into the ontological heart of historicity, and while the thematic finds its way into elements of his later thought, it nevertheless loses the immediate social dimension that it had in *Being and Time*.[163] Indeed, even in that work the concept of finite freedom remained greatly underdeveloped with regard to its social aspects. Although, as noted above, *Being and Time*'s authentic historicity does not necessitate an individual narrowing of freedom or a relinquishment of social ties, Heidegger avoids exploring the particulars of what a finite freedom entails. Despite Heidegger's insistence that pejorative-sounding terms in his account of everyday life are descriptive rather than evaluative, one can still argue that more description would be required for a full interpretation of factical life. Gadamer goes so far as to say that the concepts of authenticity and decision, in their predeterminations, entail a shattering of existing culture and *Bildung;* they circumvent a more nuanced engagement with the transmission of tradition.[164]

Gadamer connects this attitude to another phase of Heidegger's thought, pointing out that even in the earliest lectures Gadamer attended, Heidegger placed less emphasis on Aristotle's practical philosophy than on his ontology.[165] The Natorp-report, with all of its focus on the enacted situation of human life, fails to even mention *êthos,* and where Heidegger does give treatment of the concept, it is in a pejorative sense of habit, not in a rich sense of habituation and cultivation.[166] Even here, but especially after *Being and Time* in such works as the *Introduction to Metaphysics,* there is a priority of ontological questioning in Heidegger's thought, the pursuit of the source of Being over its ontic manifestations. Yet the descent to the *archê,* by including and affecting all other realms of human existence, is to signify for Heidegger the "originary ethics" – meaning that there need be no separate field of ethics, and presumably no engagement in traditional terms.[167] Despite this assertion, however, it remains the case that Heidegger did not adequately attend to the full, "originary" ethical ramifications even of his own ontology.

Gadamer finds this treatment deeply lamentable, as he takes historical understanding to be intimately connected to human formation and the cultivation of social life. The questions uncovered by Heidegger's thought, after all, pertain precisely to finite freedom as it is enacted in a community that belongs to tradition. Among its confluence of sources, then, Gadamer's hermeneutics takes up what remained ethically unaddressed in Heidegger.[168] One can locate this in Gadamer's particular treatment of concepts like *phronêsis* and historicity, but also in his broader stance on such themes as art, history, and language. In short, it is in the *Geisteswissenschaften* that Gadamer paradigmatically locates our ability to recognize and respond to the task of historical belonging, in all of its social and ethical dimensions. To be sure, these disciplines required Heidegger's stinging rebuke of their scientistic sedimentation at the outset of the twentieth century, and Gadamer's approach is certainly emboldened by Heideggerian protreptics. However, just as these lead to differing evaluations of language and art between Gadamer and

Heidegger, they also divide the thinkers' stances toward the humanistic tradition. Rather than treating freedom as a distance from that tradition – and instead of neglecting freedom altogether, as some have claimed – Gadamer identifies it with the continual engagement in transmission itself, and that means listening to what the humanistic tradition has to say.

Gadamer's relation to Heidegger on the theme of historicity is thus more nuanced than a simple relation of "stunting" or moderation – let alone an assertion of continuity over rupture.[169] To be sure, Gadamer gives a "less 'destructive'" impression, but only because he opts for a different emphasis within a similar conceptual structure.[170] To be sure, Heidegger was a radical thinker inasmuch as he sought out the root (*radix*) of our historical existence. In this regard, however, one could argue that he is in fact more diagnostical than revolutionary; he seeks an understanding, not an overthrow, of tradition. Gadamer formulates our task of historical belonging quite differently from Heidegger not because he takes tradition to be something entirely different, but because he sees a more dialogical way of engaging with it, a potential for cultivation where Heidegger sees nihilistic danger. Heidegger's account of our linguistic-historical belonging, in other words, takes Gadamer only so far. Since part of Gadamer's difficulty is that Heidegger remains too Hegelian, Gadamer must engage in an attempt at retrieval from that angle as well.

THREE

The Infinity of the Dialogue

ACCEPTING HEGEL'S CHALLENGE

In refusing to follow Heidegger's assumptions concerning historicity to their diagnostic and dismantling conclusions, that is, in eschewing any language of forgetfulness or leaping, Gadamer wishes to make room both for a less circumscribed conception of historical transmission and for a more discursive involvement with it. This accounts, on a broad level, for Gadamer's description of his philosophy as undertaking a dialogical or "ethical turn." He seeks a conception of historical involvement that addresses more frontally the potentially discontinuous experience of social life, that accounts for all manner of questionability within tradition (including that of specific traditions themselves), and that is thus more adequate than *Seynsgeschichte* to our reflective capacities as historically situated beings.

On the level of specific thinkers, this turn away from Heidegger also helps explain the importance that Hegel, despite all distance, still has for Gadamer. In one sense, this might not be considered a turn away from Heidegger at all; for Gadamer sees in Hegel a project similar in positive effect to Heidegger's, namely of overcoming the *aporiae* of modern subjectivity by moving to some higher (or ontologically more fundamental) determination. Just as Heidegger's *Kehre* uncovered a predominance of Being over consciousness (a predominance that resurfaces in Gadamer's concept of the consciousness of historical effect as being *"mehr Sein als Bewusstsein"*), so Hegel situates self-consciousness in objective spirit, and thinking as such in "the logical." Given this relation, then, Gadamer leaves it ambiguous whether his move toward Hegel represents a step "ahead of" or "back behind" Heidegger.[1] After all, this turn is not intended as a wholesale refutation of Heidegger's insights.

Another side of the ambiguity is that Gadamer turns to Hegel in spite of Heidegger's critique of reflection in metaphysics. Indeed, if Heidegger ultimately sees our position today as being "twisted-up" within metaphysics, and if Gadamer agrees with this assessment yet denies its purportedly immobilizing or silencing results, then Hegel's determinations must become a prime object of our involvement.[2] This engagement is not a problem for Gadamer, since he does not simply view Hegel as the epitome of metaphysical reflection. To be sure, there are provocative metaphysical claims in Hegel that must be revised in light of the end of modernity; Gadamer views himself as taking part in this process, and posing an insurmountable limit to reflective philosophy through the concept of historicity. What remains, however, are several interrelated aspects in which Hegel's insights remain pertinent and challenging to hermeneutical thought, and especially to the issue of historicity itself: Hegel's recognition of historicity as central to the practice of philosophy, his conception of dialectical movement and mediation, his description of objective spirit as an intersubjective medium, and his account of the openness and continuity of history. It is indeed Hegel's lasting achievement to have solidified the entire modern concern with historical understanding, including the realization of our inherent historical situatedness.[3]

The crucial point here is to see in Hegel a complementary influence to Heidegger with regard to Gadamer's concept of historicity and historical effect. If, through his Heideggerian appropriation of finitude and *phronêsis*, Gadamer stresses the continual and event-like application at work in all understanding, then Hegel's dialectic serves to bring the aspect of interwovenness, of mutual participation or Platonic *methexis*, to the forefront of hermeneutics.[4] It is through this thematic, as I hope to show in the present chapter, that the notion of dialectic – with all of its logical, ethical, and historical ramifications – comes to influence Gadamer's concept of dialogical historical understanding.

Another way to frame this contemporary significance is to raise a fundamental philosophical issue to prominence: the core challenge that Gadamer takes Hegel to pose to us is to thoroughly think through the concept of experience.[5] This concept, as I have already had occasion to elaborate in chapter 1, is frequently misunderstood as belonging solely to the realm of scientific reflection. It is taken for granted as the amassing of cases that allow one to formulate more general rules and contrive methods for the future application of past experience. Yet experience has a more original dimension, one that is rooted in human life and that accordingly extends beyond methodical strictures, and this is why it plays such a central role in Gadamer's hermeneutics. It entails knowing oneself in relation to one's situation, and accounting for the possible changes on either side of this relation. Experience is thus another term for what occurs at the heart of historical effect.

In Gadamer's view, it is one of Hegel's great achievements to have formulated, in dialectical movement, a philosophy that acknowledges the negativity of experience as the driving force of insight and that presents the movement of experience as a form of mediation between the subjective and the objective, history and truth, the knowing and the known. Since dialectic, as unconditioned or presuppositionless, always takes place from within this mediation, and permits no external determinations of its course, Hegel can be taken to underscore the importance of recognizing one's situation and being open to phenomena that one cannot determine methodically in advance.

Despite this significance of Hegel's thought, however, his proximity to Gadamer's hermeneutics remains "tension-filled."[6] There are elements of his method that, for both internal and external reasons, do not hold up to scrutiny. Hegel's influence thus remains complicated and tempered by critique. From Gadamer's point of view, therefore, our task is not so much a matter of renewing Hegel's perspective as it is of learning something from him, of preserving some truth from his thought. As Gadamer puts it, today "there is no question of Hegel discipleship, but of interiorizing the challenge that he represents."[7] Throughout Gadamer's works, this interiorization of Hegel takes the form of a "transposition" of the concept of experience, a translation of absolutizing dialectic into "the ethical dimension of the dialogue."[8] Put differently, Gadamer "wants to release Hegel's dialectic from the straightjacket of systematic grammar into the openness of actual living dialogue, into what he calls 'the logic of question and answer.'"[9]

As this indicates, and as I aim to elaborate in the present chapter, this translation or release is intimately connected with Gadamer's notion of an openness at the core of hermeneutic experience, and is therefore commonly taken to entail an opening of Hegel's purportedly sealed system of thought. According to this notion, Gadamer would be taken to agree with merely the process, not the result, of Hegel's dialectical approach. If, as one tends to believe, Hegel's philosophy accounts for the necessary fulfillment of dialectic in absolute knowing, in logical totality, and in freedom at the end of history, then this correction on Gadamer's part would amount to simply the infinite postponement of this fulfillment. It would constitute an unfolding of the absolute into the infinity of incompleteness, while remaining committed to a metaphysical conception of progress.[10] It would also – and fatally for any hermeneutics of alterity – commit Gadamer to a dialectic of consumption, in which the other cannot remain other but is always eventually appropriated to oneself. This is the reading that John Caputo, among others, gives of Gadamer's position.[11] However, this description does not adequately capture the aim of Gadamer's transposition of Hegel, and in fact runs contrary to what openness means for Gadamer. To be sure, he takes himself to open what seems to be the reflectively closed circuit of Hegel's system. He indeed espouses his own version of bad infinity – even using Hegel's term – that intends to run counter to dialectic's totalizing claims and temper them by means of the finitude that he gleans from Heidegger's influence.

Yet the ways in which Gadamer achieves this opening are frequently misunderstood. It cannot be conceived as a mere assertion of open-endedness in contrast to reflective comprehension, for Gadamer critiques the notion of a thetic or propositional starting point as well. Furthermore, far from having to pry the system open from the outside and force the logical into the concrete – Gadamer indeed denies that any such external "toppling" of absolute idealism is possible – he shows ways in which Hegel's thought itself anticipates and requires a grounding in the finite realm of language and historicality. Gadamer in fact believes that Hegel is ultimately concerned with "the same thing as we are [...] the historical dimension in which the problem of hermeneutics is rooted."[12] Thus, his release of Hegel's dialectical grammar into living

language entails making explicit something already tacitly contained in
the speculative system, and if Gadamer seeks to transpose this system
into "[t]he infinity of the dialogue,"[13] one needs to emphasize and elucidate the notion of dialogue as much as that of infinity. I will take up both
of these tasks over the course of the present chapter, and thereby attempt
to account for the challenge that Hegel poses and that Gadamer accepts.

My analysis will proceed from broad determinations into greater
detail. I will begin, in the next section, with Gadamer's evaluation of
experiential movement and situatedness in Hegel's dialectic. This will
require distinguishing between the movement of the *Phenomenology of
Spirit* and that of the *Science of Logic*, accounting for the general angle
of Gadamer's critique, and thereby delineating the ways in which Gadamer nevertheless finds Hegel to be hermeneutically significant. This
will result chiefly in the question concerning the character of historical
openness in Hegel, which I will address by turning to Hegel's philosophy
of history and right. There, I will demonstrate the closure of history to
be an unfounded reading of Hegel's philosophy, but also underscore that
Gadamer still conceives of "bad infinity" differently than Hegel's historical open-endedness. The final section will gather and summarize the
prior delineations, and give a clear picture of how Gadamer ultimately
distances himself from Hegel.

MOVEMENT AND SUBSTANCE IN HEGEL'S CONCEPTUALITY

Chapter 1 presented the notion that the consciousness of historical effect
entails an awareness of one's belonging to the transmission of tradition.
When we understand anything, in other words, we can simultaneously
become aware of the ontological fact that our understanding is situated.
There is thus a potentially reflective element to all historical understanding, in that consciousness knows itself to be part of the effect of history.
While we have seen that this knowledge constitutes an ongoing task for
any consciousness, we also saw that the relation between this knowledge
and the effect of which it is conscious bears a chiasmic structure; that
is, the two sides are always already in an intertwined relation to each
other. In characterizing historical understanding in this way, Gadamer
has already revealed a significant feature of human existence, but this

feature raises important questions. It remains to be clarified what the precise relation of consciousness to effect is, "how knowledge and effect belong together," and to what extent any awareness can "rise above that of which it is conscious."[14]

Two concerns that lurk behind these questions are, on the one hand, the danger of the impossibility of reflection due to an utterly perspectivized situation and, on the other, the notion of an absolute or total reflection, a stance in which knowledge and effect, self and tradition, would become fully mediated and transparent to each other, thus pretending to virtual omniscience over finite existence. Chapter 1 sought to address both of these positions in a conceptual manner, but Gadamer takes the latter risk to be especially prevalent in modern philosophy. To him, it is the metaphysical danger represented by Hegel's absolute idealism, the full exigency of which Gadamer hopes to steer clear of with his hermeneutics. The only way to achieve this, he believes, is by uncovering limits in human experience and setting boundaries to absolute transparency, thereby conceiving of "a reality that limits and exceeds the omnipotence of reflection."[15] However, it is precisely Hegel's thought itself that leads toward the possibility of this conception. In the movement of his dialectic, Hegel has already thought through these limits, and Gadamer takes it as his task to resuscitate their validity from within this movement. It is the possibility and character of this resuscitation that therefore requires delineation here.

When dealing with Hegel's dialectical movement, Gadamer notes that one needs to distinguish between the movement of pure thought-determinations as presented in the *Science of Logic* and the movement of phenomenal experience in the *Phenomenology of Spirit*. Though both works deal with the immanent necessity that constantly drives the experiencing consciousness forward into further determinations, they differ in what they present to us: the *Phenomenology* shows opinion coming to full congruity with what exists beyond it (and thus demonstrates ordinary consciousness coming to absolute knowledge), whereas the *Science of Logic* deals strictly with knowledge itself, where no distinction obtains any longer between knowing and content.[16] I will turn first to the *Phenomenology* and elaborate its movement before analyzing that of the logical as such.

Phenomenology of Spirit

Above, I already touched upon the significance that Hegel's dialectic bears for a reconception of experience, the concept that is so fundamental to the elaboration of philosophical hermeneutics. Yet in reality, so Gadamer insists – prodded by an insight of Heidegger's – the order of significance is the reverse: Hegel does not think of experience dialectically, but conceives of dialectic experientially.[17] It is the negativity of all true experience that drives dialectical movement. This negativity is productive (or "determinate") insofar as it does not merely negate prior knowledge, but determines this knowledge more deeply and thus raises it to a more comprehensive level. It is not a refutation of one's consciousness that would return one back to an old starting point, but a reversal within consciousness that presents a new perspective.[18] On the one hand, Hegel thereby takes something within us to undergo change through experience, or rather takes experience to amount to a changing grasp of ourselves. In the reversal brought about by the negativity of experience, we not only learn something; we become different. On the other hand, the reversal of consciousness also entails a change in the object known. What we took to be one thing, or one kind of thing, has turned out to be of another sort, or another being altogether. Hegel's *Phenomenology* describes a long series of these reversals, presenting to the reader's observing consciousness the learning experience of a situated subject. Beginning with the immediacy of pure sense perception, this subject gradually learns of its own role in shaping the determinations of its objects, and thereby gains an "absolute" perspective upon its own rationality or intelligibility. Despite the critique that Gadamer levels at this outcome, he nevertheless takes Hegel's account of the movement of consciousness in the *Phenomenology* to be quite fruitful for a conception of hermeneutically situated reflection. Indeed, he finds in Hegel an ally in the account of posttranscendental subjectivity and a prefiguration of the finitude that he himself espouses. Before attending more closely to this broader allegiance, however, it will help to first analyze several basic, significant elements of Hegel's *Phenomenology*.

One of these elements is the characterization of consciousness's movement as a mediation. What is peculiar about mediation as Hegel

[Margin note: ✳ Hegel: Dialectic of experience not Experience of Dialectic.]

conceives it is that it cannot be predicated of, nor attributed to, any particular being, but instead represents the mode of the world and of the self (consciousness and the "in-itself") in their mutual relation. From a logical or epistemological standpoint, the mediation expresses the necessity of moving beyond inadequate forms of knowledge.[19] Viewed ontologically (in terms of the subject's finite historical existence), it is a mediation between the subject's experience of history and history as an objective force that carries subjects. The two stand in an "infinite relation [...] whose terms are not given."[20] The result is that there is no fixed being that then subsequently "has" movement; mediation is the process of the whole, and Hegel's description of the elemental "fluidity" (*Flüssigkeit*)[21] here in fact bears some resemblance to Heidegger's early aims presented in the previous chapter. It is also not amiss to find here a parallel to Gadamer's sense of historical transmission. After all, as intertwined with history, we inherently move; we must also intrinsically mediate between our past as it is handed down and our present situation and concerns. Mediation is thus not a superadded aspect of our historicity, but characterizes the medium in which – or better, the substance *as* which – all historical transmission already moves. I will treat this substantiality in more detail shortly.

This brings Gadamer to the element that drives the whole transmissive process, to the "motor" of historical mediation. He locates at this level the synthesis of reconciliation (*Versöhnung*), which he labels "the secret of Hegelian dialectic."[22] In showing this process to lie at the heart of consciousness's experience, in the overcoming of alienation on its path to knowledge, Hegel underscores his bold and optimistic claim that thought, through difficult work, can make itself at home in the world. Yet it is presumably "secret," in Gadamer's view, because it is easily missed or construed to be something it is not. Indeed, there is much room for misunderstanding Hegel here, and Gadamer takes a clear position in his defense.[23]

On the basis of what we have already stated about mediation, Gadamer notes that reconciliation need not be viewed as a dominating envelopment of alterity by a logic that would appropriate and supersede the other, and that would accordingly possess the capacity for this supersession in advance. It is not the caricature, typical of many Marxist readings of Hegel, that depicts a reason bent on subsumption under concepts. Rather, what Hegel aims to capture with this notion is the experience of historical consciousness engaging with its particular situation and coming to terms with it. In this sense, transposed into Gadamer's terminology, reconciliation embodies the "task for each individual" to understand "what is happening to us," and thus speaks to the finite, ethical, and hermeneutical aspects of human life.[24] When we confront history in this way, our past is encountered as if it were an external nature to which we must reconcile ourselves, and this will mean to some degree determining and appropriating it.[25] Even if one can still debate to what extent this appropriation can or should occur, it should now be clear that even in Hegel, this arises from the initial indeterminacy of the situation itself. What this understanding of reconciliation thus reveals is that the awareness which Hegel takes to eventually result from this task, namely the insight that "what is rational is actual; and what is actual is rational,"[26] is not declaratively posited in advance – this would excuse a fatalism that Hegel could never espouse – but won through precisely those difficult reversals that consciousness experiences.

Nevertheless, Hegel's characterization of this rationality quickly raises some of the core difficulties of his concepts, and the point at which Gadamer distances himself quite clearly. Hegel takes the path of the experiences of consciousness to culminate in an absolute knowing; he also takes the philosophical engagement with history to yield insight into its internal necessity and *telos*. Thus, for Hegel it is conceivable that one could fulfill or complete experience and, while not halting the advance of time, still cease actually experiencing in the full sense of the word; one would come to rest in the highest knowledge of what is and is not possible. Yet for Gadamer, the very notion of experience reaching a culmination is antithetical to its nature: "The dialectic of experience has its proper fulfillment not in definitive knowledge but in the openness to experience that is made possible by experience itself."[27] This claim is based on Gadamer's insight – drawn from the work of Francis Bacon – that experience cannot be made into an actual science. It bears its own universality that is required for, but not identical to, that of science.[28] The fact that experience bears scientific results is overshadowed and continually put in question by the occurrence of new experiences.

Thus, the fulfillment of hermeneutic experience would amount to the insight into one's own finitude and limitations: "that all foresight is limited and all plans uncertain."[29] To truly think dialectic experientially, therefore, would mean to situate it within those limitations as a stance that is both already brought about by indeterminate experience and always open to further indeterminacy of this sort. This latter point challenges any notion of fulfillment as actual completion. Gadamer's notion of something like completed experience is thus still thought in accordance with Hegel's ideas of reversal and negativity, but this result of openness is not a closure or a final transparent conception that consciousness has of itself. Crucially, however, Gadamer's openness does also not simply assert an infinitely ceaseless experience in a futural direction. Instead, it is an open relation to the alterity of experience in both its provenance and its futurity, and herein lies the hermeneutic inflection of bad infinity. To be truly experienced, for Gadamer, accordingly entails inhabiting a "fundamental ethical comportment [*sittlichen Grundhaltung*]" of openness for the other and what is foreign.[30]

As central to Gadamer's notion of an infinite dialogue, this openness bears further examination. Yet even here, Hegel remains useful. Despite holding his conception of hermeneutical-experiential openness over against dialectic's teleological force, Gadamer detects, even in Hegel's account of how absolute knowledge takes shape, a strong account of this ethical comportment. He finds this most clearly in Hegel's description of ethical life in the "Spirit" chapter of the *Phenomenology*, where logical categories play out in the realm of intersubjectivity. While Gadamer does not ever present a singular, sustained interpretation of this chapter, it is possible, by recounting some key aspects of Hegel's description, to piece together and clarify the various positive assessments that Gadamer makes concerning objective spirit throughout his works.

Prior to the "Spirit" chapter, Hegel has already shown, largely through the dialectic of master and slave, the necessity of mutual recognition in the life of ordinary consciousness. We are never merely self-related, and indeed require others in order to function as individuals to begin with. In a further contextualization of self-identity, Hegel now demonstrates that the norms and principles by which we organize our relations and that we initially take to stem from within our consciousness actually have "a 'life' of their own."[31] The overall trajectory of the analysis is therefore a movement "away from an established ground to a situation of subjective ungroundedness."[32] As Hegel describes it, the course of this development is

> essentially the movement of the self to set aside the abstraction of *immediate existence,* and to become conscious of itself as a universal – and yet to do so neither by the pure alienation and disruption of itself and of actuality, nor by fleeing from it. Rather, it is *immediately present* to itself in its substance, for this is its knowledge, is the intuited pure certainty of itself; and just *this immediacy* which is its own reality, is all reality, for the immediate is *being* itself.[33]

To get to this point, however, spirit must uncover this immediacy. At the beginning of the chapter, the ground has already partly receded: we find consciousness in a world that is already organized, a situation not brought about by the subject's own judgment, but where the subject is rather "submerged in the formal universality of legality or law."[34] This realm, which Hegel labels the "ethical order" (*Sittlichkeit*), is still grounded inasmuch as it is dominated by a strong communal sense of custom based on the preservation of what are taken to be given universal laws. The individual puts her trust in this communal ethos, performing her role as duty prescribes it. Duty, here, is something that is accepted as a divine precept or a law of nature, something simply perceived, rather than being a willed choice derived from a sense of obligation. Yet, as Sophocles points out and Hegel underscores, one can perceive various and conflicting duties: to bury the dead or to obey the king. In this divergence, the individual cannot resort to mere trust in the ethical order. Even being granted a "legal status" is not enough to stabilize the ambiguity; the "empty unity of the person is, therefore, in its *reality* a contingent existence, and essentially a process and an action that comes to no lasting result."[35] The ethical order accordingly turns out not to be natural at all: the duties that form the ethos arose historically and are subject to the contingencies of custom and desire. Given their now evident insufficiency to determine the subject's actions, she must resort to her own will and commitment to action.

Yet having recognized that the actual or given, even in the form of the self as will, is not sufficient to determine what should occur, the next move is for consciousness to embrace the artificial nature of obligation and commitment and to seek out an alternate context for subjective life and social development. This is found in the realm of culture (*Bildung*), where one participates in the formulation and cultivation of higher ideals. By choosing these ideals, one undergoes a conversion from immediate existence to better judgment, and takes on an identity that, though universalized, one now treats as the actual self. Since one is responsible for this choice and cultivation, but takes the ideals themselves to apply universally, one can hold others accountable to the same standard, for they are equally free and responsible. Here, then, is another form of binding communal or spiritual life, yet one that is enacted consciously rather than blindly, and that therefore resides at the level of universal rationality rather than compulsive immediacy: "This *equality* with everyone is, therefore, not the equality of the sphere of legal right, not that immediate recognition and validity of self-consciousness simply because it *is*; on the contrary, to be valid it must have conformed itself to the universal by the mediating process of alienation."[36] Through this elevation to the universal, however, the specificities of individual existence are radically reduced in significance. The self loses its particularity in raising itself to the level of culture, or at the very least finds itself continually overshadowed by the ideals it has yet to reach. Culture thereby "acquires the significance of an objective *being* which lies beyond the consciousness of the self."[37] Yet Hegel's point, as always, is that the universal must become concrete.

After demonstrating these shortcomings of the ethical and cultural positions, then, Hegel describes the situation in which he takes this concretion to actually be possible, and calls this the realm of "morality" (*Moralität*). To live in morality, according to Hegel, is to embrace one's social situatedness – not the purportedly natural givenness of ethics or the idealistic (and alienating) enculturation of the individual – as the beginning and end point of any universal determinations. This situation of "*concrete* moral spirit" amounts to a type of finitude, a limitation of how the good can be conceived or come about.[38] Since it is not considered established or given in advance, it is something that must first be accomplished. Hegel is thus describing spirit's recognition of its own activity in establishing its community. He names this recognition "conscience" (*Gewissen*): "the common element of [. . .] two self-consciousnesses,

[...] the substance in which the deed has an *enduring reality*, the moment of being *recognized* and *acknowledged* by others."[39]

To be sure, the entire sphere of spirit is a situated world that exists prior to one's will: first as law and custom in the ethical realm, then as universal ideals in the realm of culture, and then as intersubjective responsibility in the moral realm. Yet as much as this seems to take the emphasis off individuals' achievements, it does so only to place this power within a truly social context. Far from being an externally enveloping, destabilizing, or ungrounding force, spirit is recognized by the individual as his own inherent-coherent element and ongoing project: the "we" that is accepted here is one "that needs to be performed through the singular actions of particular selves."[40]

Even in this coherence, however, Hegel acknowledges an important limit. Despite being certain of its embeddedness in social existence and its commitment to a life of recognition, the self situated in the moral sphere has no guarantee that its relation to others will be adequate, nor that their actions will properly recognize the self. The only option, then, and what amounts to a concrete necessity, is to attend and respond to particulars in the full awareness that perfect relations are impossible.[41] This amounts to a recognition on consciousness's part that it actually *is* spirit, that it belongs intrinsically to an intersubjective world and, in order to be at home there, must reconcile itself with the entirety of this world. Here the goal of absolute knowing, of complete self-knowledge, surfaces again. For in spirit's reconciliation of its behavior with its inner necessity, it knows what it must do and can realize its aim of becoming fully self-determined.

One could say that history enters into full force in this chapter of Hegel's *Phenomenology*. To be sure, the entire book presents history and consciousness as linked inextricably: history is precisely the path of spirit's gradual self-comprehension. Yet up to this point, the historical was a category of consciousness's seemingly blind subservience to its past (as in the natural-ethical). Now, it is the realm out of which the moral society lives out its futural intersubjectivity. Through this presentation, Hegel demonstrates nothing less than the fact that "the substance of knowing is history."[42] That is, history is acknowledged not just as the medium through which consciousness is mediated and achieves its aims, but as the very texture *as which* consciousness recognizes itself. The self-knowledge entailed in absolute knowing is, among its other determinations, a self-recognition of spirit as historical enactment.

Gadamer takes this recognition of spirit's intrinsic historicality to be Hegel's "foundational insight."[43] His allusions to Hegel's "Spirit" chapter tend to focus on this historical-ethical substance, gleaning wide-ranging implications from it. To begin with, Hegel serves as an indispensable hermeneutical ally here, for he presents a revision of transcendental subjectivity that accounts for broader a priori structures that nevertheless are, in effect, historical.[44] In helping account for subjectivity's belonging to the higher dimensions of objective spirit, Hegel is highlighting something that we are not accustomed to, nor particularly good at, recognizing today: that objective spirit is something we all live out of, and that, among other things, this refutes the tenability of inward and abstract moralism.[45]

In following Hegel by stressing that spirit is a "collective achievement,"[46] Gadamer underscores the communicative and dialogical character of ethical substance, indeed identifies spirit with language itself.[47] This solidifies Gadamer's intention to transpose Hegel's thought into the finite historical and linguistic realm. Yet here we have seen indications of this finitude in Hegel's own concepts. Hegel himself, after all, makes the identification of language and spirit.[48] He even extends this, effectively equating spirit with the entire intersubjective transmission of tradition, when he states that "spirit is the substance of history."[49] Gadamer makes a similar connection when he speaks of a form of tradition, namely that of the written word, as "pure spirit."[50] It is presumably pure because its ideality cannot decay in the same way that buildings and artifacts can. It would mean, however, that these latter works, too, are spirit. This underscores that spirit, in Hegel as well as Gadamer's conception, is not only a collective conversation of which we are inevitably a part because of our situatedness in the same world; it is also, and perhaps foremost, an ongoing presence that addresses us and demands our continual involvement.[51]

In characterizing the demands of the historical situation as a task without guarantee, Hegel prefigures much of Gadamer's own account of experiential finitude. Indeed, by formulating the possibility of spirit's recognition of these boundaries, Hegel comes close to capturing something akin to Gadamer's notion of the consciousness of historical effect. The latter, after all, recognizes its unity with the transmission of history, yet through the awareness of prejudice and horizons understands this unity to be an intersubjective task that is irretrievable and ongoing. The difference from Hegel here – and it is indeed a significant one – is that Gadamer denies the possibility of full reconciliation between self and tradition, and thus eschews the finality with which absolute knowing seems to grasp its infinite situation. In Gadamer, there is thus at work an infinity with a different direction, an "inner infinity" or deeper finitude, than Hegel is willing to admit. Instead of merely dwelling in the open-endedness of unpredictable intersubjectivity, spirit is more fundamentally opened and ungrounded: it has always already been situated and affected, and cannot retrieve this origin. Whereas absolute knowing can attain certainty as to how it must think and act, Gadamer stresses that "[w]e arrive too late in the event of understanding if we want to know what to believe."[52]

Science of Logic

Gadamer, perhaps surprisingly, draws very similar conclusions from his reading of Hegel's *Science of Logic*. It is surprising, since Hegel takes the *Logic* to operate at such an advanced and sealed level of knowledge that no opening or human grounding of this system seems possible. However, if one considers the *Logic* not as a further development of Hegel's thought that runs sequentially subsequent to the *Phenomenology*, but instead as a parallel to it, Gadamer's conclusions make more sense.[53] The *Logic* thus merely makes the metaphysical assumptions of the *Phenomenology* explicit on their own.

Given that no strictly subjective experiences are at work here, however, this raises the question as to what sort of movement this dialectic actually undergoes.[54] In pursuing this question, Gadamer notes first that the *Logic* is not a posited, solid totality. Unlike the sense-certainty with which the *Phenomenology* sets out, the *Logic* does not begin by *positing* immediacy, but instead simply allows an indeterminate immediacy to present itself. Like the *Phenomenology,* however, the stages that follow are not necessary in any universal sense; they are necessary with respect to dialectical self-articulation and the stage at which thinking finds itself.[55] The movements are "correct," but not exclusively so; the *Science of Logic* could be rewritten from another rational standpoint, and still cover the same concepts.[56] What is more, the entirety of the *Logic*'s movements culminate in a reality "that exists only as self-communication [...] that has the mediation [...] of its sides as its very substance."[57] Although some read this as a statement of complete and final reflectivity, Gadamer draws the conclusion that, while the *Logic* is a dialectical whole, it represents a science that cannot be completed.[58]

Gadamer's deeper reasoning for this conclusion lies in his assertions that the *Logic*'s self-communication is rooted in the movement of language, and that human linguisticality is thus the "carrier" of speculative content, coextensive with reason.[59] His stance amounts to a Hegelian critique of Hegel's own dialectic: he shows that the propositional form, while advancing beyond the predicative, still "remains one-sided and ultimately incomplete as long as it fails to take account of its own linguisticality."[60] To be sure, Hegel acknowledges the significance of language throughout his philosophy, but he takes it to possess an exteriority that makes it an expression of thought rather than a region coextensive with it. This entails that consciousness could, in theory, withdraw from language as from a chosen medium for thinking. Language, then, would merely be a "casing" for thought. Yet even when placed in the shell of a propositional statement, Gadamer asserts, the linguistic valence exceeds this supposed container. For language to carry in this way, and to extend past propositional terms, means that it moves at a level beyond grammar, dialectic, or concepts. Thus, while Hegel on occasion refers to the "instinct of language," he still thinks the movement of language as tied somehow to statements.[61] Over against this, Gadamer emphasizes our situation within a movement of language that is not completely illuminable, that remains infinitely out of reach.[62]

Therefore, just as an absolute knowledge of the historicity of consciousness is a "hybrid" notion for Gadamer, so he deems it impossible to give an account, in thought, of what gives or carries thought.[63] Even though dialectic attempts this (as an attempt at escaping finitude), it can never succeed. Citing both Heidegger's concept of the *Lichtung* and the indistinguishability of philosophy and sophistry in Plato's *Sophist*, Gadamer notes that language will always conceal as well as reveal.[64] Thus, Hegel's *Logic* is not as closed as many think. Hegel even seems to tacitly acknowledge this finite character of logic when he names its realm "the logical"; in Gadamer's reading this is not the totality of all conceptual thought, but the dimension that underlies all thought.[65] If this dimension cannot be subsumed in thought, then reflection cannot come to be at home in any permanent way. The logical resides in, or is simply equatable with, "the word," and since the word occurs as a conversation over time, the logical – just as the dialectically experiential – has its seat in the transmission of tradition.[66]

In spite of Gadamer's critique, then, there remains a deep parallel to Hegel here, and it concerns the notion of experiential movement as such. For Gadamer, the movement of human linguisticality, of conversation, is immanent and carries itself out, just as the concept communicates (with) itself throughout the *Logic*. Thus, analogously to the way in which Hegel's speculative proposition is suspended within the *Logic* through the unfolding of the concept, so for Gadamer linguisticality unfolds as the ongoing questioning of matters at hand in our historical situation, and is suspended, so to speak, in the universality of our hermeneutic finitude. This suspension, as we have begun to see, is conceived by Gadamer not as monological or propositional but precisely as dialogical: it is the continued logic of question and answer between self and other, or self and text. Gadamer nevertheless refers to language as a speculative "middle," though, since it relies on the self-movement of thinking that relates to beings as a whole and simultaneously brings this whole into language.[67]

These are the core means by which Gadamer aims to transpose Hegel's dialectic into the historical and dialogically ethical realm, and to resuscitate limits to reflection from within the movement of Hegel's dialectic. Gadamer's adaptation of Hegel's conception of experience, in both the *Phenomenology* and the *Science of Logic*, would necessitate an openness for the differential meanings of language, for the continued effect of the past, and for being put in question by others. It is, then, an openness constituted in part by its futural indeterminacy. Gadamer, in fact, finds within Hegel's own thought several indications of this indeterminate anticipatory limit: the movements of the *Phenomenology* and the *Logic* have revealed a hermeneutical-ethical dimension where the ceaseless self-communication of the absolute idea finds its counterpart in the intersubjective but unguaranteed recognition of spirit.

Despite all of Hegel's emphasis on spirit's culmination in self-transparency and free self-determination, then, there remains an openness within his system. Whether this openness amounts, in Gadamer's eyes, to a hermeneutically adequate acknowledgment of our historical situatedness, remains to be seen. I have already indicated that he takes Hegel's stance to only grasp part of the truth; aside from a futural or "outer" infinity, another aspect of openness concerns its irretrievable "inner" infinity, and this is something that Hegel leaves unaddressed. The full extent of Gadamer's critique, his conception of infinite dialogue, will become clear only after dealing more extensively with Hegel's conception of history itself. In the next section, I will therefore turn to Hegel's description of the historical project of freedom, coming to a better understanding of both his and Gadamer's stances with regard to the openness of historicity.

SELF-KNOWLEDGE, FREEDOM, AND
THE OPENNESS OF HISTORY

History, as philosophers have liked to point out, has an ambiguous meaning. It can denote, on the one hand, the chronological succession of past events, the totality of such a process, or even the ongoing datability of occurrences.[68] In short, it envelops everything that is considered as "having been." On the other hand, the word "history" indicates the description and study of this past totality, and as a discipline is labeled "historiography" precisely in order to distinguish it from its historical subject matter. From a philosophical standpoint, however, it is unclear what this discipline teaches us, what truths are attained through historical investigation.[69] It may therefore be quite understandable that much of the philosophical engagement with history has limited itself to an assessment of historiography itself, investigating past accounts and deliberating about their sequence, accuracy, or completeness.[70]

Yet Hegel's philosophy of history represents an interesting critique of this restriction, and he challenges it by calling into question the very dichotomy on which it is founded. He notes that our understanding of history is ambiguous for the very reason that its two meanings share a "common inner principle."[71] This principle finds expression in the facts that history, as the totality of human achievements, includes all past historiographies, and that any account of history, no matter how contemporary, is at the same time also a product of history. This apparent unity of history, the interrelation of inquiry and its object, raises the question as to its overall character, as well as to what we can learn from history taken in this unified way. Seen from the perspective of the concept of historical effect, which also entails an intertwined unity between self and tradition, it poses the question as to what sort of reflection upon history is possible. Gadamer's response is to speak of an infinite dialogue, whereas Hegel's answer, stated far too succinctly, is that a philosophy of history reveals the history of historical consciousness, that it therefore shows spirit's coming to know itself, and ultimately fulfills the Delphic dictum "Know thyself."[72]

In what follows, I will investigate what this highly condensed answer means, and how it relates to Gadamer's position. The first step toward clarifying what Hegel means by history as self-knowledge is to grasp how the question of history even arises for him, and to elaborate what role it plays in his investigation of spirit in the *Philosophy of Right*. This initial task will lead to a closer scrutiny of the notions of necessity, freedom, and contingency, through an analysis of several key passages in the "World History" section of the *Philosophy of Right*. From here, I will be able to assess Hegel's and Gadamer's positions concerning the infinite character of historical openness.

History as Self-Knowledge

Hegel prefaces his *Philosophy of Right* by elaborating the role that philosophy plays in the present, especially with regard to the establishment or justification of law. By delineating several positions that he views as untenable, he gradually uncovers the need to engage philosophically with history. Near the end of the preface, a complex analogy summarizes these distinctions and notes the significance of a truly philosophical position in, and toward, the present condition of the state: as true philosophy is said to bring one to God, thus avoiding the mediocre path that in fact leads in the opposite direction, so philosophy also provides a "warmer peace" with one's time, distinguishing it from the respective alternate stances of "approximation" and "cold despair" that by implication would lead away from the present – although a third alternative might still entail a compliant "peace with actuality."[73]

The first position that Hegel rejects here is that of "knowing as an approximation of truth,"[74] a phrasing that clearly targets Kant's doctrine of regulative ideas. According to this notion, human reason posits ideas that, although not concretely instantiable, nevertheless "approximate the unity that is possible empirically."[75] Regulative reason thus seeks, "as far as possible, to bring unity into the particular cognitions, and thereby to *bring* the rule *close* to universality."[76] In this conception of truth and morality, the present is always only on the way to complete knowledge or perfect justice; the practical ideal will never be experienced concretely. Indeed, as Hegel suggests in his analogy drawn from Bacon, such a philosophy would be perpetually moving *away* from the present, as "the true could only be a problem yet to be solved."[77] From this standpoint, truth and freedom are found in thinking alone, in abstraction from the present, in a formalism that is "unable to make a link with the actual development of ethics as practiced."[78] In this stance, "thinking then knows itself to be free only insofar as it diverges" both from communal experience and from matters of the state.[79] It is precisely this cool detachment from concern with the actual, the satisfaction with one's thinking even in the bleakest confinement, that Hegel criticizes as enabling a cold despair.

Hegel notes that the "atheism of the ethical world" entailed in formalism risks opening a gap in worldly experience in which any practically oriented rationality must devise its own theories.[80] This is evinced in the romanticism of Hegel's contemporary Jakob Friedrich Fries and his liberal adherents, which, in a certain sense, seems opposed to any formalism, precisely by embracing the spirit of friendship and the *sensus communis.* There is an apparent warmth to this stance, not least in its evocation of bonfires and *Bruderschaft.* However, there remains an equal lack of any thought-out ethics in this realm as well, and as with abstractive thought, every practical rule has the same null value. The "most comfortable of all methods," this path of more natural freedom views any law or custom as a burden to subjectivity and willfulness, and one gives oneself at ease with asserting ideas "as facts of consciousness."[81]

Though this position might already be said to embody the acquiescence that makes peace with actuality, Hegel seems to be addressing an even less radical crowd in the third alternative of his critical analogy: those who are unconcerned with the present, and eagerly accept "publicly familiar truth" as valid.[82] In his introduction to the *Philosophy of Right,* Hegel underlines that the familiarity of positive law *is* precisely its validity, but he notes further that, since such law cannot be natural in an absolute sense, any acceptance of positive law is irrational if it cannot – or will not – account for the reason why one follows certain customs over others. Hegel emphasizes this point by taking issue with the traditionalist excuse that the law is right simply by virtue of its consistency over time. It is the nature of law, rather, to be contingent and to adapt and change.[83]

Challenging the notion, then, that the truth and right of a law can be grounded in either its pragmatic or traditional justification, Hegel initially points out that historical developments are not necessarily just. Even if these developments prove to be just, however, traditional or practical explanations of existing laws are not philosophical justifications. Knowing all of the genetic-explanative reasons for a rational law does not amount to a grasp of why it is right. Drawing on Montesquieu's claim that justification stems from viewing laws as part of a larger framework, such as a nation's character, Hegel intends to show why we must seek the *basis* for our familiarity with positive law, the reason for accepting a law as true and right.[84] In his own philosophical project of showing the rational basis of the present, he thus seeks a "warmer peace," a "reconciliation with actuality."[85]

This reconciliation not only involves looking to national identity (including economy, religion, geography) as the horizon of the law, but also entails orienting oneself toward the past, trying to find the necessary developments leading to what is rationally valid in the present, and grasping all of this in a reinterpretation of the state that already exists in the world. We must, according to Hegel, come to see our own development as part of the larger project of free thought and make a home here and now for the concepts of freedom and right. This is precisely what Hegel means by achieving the idea of right, and also explains his allusion to Goethe's sonnet, "Nature and Artifice."[86] In order to understand ourselves, we have to enter the circle of philosophy in and through our own time. As present laws and rationality are products of history, however, grasping the present inherently means turning to the past, and engaging with its own rational development.

If the task at the outset is to find what is rational in our history, however, this seems to indicate a metaphysical stance on Hegel's part, an a priori presupposition that history operates rationally. Indeed, he states as much in his introduction to the *Philosophy of History*: "[T]he thought that Reason rules the world, and that world history has therefore been rational in its course [. . .] is a presupposition in regard to history as such."[87] Hegel immediately rescinds and explains his demand for this assumption, though, stating that it will actually first arise as a *result* of an empirical philosophy of history, one that he has already undertaken and can therefore already view as a totality.[88] We should briefly inquire into this philosophy of history, then, to glean how it understands reason and takes itself to remain presuppositionless.

One can see Hegel's philosophy of history as the dialectical culmination of several other methods of historical inquiry, the last of which are a critical history and a specialized history of ideas. Critical history, which Hegel describes as a "history of historical writing," entails an important step beyond naïve, universal history, for it is aware not only of the subject's inherent role in shaping historiography – this was already emphasized by the pragmatic history that sought to appropriate historical facts or consistencies for moral instruction in the present – but also of the historical narrative itself as an event in the totality of history.[89]

It is of crucial significance that this critical stance takes the historical consciousness – the spiritual content – of past ages into account, for here it becomes evident that human history is an involvement of spirit with itself on at least two levels: first, the initial historian's account was already either a self-representation (original history) or an engagement with one's history as such (universal history); second, the critical historian can now survey and reflect on these self-conscious involvements. This heightening of historical awareness – albeit a static elevation that does not yet provide a sense of development – gets one closer to understanding what a discovery of reason in history might mean: it would be the consciousness, on the part of the historian, of a spiritual(-historical) stance that pervades all of human history, and that she herself takes part in. However, since the critical historian is still at the center of this interpretation of history, her account risks simply being an idiosyncratic survey of past positions, a narrative that Hegel warns is susceptible to "subjective fancies."[90] Therefore, we must find a broader, objective scope for history, as well as a thread internal to its development.

Even an objective history of ideas that traces developments of specialized areas of thought throughout time, however, risks becoming mired in a certain externality if it does not attend to what is precisely historical in its subject matter. It would not suffice to state that one idea followed another; a fully rational account of history would instead have to show the inner connections between ideas and ages, their historical – even conceptual – relatedness.[91] Though Hegel, in the *Philosophy of History*, mentions only in passing the histories of art, law, and religion, the history of science provides a perfect example of this relatedness. An externally historical account of mathematics, for instance, might state that calculus was developed later than geometry or algebra, and that it represents a deeper mode of mathematical formalization. However, there are reasons internal to its temporal genesis, reasons having to do with the very historical iterability and perfectibility of mathematics itself, and these must be accounted for in its history.[92] The ideas in this history are thus developmental; moving, in the case of science, toward aims of higher formalization, and more precise prediction.

Hegel gleans a similar internal development from the standpoint of world-philosophical history that he synthesizes out of the critical and specialized histories. Just as science has an idea of its goal and moves progressively closer to it, so historical consciousness appears to progressively objectify or concretize its matter as well. It attends to the way that spirit's self-consciousness has developed, and seeks the reasons why this has occurred. The material of historical consciousness, as we have seen through the critical lens, is precisely humans' self-consciousness of their historical situation, and Hegel takes this self-consciousness to necessarily increase over time. This means that in history – unlike in art, religion, or philosophy – spirit is both "internality and externality," and that reason comes to know itself in its spiritual *actuality*, rather than through imagery, feeling, or pure thought.[93] To find reason in history, then, means for Hegel nothing other than to discover empirically the common inner principle of history mentioned at the outset of this section: through its dealings with history, spirit comes to know itself, and consciously shapes its identity over time.

If this empirical account of reason's history dispels the charge of metaphysical presuppositions, Hegel nevertheless characterizes the progress of self-consciousness quite strongly, noting that it is bound to happen when people start shaping their lives and taking the future into account. This can be misunderstood as the claim that there is constantly and everywhere progress in humanity, and that Hegel espouses a deterministic or mechanistic view of history. What it means for Hegel, instead, is that there is progress in spirit's vantage point, progress that becomes evident as soon as one looks to the actual development of historical consciousness: from private assessment of one's immediate life (original history), to the inclusion of distant historical lessons in one's own social situation (pragmatic history), to an awareness both of history's own self-conscious and self-determined development and of being a product of that very development (world history). From this development, it seems possible to conclude that historical consciousness seeks and eventually attains full self-consciousness. Against the metaphysical claim that history runs according to the plan of a hidden Providence, then, Hegel asserts that we can know the force that shapes history, since we are that very force.[94]

Far from being an exterior force upon history, the progress leading to the world-historical perspective that Hegel views as the crowning achievement of historical consciousness is really a conscious and self-determined gathering of various historical insights developed over the course of human civilization. That this stage of historical awareness was reached through consciousness's own determination seems itself a refutation of the notion that Hegel believes history to have a naturally determined course and *telos*. To be sure, the self-knowledge that Hegel sees on a global scale already occurs naturally within every society, and might therefore perhaps be said to be a given starting point. The rise in self-awareness, however, is anything but automatic, and two culminating points of the *Philosophy of Right* help establish this: first, the progress of historical self-consciousness has its source solely within consciousness itself, more precisely in consciousness's freedom; second, every culture struggles toward self-consciousness in and through their own historicity, and only world history allows a perspective broad enough to draw complete self-knowledge from these struggles. In order to clarify these points, I will next elucidate Hegel's conception of world history as "the necessary development, out of the concept of spirit's freedom alone, of the moments of reason and so of spirit's self-consciousness and freedom."[95]

The Project of Freedom

As the discussion of Hegel's *Phenomenology* above showed, consciousness develops because it is never simply immediate to itself. Drawing on Fichte's insight that the self is its activity, Hegel concludes that for consciousness to know itself as active, its object must not be able to be fully subsumed under consciousness, to become static. This also means that self-consciousness always involves mediation, be it through objects, through other consciousnesses, or through history itself – which, as we saw is for Hegel the substance of knowing. That this mediation and development is nevertheless *self*-determined, and not simply given over to the objects of consciousness, rests on the fact that consciousness always returns to itself, albeit in a changed way. By continually understanding itself differently, consciousness changes itself, and produces itself over time.[96] Because of this, Hegel claims that any consciousness that experiences history must necessarily advance.

Yet how does this advance occur "out of the concept of freedom"? Hegel underscores that right is rooted in the freedom of the will, which is as basic to human nature as gravitation is to bodies. As such, it is the foundation on which consciousness can even first begin to determine itself. The process of actualizing freedom, of mediating it from a natural state of being "in itself" to also being "for itself" as a "second nature," is a movement of specification, and therefore also one of limitation.[97] After all, a freedom that is purely negative and unspecified has not been mediated through anything, has no identity, and therefore no grasp of itself. To be fully free, however, is to grasp oneself completely, and Hegel's account of the movement from personhood to the sovereign state in the *Philosophy of Right* conveys spirit's apprehension of itself in its self-limitation. Thus, though nature may be the foundation for freedom, it is not until a people consciously takes up a purpose and enters history that freedom becomes a concrete project for consciousness. With the story of freedom and the story of history overlapping in this fashion, it should be clear that a culture can be historical and free only once it knows itself and understands its unity throughout all of its endeavors.

The modern constitutional state represents for Hegel an advanced form of social organization that possesses this self-awareness on multiple levels. It embodies the point of realization when spirit "has come to know that it has itself over against itself as an external world whose determinations are none other than spirit's own determinations."[98] The state is thus conscious both of its historical origin in its struggle for freedom and of the historically significant effect of its actions. Analogous perhaps to the sphere of morality in the *Phenomenology*, it is the "objective will," the free individual, a self-contained and self-determined product of reason. However, the state is not the ultimate horizon for self-understanding. At most, it is an important moment within the broader perspective of world history. If we follow the necessary progression of freedom, we find that, contained in the concept of state sovereignty itself, there arises the issue of "relationships among self-sufficient states."[99] While the state epitomizes the self-knowing entity, then, it is nevertheless present with others on the world-historical stage, and it must grasp itself within this sphere.

The difficulty in this demand, however, is that the realm of international relations is "a maelstrom of external contingency and the inner particularity of passions, interests, aims, of talents and virtues, of power, of wrong, and of vice."[100] The lack of any possible arbitration at this level – Hegel denies the possibility of a Kantian league of nations due to the lack of a universal will[101] – seemingly exposes the state to sheer chaos. Yet simply because there is no law at the international level does not mean that all is given over to arbitrariness. To understand oneself as an individual nation on a global scale means to view oneself under the "higher praetor [of] universal spirit that is in and for itself – the spirit of the world."[102] It means to view humanity as a whole as the proper horizon of action, to see the finite concerns of nation-states as moments in the course of world history. By inhabiting this stance, spirit knows itself as a "total human project."[103]

It is only within the world-historical horizon, then, that the claim concerning reason's rule within history finds full explanation and validation. In fact, it is world history's character of self-knowledge that justifies its position, else all would remain pure contingency. World history is thus less a designation of sheer chronological succession or a detached perspective on human development than it is the intersubjective standpoint of spirit toward itself. As a kind of theodicy, a justification of the path of history, the vantage point of world history reconciles spirit with the necessity inherent in its prior development, and with the contingencies that remain in the present.[104] This reconciliation is fully achieved only when – through a philosophical-historical investigation – one becomes aware that history had an implicit goal, and that this goal – spirit's self-consciousness – has been made explicit and actualized.

One can see in this reconciliation Hegel's reason for insisting on a historical dimension to the investigation of right. Far from being a mere traditionalist justification of contemporary practices or a complacent demand for resignation in light of world events, Hegel's inquiry intends to demonstrate that "self-understanding has practical consequences."[105] Just as the *Phenomenology* sought to demonstrate that the substance of knowing is history, so Hegel's *Philosophy of Right* conveys the possibility of knowing oneself on a world-historical level – indeed, that the time has come for such knowledge – and underscores that this knowledge is self-justifying. As crucial as it is for a state to possess an awareness of itself as a free "whole within the world," it must also know the limits of its freedom and understand "the character of the content of the ethical world that is now present and actual."[106]

Having reached this culminating level of spirit – the so-called end of (world) history – the task of philosophy would seem to be complete.

Echoing the status of absolute knowing, consciousness has become fully aware of its position in the world, of its reach, duties, and limitations. Indeed, because of these limitations – since the self-knowledge involved in this completion is itself historical, since "any code is incomplete,"[107] and since "the reality of justice can always be overturned if enough individuals choose to do so – the history of freedom is an open one in practice."[108] Not merely a recollective stance in the present, the orientation toward right is thus also a futural one, and although Hegel does not make any claims about the future, it is clear that any further developments will be part of spirit's self-determination.

Modes of Openness

We thus have an account, in Hegel, of a consciousness that is aware of both its past development and its present situatedness, and is committed to a potentially infinite future evolution, to the ongoing project of freedom. It should now be quite clear that this awareness, though reached at a certain point in time by a given state, does not in any sense constitute an "actual end of history," a ceasing of historical existence.[109] It is, instead, the recognition of an open-endedness, an infinity, inherent in self-determination. Contrary to many of his detractors who see a metaphysical imposition here, the absolute standpoint that Hegel claims to grasp is thus actually rather thin, and pertains *to* history rather than existing *above* it as the purported knowledge of our destiny. The claim is, quite bluntly, that we have no fixed identity; we are free to be who we want to be, and will always struggle in living out this desire.[110] Some have taken this stance to involve an actual achievement of infinity: freedom is then nothing but the living-out of an already attained totality, the boring perpetuation of "economic calculation, the endless solving of technical problems, environmental concerns, and the satisfaction of sophisticated consumer demands."[111] Yet this reading assumes the level of state-consciousness to be final and fixed, and Hegel himself seems to have something more adventurous in mind. While he does emphasize the necessity of binding oneself to some community that carries out the project of freedom, this is not a bond imposed from without. Indeed, against this rather conservative reading of Hegel, he clearly asserts the inevitability of change and the necessity of adapting to history in the pursuit of freedom.[112]

With these assertions concerning the open-endedness of history, Hegel seems to stand in some sort of proximity to a hermeneutical position. At least, the notion of an infinite project of freedom seems not to violate any concepts that Gadamer has put forward. Gadamer, after all, stresses the ongoing conversation in which human sociality is embedded, and lauds Hegel for his recognition that freedom, even as the acknowledged core principle of human history, will always need actualizing.[113] Spirit will always be in the process of making itself at home in the world, residing in what Gadamer calls its "space of freedom," the indissoluble "contradiction between what is real and what would be rational."[114] To this extent, there can be agreement between the two thinkers concerning one aspect of bad infinity: on concrete human existence as a futurally directed, infinite dialogue.

However, there is another aspect to bad infinity, its inward attention to a finitude that can be grasped as an infinity in the sense of inexhaustibility. In response to Hegel's adamant rejection of this aspect, Gadamer underscores the irretrievability of our origins in language and history, and underscores the necessity of always again facing the demands of the past to be interpreted and applied. This may indeed sound quite futural, and can easily be conflated with the external direction of bad infinity, but something more immediate is at stake; the inner infinity concerns the very familiarity through which one stands in continuity with tradition. That is not to say that one cannot to some extent comprehend one's historical situation and situatedness – Gadamer indeed takes our present space of freedom to be "filled with reality by prior familiarity"[115] – but it excludes any complete grasp of this familiarity. Thus, whereas for Hegel there can be a total mediation of the past that surmounts its prior alienation and at the very least solidifies its meaning for the present, such a finality, however temporary, is not possible in Gadamer's view. We may achieve momentary mediations with regard to objects – as when grasping the truth of an artwork – but with regard to transmission as such we must always reenter the process of understanding anew; no interpretation is final, and there will always be revision because the unitary horizon of historicity cannot be subsumed.[116]

Hegel's notion of completion – and of any absolute "pastness" – thus remains an insurmountable issue for Gadamer. Even when defined as an open-ended project, the recognition of self-determination that absolute knowledge entails on spirit's part remains a difficulty for any adequately hermeneutical description of our situation. While the substance of knowing is history for Hegel, he still sees this substance as an object that can, in theory, be fully grasped: it is spirit that can know itself. And while this self-knowledge does not entail that history itself would cease, it involves a surpassing of our finitude through the sublation of our historical ground: our "becoming conscious of what we are by becoming conscious of the whole process whereby we produce ourselves."[117] As related as this might sound to Gadamer's concept of the consciousness of effective history, he denies the possibility of ever grasping our historical situatedness with this level of finality, clarity, or determinacy. Concerned to maintain an accurate conception of our historical involvement, that is, one that accounts for the openness of experience, he simply cannot follow Hegel in this one-sided direction. With all of his emphasis on negativity, limitations, and unpredictability, Hegel still takes consciousness to accrue in the course of history. He views the determinate negations of spirit as engendering constructive progress in the long term. For all the emphasis he places on concretion in this developmental dynamism, he still seems to neglect the fact that historical engagement – as a precursor to any level of self-consciousness – would be the task of every singular individual. Perhaps this helps explain Gadamer's less than optimistic outlook concerning the progress of historical self-consciousness; he is aware of the eminently ongoing task of understanding not just as an anonymous historical process, but as a highly individual demand.[118]

CONTINUITY AND RUPTURE

Gadamer thus seeks to transpose Hegel's thought into a hermeneutically open position that is rooted in the concrete experience of transmission. Because it is a transposition, there are ways in which this stance still remains close to Hegel. The latter's insights into historical mediation and its movement represent crucial foundational points for philosophical hermeneutics. Indeed, the relation that Hegel describes as the unity of substance and subjectivity bears important similarity to what Gadamer describes as the intertwining of understanding and tradition in historical effect. This relation accounts both for the continuity that we inherently share with the transmission of tradition and for the fundamental interpretive and intersubjective task of grasping the continuity in more explicit and reflective terms. This proximity to Hegel explains Gadamer's remark that his philosophical hermeneutics aims to "retrace the path of Hegel's *Phenomenology of Spirit* until we discover in all that is subjective the substantiality that determines it."[119] It might initially sound far too deferential to Hegel, with its passive language of seemingly external determination. However, if one recalls the sense of negative determination (or determinate negation) that Hegel espouses, one can see that Gadamer is here locating, in substantiality, the continuity that constitutes the movement of transmission. In other words, through his account of dialectical movement, Hegel is urging us to acknowledge and reconcile ourselves to our ongoing historical situation.

It is precisely in the characterization of this situation, however, that an irreconcilable tension divides Gadamer and Hegel. The tension concerns the nature of tradition's continuity, and our relation to it. Since we belong to the movement of tradition, it is a question of self-relation, and Gadamer reads Hegel as a thinker who intended to overcome, but always remained embroiled in, the problems of self-consciousness.[120] While recognizing our historicity, Hegel also states the criterion of experience to be transparent self-knowledge or the full awareness of the assured continuity of tradition, thereby positing something that "does not do justice to hermeneutical consciousness," and that does not account adequately for our historicity or our finite experience.[121] Gadamer's concept of the consciousness of historical effect thus shares similarities with absolute knowing, but stays open or undecided in crucial ways that, as we have seen, are only hinted at in Hegel. Despite the validity of the structure and even the open-ended direction of dialectical movement in Hegel's analyses, then, Gadamer emphatically stresses the need to admit of an openness in another direction, an experience of "inner" infinity that "exceeds the omnipotence of reflection."[122]

This experience is precisely that of a limitation at the heart of our historicity. To be sure, as the mere recognition of the necessity of further

experience, this would sound strictly future-oriented and like a demand
for open-ended interpretation in the style of Hegel's historicity. However, the limitation is far more than a project that, once begun, would
remain uncertain in the precise manner of its development. It is really
the assertion of the impossibility of immediate or thetic beginning, an
insurmountable "occlusion in temporal becoming."[123] While we can become aware of and grasp our situatedness within an ongoing historical
transmission, we can never retrieve the pure outset of this embeddedness. Furthermore, our certainty of belonging to history is an ongoing
task rather than a one-time achievement. There is thus discontinuity
even within the present of our historical belonging, and when we go
through a transition from one epoch or age to the next, this does not involve a complete mediation of the old and the new in the present. "What
defines the 'maturation' of time is, instead, the real undecidedness and
open infinity of the event itself."[124]

Gadamer sees clear limits in the extent to which we can be conscious
of historical effect, and his conception of historical continuity thus includes an aspect of opacity or discontinuity that Hegel fails to consider
adequately and that he denigrates by labeling "exteriority" or "bad infinity." In Gadamer's view, "what Hegel calls bad infinity is a structural
element of historical experience as such."[125] Philosophical hermeneutics
aims to resuscitate this infinity, but with a "decisive modification."[126] It
is not some unknown force that, in contrast to reason's internal development, would determine our historical movement from the outside.
Rather, it is a course that we all follow, yet that can never be lifted into
total presence: Gadamer calls it the "path of language."[127] It is this path
that he has in mind when he considers tradition as language and as a
thou.[128] The way that it supersedes our reflection is not through overt
domination, but through the sort of alterity that happens to us through
experience and demands a response. The most adequate response that
one can give is to listen and remain open, for the inexhaustibility of interpretation and the inability to contain the other prohibit any finality. This
inconclusiveness (*Unabschliessbarkeit*) entails that our understanding
will always remain a dialogue, rather than a dialectical progression.[129]
Far from allowing us to formulate regulative ideals, it actually rules out,
as I will underscore in the next chapter, any conception of historical

understanding as the engagement in infinite tasks of Kantian or Neo-Kantian inflections. Yet the fact that historical understanding is tinged with discontinuity does not mean that we should not "*seek* for a type of reconciliation of pluralization and differences without ignoring or repressing the otherness of the Other."[130] As already stated in chapter 1, Gadamer does not proscribe identity or continuity nor assert their opposite; he merely claims that one cannot presume continuity or rupture in advance as directives of experience. It is only in the finite, particular experience of historical effect that one can claim to find continuity or discontinuity. In my concluding chapter, I will show how this experience of tradition is central to, and constitutive of, the historical human sciences.

In describing the past's occurrence to us as an inescapable address that deserves an open ear, Gadamer's formulation of our irretrievable belonging to tradition opened him to accusations of conservatism. Later in his career, perhaps in light of these reproaches, he elaborates on the opaque core of historical effect and decisively broadens his conception of tradition's alterity. Far from demanding our acceptance or deference to a specific tradition, Gadamer could now be said to "embrace the withdrawal of heritage as the very source of new meaning and experience."[131] Thus, it is not the specific Western tradition in which we are situated that constitutes our conversation and undergirds the occurrence of history. After all, traditions fade and lineages break; as he already underscored with respect to our individual lives, there is discontinuity and rupture. Gadamer's point is that we do not need a unified or univocal heritage in order for transmission itself to be effective. The rupture of the Western heritage is itself a new opening for historical understanding, shedding new light on ways to engage with and interpret the past. This is a form of freedom, a space in which the artist, for instance, can distance himself from "the pre-givens of substantial content" in order "to present everything that the human being at all has the capacity to inhabit."[132] Here we see that Gadamer is not dogmatically attached to a formulated past, to a given social structure or heritage. Even – or especially – the breakdown of a tradition reveals a solidarity that reaches beyond cultural entrenchments to the essence of human historicality as such.

Contrary to many anti-Hegelian critics who still operate with a notion of a singular history, then, Gadamer disputes the idea of a unified tradition in this sense. Yet even in this notion Gadamer still remains partially indebted to Hegel, for he gleans his notion of communicability across ruptures from Hegel's discussion of the pastness of art in the *Lectures on Aesthetics*. We thus see how Gadamer continues to accept the challenges of Hegel's thought. Gadamer's engagement thereby perfectly embodies what it means to let tradition address us, and how this occurs not once but continually. Robert Pippin is indeed correct in stating that Gadamer's appropriation of Hegel is historically situated and that we cannot encounter Hegel in the same manner today.[133] Yet this is precisely Gadamer's point; we will always understand differently.

FOUR

New Critical Consciousness

REFLECTION AND JUDGMENT

The previous chapter elaborated how, in turning to Hegel, Gadamer hopes to alleviate the ethical gap he finds in Heidegger's conception of historical involvement. Hegel's elaboration of ethical substance offers Gadamer an attractive vision of concrete, lived freedom, emphasizing the historically transmissive, intersubjective character of this project. Yet Gadamer's reading of Hegel is far from deferential even on this point. On the one hand, it echoes and intensifies the angle of critique directed at Heidegger, pushing even further into the realm of situated social life and of ongoing historical interpretation that diagnoses of *Seinsvergessenheit* and aspirations of absolute knowing intend to finalize or overcome. In this respect, both dialectic and Dasein-analysis must still be translated into the infinite ethical dialogue, that is, into the task of hermeneutic historical transmission. On the other hand, the "bad infinitization" of dialectical movement, the crucial uncovering of irretrievable historicity, occurs by way of the finitude gleaned precisely from Heidegger, and constitutes an application of this concept to intersubjective existence. From this angle, the trajectory of Gadamer's that I have laid out thus far can be read as an attempt to elaborate what an "originary ethics," first mentioned by Heidegger in the "Letter on Humanism," might be.[1] It is a matter of understanding the different senses and possibilities of freedom that arise from a historically hermeneutical interpretation of human existence.

While thus indeed rooted in a common concern for the elucidation of what Heidegger had called "finite freedom" in *Being and Time,* Gadamer's path of developing this ethical dimension, as one might expect, takes its own course. It draws from vastly different sources, and is connected to the thematic of humanism that Heidegger not only eschews, but intensely condemns as belonging to the metaphysical tradition. What is more, since Hegel provides Gadamer with only an ambiguous relation to freedom, a stance that is at once both "behind" and "in front of" Heidegger, Gadamer draws on another thinker who confronts this issue with thorough systematic force. This thinker is Kant, who for Gadamer represents both a figure of great significance for the description of our finite historical nature and a missed opportunity in the full interpretation of this description. Much as with Hegel, then, Kant is significant in terms of both his contributions and his shortcomings.

In one sense, Gadamer's involvement with Kant continues the assessment of reflective consciousness in which Hegel played such a pivotal yet ambiguous role. The issue is not, after all, whether or not reflection as such is possible. The matter lies in characterizing this reflection, in pinpointing the degree to which we can elevate ourselves above our situation; and while Hegel ascribes a mediated and intersubjective aspect to this process, he also asserts the possibility of its completion. Gadamer, through the concept of the consciousness of historical effect, denies this possibility, underlining instead the task of a continual and revisable (indeed, fallible) interpretation that can be considered both historical and critical. The fact that Gadamer stresses the need for a "new critical consciousness"[2] as part of the hermeneutic task signals his indebtedness to Enlightenment thinking on this issue, and he even explicitly states that "the Kantian warning retains its justification precisely here," where the question of our historical reflection is at stake.[3] The warning, of course, is Kant's caution against reason overstepping its bounds, and Gadamer applies it directly to Hegel's absolute knowing. Elsewhere, Gadamer compares his overall aim in *Truth and Method* to Kant's project in the *Critique of Pure Reason:* philosophical hermeneutics inquires how understanding is possible in "all human experience."[4] It is in part through this broad, critical relevance of Kant that we can expect to find out more about how Gadamer characterizes historical effect as a "hermeneutic universe,"[5] and how the consciousness of historical effect amounts to our task within this universal element.

Yet there are more minute pathways through which Gadamer takes Kant to contribute hermeneutically significant insights. In his third *Critique*, Kant recognizes the unique role that judgment plays in our cognition, ascribing it a place beyond the truth of laws and concepts. His descriptions of how we experience beauty do much to prepare Gadamer's own account of aesthetic experience, which in turn plays an exemplary and expository role in the latter's account of hermeneutical truth as a linguistically and historically situated occurrence. Moreover, Kant also alludes to the social and moral import of beauty, touching upon thematics that align closely with Gadamer's own concerns. On the whole, however, Gadamer laments that Kant retreats from the most powerful implications of his insights, both in matters of aesthetics as such and in terms of historical situatedness. While Gadamer's approximation of certain Enlightenment positions is less well known, he certainly cannot be accused of following in Kant's footsteps.[6] To Gadamer, Kant's relevance seems more that of an impetus for further inquiry into the power of judgment, a supplement to Aristotle's insights on *phronêsis*, and a signpost toward more radical conclusions regarding the cultivation of judgment and historical sensitivity. As these conclusions form the focus of the next chapter, my presentation of Gadamer's involvement with Kant will prepare for the subsequent discussion of those topics.

The present chapter will begin by situating Gadamer's concern for Kant both within the trajectory of *Truth and Method* and within the context of Gadamer's work as a whole. Here I will describe the hermeneutic and humanistic issues that drive Gadamer toward an involvement with Kant's third *Critique*, and how the latter work is thought to aid in the resuscitation of those issues. In order to assess this possibility, I will next analyze those concepts and passages from the *Critique of Judgment* that pertain most proximately to Gadamer's reading. In the subsequent presentation of this reading, I will treat Gadamer's interpretation both through his own writings and by means of recent debates on the issue. On this basis, I can return to a broader alignment of hermeneutics with Enlightenment thematics and to the humanistic concerns that form the subject matter of the next chapter.

THE NECESSITY OF KANT

There are at least two interrelated reasons why Kant's philosophy is of "necessary concern" to Gadamer. First, from the broad perspective of contemporary hermeneutics in an age of plurivocity and mutual suspicion, there is simply no getting around the question of reason's reflective capacity: the status of its freedom with regard to its historical situation, and in relation to various forms of authority and coercion. This is an issue arising eminently from Kant's conception of Enlightenment, which announced the need for a "free and public examination"[8] of religious and political claims to authority, and which subsequently developed the rational grounds and methods for this examination. As already elaborated in chapter 1, Gadamer responds critically to such accounts of autonomous reason, which he considers an implicit demand for complete historical detachment, and which he takes to embody an overall "prejudice against prejudice," that is to say, an attempt to inherently discredit any claims arising from tradition or potentially authoritative sources.

Nevertheless, Gadamer's relation to Enlightenment aims, and to Kant specifically, is not strictly antagonistic. In fact, while criticizing the epistemologically limiting framework, Gadamer sees a fundamental proximity to Kant's inherently liberating intentions, claiming that "[w]hat Kant calls Enlightenment in truth corresponds to what hermeneutics has in view."[9] There is thus a parallel to be traced between Kant's announcement of the social project of *sapere aude* and Gadamer's account of the task of engaging dialogically with historical effect. Since such a reading of Gadamer's proximity to Kant runs contrary to typical interpretations of Gadamer's position, it will need further justification over the course of this chapter. To even arrive at this level of explanation, however, we must concern ourselves with the thematic of judgment and reflection, and this requires addressing the second of Gadamer's reasons for engaging with Kant's thought.

This second, narrower reason pertains to Gadamer's overall aim, in *Truth and Method*, of elaborating and reviving a form of truth not captured by the methodical strictures of modern natural science. In previous chapters, we have seen how this truth beyond method bears a historical, linguistic character, and pertains to the practices that one might gather under the term "ethical life." Historically speaking, this conception of ethically pertinent truth was quite pervasive prior to the development of modern science and, connected as it is to practical concerns, has strong roots in the humanist tradition – especially in that tradition's ideals of cultivation (*Bildung*), tact, judgment, and the communal or common sense (*sensus communis*). Drawing on sources such as Shaftesbury and Vico, Gadamer aligns common sense with *phronêsis*, stressing that it is a knowing that shapes moral existence, and therefore has its place in the social-ethical realm. Put in Hegelian terms, it is a sense, acquired and honed in communal life, that is crucial to reconciling oneself with the substance of this community. Looking both to the communal and historical ideals for guidance, common sense gains and sustains a "sense of what is right."[10] It thus also reflects the situation of the human sciences over against the natural sciences, for the object of the human sciences – moral and historical life – is precisely determined by the *sensus communis*.

Gadamer underlines that taste, too, possesses intrinsic moral and social dimensions, and was characterized prior to Kant as its own mode of knowledge. Capable of evaluating the particular in relation to a whole that is not pregiven, it applies even beyond the confines of aesthetics. Indeed, all matters of morality and law demand this approach, and taste thus operates in a community as something central, but not subservient, to it. Taste in this social sense entails having the proper distance from things in order to make good judgments, and is thus not a merely private or subjective stance. Gadamer elucidates the history and interconnection of these concepts very early in *Truth and Method* as an outline indication of what he seeks to retrieve. Yet since a rupture has occurred with regard to the tradition of these concepts, since they no longer shape our lives to any decisive extent, their sense of truth no longer finds much – if any – purchase in the present.

On the surface, this discontinuity might not seem problematic, and Gadamer's aims of retrieval not that difficult to achieve. After all, by describing the reasons that a past age had for employing the experiential notion of truth, Gadamer is seemingly already allocating these reasons a place in present discourse. One might therefore consider it merely a matter of adequate argument – strong evidence of their value, for instance – to revive these particular ideas and this specific conception of truth. At another extreme, the rupture would not be problematic if one could envision, as Heidegger does, a new beginning with regard to truth. It would be a matter of leaving the past tradition, as well as the present's problematic technological-scientific conceptions, behind. Even further along these lines, it might not even strike one as imperative that a philosophical project aiming to describe the truth of practical life has to deal with this truth's historical existence at all; it need only be proven to exist on logical or argumentative grounds, perhaps even by appeal to transcendental structures.

Gadamer's entire point concerning these approaches is that they are not adequate to the presentation, let alone the grasp and retrieval, of experiential truth. They apply foreign standards to that concept of truth that he is trying to delineate and that he believes makes its own convincing claims. To ameliorate our presently impoverished or limited situation with regard to the understanding of truth, then, it cannot be enough to simply announce the adoption of an older truth-conception. This would amount to antiquarianism, an importation of the foreign into the familiar without a clear understanding of its provenance, relevance, or mode of existence. The entire issue, as the previous chapters have helped to illustrate, is that this humanist conception of truth entails recognizing an alternative human ontology to modern subjectivity. It entails taking finitude as one's starting point, and engaging the ruptured tradition from this vantage point. With historicist options ruled out, Gadamer's solution is accordingly to engage with, and performatively retrieve, the very experience of truth that he wishes to resuscitate: he will return to the humanist ideals, but only by retracing the way in which they lost their traction and were relegated from the realm of truth to that of art and subjective feeling. It is only through this retracing, Gadamer believes, that we can experience and understand their claim to truth, which is also the truth of ethical life and "the human sciences as a whole."[11] The retrieval of these ideals can, in addition, serve to define and delimit the capacities of Enlightenment reason.

Gadamer therefore needs to address the subjectivization of truth, which occurred largely through the field of aesthetics in the past two hundred years and lives on today. Kant ends up being the most important figure in this regard, for even if he is not directly responsible for the development of aesthetic consciousness, he nevertheless prepared its way as the initiator of what Gadamer calls "aesthetic differentiation."[12] While still tied intrinsically to the concepts of taste and genius, this abstraction – indeed an uprooting of art from its social and hermeneutic soil – ultimately stems from Kant's narrowing of the *sensus communis* to a domainless and therefore truthless judgment of taste. By employing and narrowing the scope of the central humanistic ideals, then, the *Critique of Judgment* presents a direct connection back to that earlier tradition. Thus, given what we have said about the type of retrieval that occurs here, Gadamer's "analysis of Kant is a bridge that connects Gadamer's own project with the project of humanism."[13] In order to grasp this bridge-function of Kant's third *Critique,* I will first elaborate its key concepts that are relevant to Gadamer's analysis.

UPROOTING TASTE IN THE THIRD *CRITIQUE*

The judgment of taste, as Kant delimits it in the "Analytic of the Beautiful," can be described as "homeless" or "uprooted" insofar as it has no legislative domain, nor even, like its close relative the empirical judgment, a residence (*domicilium*) in nature. However, although it does not rest on concepts or sensations, taste is nevertheless taken to be valid for everyone, and resides in all judging persons in the form of a subjectively universal principle, the concept of purposiveness. The judgment's universality is rooted in the idea of a common sense, an ideal standard that serves as the condition for communicating the pleasure felt in the free play of cognitive powers. Thus, though Kant's account delimits a place for taste, it is at most a transcendental one. Gadamer ultimately wishes to press Kant on whether his conception of the *sensus communis,* displaced as it is from the historical-linguistic realm of tradition and sociality, is enough to account for the understanding experience of art, in which the artwork reveals a connection to the world and to our place in it. My inquiry in this section, then, takes place in two steps. First, I will clarify where Kant takes taste to reside, inquiring in more detail about the universality of the judgment of taste, its "voice," and its grounding in a common sense. On this basis, I investigate the commonality that Kant takes taste to establish. Here I am concerned with questions regarding the cultivation of taste, its moral dimensions, and the activity of the genius.

Domains and Powers in Kant's Critical System

In the second, revised introduction to the *Critique of Judgment,* Kant delimits the respective domains of the cognitive powers, the separate fields for which they are legislative. These domains had already been securely established in the first two *Critiques,* and Kant here merely indicates cognition's different orientation with respect to these areas. The understanding, we are reminded, gives laws to the domain of appearances by supplying these appearances with the "concepts of nature." We are limited in our theoretical endeavors to the natural domain of "the objects of all possible experience," since the understanding's legislation restricts itself to phenomena.[14] Reason, on the other hand, gives laws to the "practical sphere," the domain of possible human action, by means of the "concept of freedom."[15] We are free in this domain, as nature does not determine us to act in any certain way. In our practical pursuits, we are detached from nature and think of ourselves as belonging to the intelligible, supersensible realm. The legislation that reason exercises here takes the form of the categorical imperative, the law by which the will ought to be determined and which each rational subject gives to himself.

Despite these differing legislative orientations, however, Kant points out that the domains of understanding and reason rest upon common ground. Both cognitive powers can be logically thought as being operative within us, as the first *Critique* has demonstrated, and thus both may inhabit the territory of possible experience. Moreover, this territory is itself situated within a larger realm, the unbounded realm of the supersensible. Yet this realm is inaccessible to the legislative grasp of either cognitive power, since within the territory of possible experience, the cognitive powers mutually inhibit each other's complete (i.e., theoretical) knowledge of the unbounded realm. Understanding's concepts permit of intuition of appearances without knowing their supersensible substratum, or noumena, and reason can think things in themselves without any hope of intuiting them. While remaining the basis of all possible experience, then, the supersensible realm cannot become a territory or domain for cognition. We can occupy this realm with practical ideas, but no permanent, theoretical advance from the knowledge of the sensible world to that of the supersensible is possible.

Nevertheless, as already indicated, the cognitive powers share the same territory of possible experience. The supersensible concept of freedom, reason's legislation to the domain of human action, is precisely intended to have an effect in the sensible world. In acting, we step purposively into nature. If this is to be the case, however, it must be possible to think the laws of freedom harmonizing with the a priori lawfulness of nature, to imagine our practical purposes as compatible with, and feasible in, the sensible world. Thinking this harmony of freedom and nature, supplying a "basis *uniting* the supersensible that underlies nature and the supersensible that the concept of freedom contains practically"[16] entails, for Kant, judging nature as if it were itself purposive. The concept of the basis, the principle of purposiveness legislated by such a judgment, would not possess its own domain, however, as it reflectively gives its a priori rule to itself rather than to nature or to freedom. As we will see in more detail below, reflective judgment thus determines the subjective feeling of pleasure – which unites the cognitive power with the power of desire – instead of imposing any concepts on nature. Judgment of this kind accordingly falls completely outside the bounds of cognition, as it merely mediates between nature and freedom, and makes a movement between the two possible.

In order for the harmony between nature and freedom to arise, we not only must think of nature as being purposive, but must experience it that way as well. Indeed, one always already treats nature as if it possessed a higher unity, one intends it as purposive. When this intention is fulfilled, when purposiveness "appears," the experience gives rise to pleasure. This pleasure, while remaining a subjective feeling, also makes a claim to universal validity. To understand this a priori validity of reflective judgments, it is necessary to clarify precisely how purposiveness is experienced. As I am concerned here only with matters of taste, I will restrict the investigation to reflective aesthetic judgments regarding beauty.

Judgments of Taste

As already stated, the aesthetic judgment makes no cognitive claim. Whereas cognition of objects requires sensory intuition and its subsumption under concepts, the aesthetic judgment apprehends the object only in its intuitive form. Furthermore, it takes no interest in the object's existence, and even someone on an "uninhabited island" should be able to declare something beautiful.[17] In this formalistic stance, there is not even reference to the sensory content, the material aspect of the appearance. Since the judgment ignores objective presentations, the apprehension of the object's form is singular and relates solely to the subject.[18]

In a movement of simultaneous receptivity and active detachment, the imagination takes up the form of the object and compares it to the power of understanding. In this comparison, which entails a relation to, but not an activity of the understanding, the form is set in accord with the subject's cognitive powers. The resulting free play of imagination and understanding is the source of the experience of subjective purposiveness, since it appears as if the form had been tailored, as if on purpose, to our cognitive powers. This purposiveness, Kant stresses, is furthermore felt as pleasure. Pleasure is thus not simply the consequence of the conformity of the object's form to the cognitive powers. To feel the free play *is* to feel pleasure.

Kant defines taste as the "ability to judge by such a pleasure (and hence also with universal validity),"[19] indicating on the one hand that taste is not a merely private capacity, and on the other that pleasure – and the purposiveness involved in giving rise to it – plays some role in this validation beyond individual limits. To say that some object is beautiful may indeed merely be a claim regarding the object's form and the subject's singular apprehension thereof, but this judgment nevertheless asserts a bindingness for everyone. It is worth recalling, on this note, that the necessity of the judgment of taste is not a conceptual universality. As a singular judgment, it does not identify anything as true, nor does it make any cognitive claims concerning the object. The question, then, is how it asserts its validity. Wherein is its universality grounded? In describing the second moment of a judgment of taste, Kant reiterates that its universal validity is not objective or logical, but rather subjective, "for although it does not connect the predicate of beauty with the concept of the *object*, considered in its entire logical sphere, yet it extends that predicate over the entire sphere of *judging persons*."[20] We may, therefore, not be able to logically prove an instance of beauty or give a rule as to its judgment, but we go beyond private sensation in pronouncing a judgment of taste. We speak it in a "universal voice" that applies to all people capable of judgment.[21] Shortly, this voice of taste will turn out to rest upon an even deeper ground, a common sense that constitutes the very possibility of communication, and thus grounds taste's universality.

Noting that any communication must somehow pertain to cognition, that universality is impossible if not tied to knowledge in some way, Kant suggests that the universal communicability of taste is "nothing but the mental state in the free play of imagination and understanding (insofar as they harmonize with each other as required for *cognition in general*)."[22] Put differently, because one's imagination and understanding are in harmony in the judgment of taste, in "that proportioned attunement which we require for all cognition," one has the capacity to communicate universal validity in the judgment of taste.[23] As Kant puts it, since "cognitions are to be communicated, then the mental state [...] required for cognition in general [...] must also be universally communicable."[24] The paradox in the judgment's universality, however, lies in the fact that the subject cannot reflexively know his or her mental state as one that is required for cognition in general. There is no conceptual, objective view that one can take to ascertain one's position with regard to knowledge as a whole. Rather – stressing again the character of aesthetic judgment as reflective – we must sense the necessity of the judgment of taste from a subjective standpoint: the "unity in the relation [between the cognitive powers] in the subject can reveal itself only through sensation [*Empfindung*]."[25]

In order to be able to speak with a universal voice, therefore, we must be able to sense the validity of judgments of taste. Kant locates this ability "to compare our own judgment with human reason in general"[26] in a common sense, which he takes care to distinguish from the conceptual, though frequently obscure, "common understanding [*gemeinen Verstande*] that is sometimes also called common sense [*sensus communis*]."[27] When the object's form accords with our cognitive powers, and the form proves to be harmonious with the free play of imagination and understanding, common sense allows us to feel the harmony of the cognitive powers in their universal relation *as* a universal relation. By virtue of this sense, we can reflect on our own judgment, take into account "the merely possible judgments of others,"[28] and "judge a priori the communicability of the feelings that are connected with a given presentation."[29] The common sense is thus the condition of the possibility of feeling the unity of powers, and the condition of communicating anything about them.

Explicating the fourth moment of judgments of taste, and drawing the "Analytic of the Beautiful" to a close, Kant describes judgments of taste as exemplary instances of this common sense. It is a sense that serves as the basis for communication, but that cannot itself be communicated, for we cannot state it as a rule or a concept. The binding necessity of judgments is thus a necessity of exemplarity. All we can state are the judgments, not the condition underlying them. The singular judgment thus serves to exhibit vocally the universality of the common sense, while the latter remains a presupposed "ideal standard" that is exemplified in these instances. As Kant grounds taste on – indeed identifies it with – the common sense, it bears investigating what kind of commonality this sense establishes. This involves such issues as the cultivation of taste and its connection to morality, nature, and genius.

The Ideal of Taste

In the final paragraph concerning the fourth moment of taste, Kant raises the question whether common sense, and therefore taste, is an "original and natural ability, or [...] only the idea of an ability yet to be acquired."[30] Though he defers an immediate response, and nowhere supplies an outright answer, various indications point toward the latter conception. Manfred Kuehn reads the matter this way, noting that "common sense as taste is intimately connected with practical reason and can ultimately be understood only in relation with it."[31] The passage that supports this thesis most strongly is found in the closing sentence of the "Critique of Aesthetic Judgment." Here Kant speaks of an "unchangeable form" of taste that will take shape only upon the propaedeutic cultivation of our "moral feeling."[32] As the culmination of our moral development, the "universal human sense"[33] of taste is something that ought to be brought about. It is thus tied intrinsically to practical reason.

One can find similar indications of taste as an ideal much earlier in the *Critique of Judgment*. A thematic and structural shift, indicative of Kant's view, already occurs in sections 16 and 17, in which Kant leaves pure judgments of taste behind in favor of fixed or accessory beauty. He describes the ideal of taste – by which we model our own ability of taste – as an "archetype"[34] that we ourselves generate. Yet, as rational, this idea can neither be intuited nor, since it pertains to judgment, be conceptualized. Only an ideal of beauty, therefore, can present this idea. It is at this point that Kant rules out pure judgments of taste as capable of presenting ideal beauty, and thus as presenting the idea of taste that we seek. Only mixed judgments of taste can ever hope to present ideal beauty, since they are "partly intellectual,"[35] or connected to concepts of objective purposiveness. Judging ideal beauty thus entails connecting an interest to it, an intellectual interest that pure judgments of taste – bearing no intrinsic connection to morality – lack.

Due to our interests in the ideal, Kant believes that mixed judgments of taste have a certain priority in life, that "we regard some products of taste as *exemplary*."[36] Kant acknowledges that, in order to "find the rule [...] within himself,"[37] one will attend to examples in experience. He distinguishes "[*f*]*ollowing* by reference to a precedent" from "imitating,"[38] as the example should serve as an influence rather than a basis for a judgment, and any empirical determination of our taste would constitute a breach of its autonomy.[39] Thus, while taste might be extended and cultivated by way of examples, the basis for its judgments remains entirely in the sphere of subjective universality. It is in connection with this apparent linear order that Kant stresses the prior development of morality as a prerequisite for taste. Pointing out that "direct interest in the beautiful in nature is actually not common,"[40] he stresses numerous times that taking a direct interest in nature's beauty presumes previous moral training: "one can do so only to the extent that [one] has *beforehand* already solidly established an interest in the morally good."[41] With regard to this establishment, one could point out the general necessity of human self-determination, that is, acting with respect toward the moral law. With sufficient honing of our human propensities, we thus might be capable of appreciating exemplars of beauty.

Nonetheless, Kant underlines the unique character of direct interest as one that is not common. As a special relation to the beautiful, it is not simply the result of a linear development. Rather, there seems to be a reciprocal furthering of taste and morality, as indicated by the notion, in section 59, of "Beauty as the Symbol of Morality." In symbolic hypotyposis, Kant notes, an analogy is established between the respective forms of reflection in judgment and reason. Instances of beauty, and the mixed judgments that pertain to them, help us in realizing rational ideas concretely, and thus arouse – and connect with – our direct interest in the moral. As Kant puts it, such judgments help us "transition from sense enjoyment to moral feeling,"[42] "from sensible charm to a habitual moral interest without making too violent a leap."[43] We can conclude, therefore, that while ideal taste presumes our completed moral development, this moral feeling is itself cultivated through exemplars of taste.

Kant takes care to discern precisely what kind of interests we connect with judgments of taste. He notes that it is very *"interesting"* to have taste in society, believing that we take a social interest in the beautiful because our judgment allows us to communicate our feelings about beauty to others, and this in turn furthers our sociability.[44] This alignment of our interest, however, makes taste subservient to inclination, and limits our interest to the empirical. There is thus no intrinsic or direct connection to morality, no movement between appearance and freedom. A direct interest would be one that arises with, and connects to, examples of purposiveness as instances of ideal beauty.

One source of such examples is nature. In fact, for Kant, nature (or what we consider natural) is all that we can take a direct interest in.[45] The fact that nature can display a purposiveness without having a purpose, that it can show a "voluptuousness for the mind," means that one "cannot meditate about the beauty of *nature* without at the same time finding [one's] interest aroused."[46] Taking such interest directly indicates our attachment to morality, for we thereby display our desire that the ideas of practical reason find objective realization. Another exemplary source may be found in art, for fine art possesses the capacity to "have the *look* of nature even though we are conscious of it as art."[47] The genius, as a creator of original and exemplary beauty, and as one inspired – indeed, gifted – by nature, evokes an interest similar to the one we have in nature. Having the incommunicable ability to discover and express aesthetic ideas, the genius can pass them along to others, communicating "the mental attunement that those ideas produce."[48]

What remains incommunicable, however, even to the genius himself, is the natural gift of producing art. In his inspiration, something exceeds the genius's ability to know how he expresses his ideas; this talent comes to him from nature. Since the genius's exemplarity is at the same time his "*free* use of his cognitive powers,"[49] a judging of beautiful art, then, entails feeling a purposiveness that is at once natural and tied to the realm of human freedom. As with the exemplars of beauty treated above, however, the genius's art is not something we can learn or copy. The most we can hope to glean from our experience of fine art, for Kant, is a sense of the genius's ideas. We can abstract from the artists' products, collecting "models of fine art [as] the only means of transmitting these ideas to posterity."[50]

The preceding analyses show that taste and morality are inextricably and reciprocally linked for Kant. In this regard, the ideal of taste, common sense, stands as a universal goal which, while not communicable itself, provides the basis for any communication. Exemplary natural beauty serves to evoke this common sense. Similarly, the fine art of the genius provides us not with the ideal itself, the rule by which to achieve beauty, but with models that serve to cultivate our direct interest in the moral and guide our taste. Through taste, then, for Kant, we may indeed find ourselves in a moral-aesthetic community, but it is one that does not require any empirically social or historical basis.

BETWEEN ENLIGHTENMENT AND HUMANISM

Questioning Aesthetic Consciousness

As mentioned above, Gadamer situates his critique of Kant's aesthetics within a broader elaboration of the notion of aesthetic consciousness, along with what he views as its attendant modes of abstraction, culti-

vation, and lived experience. While these points of contention in fact
fall more squarely on the shoulders of Schelling, Goethe, or Schiller,
Gadamer nevertheless pinpoints in Kant the initial conception of art
that gave rise to aesthetic consciousness. By denying taste a place in
any region of knowledge, and separating it from empirical-historical
sociality, Kant prepares the way for aesthetic abstraction, a tendency
to ignore all that is not an aesthetic quality in the work of art. This has
had the consequence, according to the analysis in *Truth and Method*, of
relegating art to a subjective or "artistic-instinctive"[51] realm, eventually
eradicating any cognitive claim in art whatsoever.

The most important insight to be gleaned from Kant's account of
taste, so Gadamer maintains, is that it reveals the imagination to be
productive without the guidance of concepts or rules. However, while
we have seen that Kant certainly retains an intrinsic moral connection
to taste, Gadamer contends that Kant ends up removing the domain of
taste, and thus also that of common sense, from its properly social and
cognitive element, from "out of the center of philosophy."[52] Since the aesthetics of taste is formal and reflective, when Kant calls it the "common
sense" he is really not touching at all upon the humanistic social or moral
aspects of that term. Both taste and common sense reside, for Kant, in
a transcendental reflection, making any claims of sociality or tradition
upon taste impossible or at least invalid. From a Kantian angle this is
entirely unsurprising, as the moral sphere is not empirically determined.
Yet these social claims, according to the humanist tradition Gadamer
seeks to revive, are precisely the means by which taste is taken to arise
and shape itself. Thus, the issue is not only that Kant narrows the *sensus
communis* from a broader range of judgment to an aesthetic judgment
of taste, but that he also narrows taste itself to being strictly formal and
without substance. Its universality stems from a largely negative definition, being described by what it abstracts from (subjective attractiveness,
specific faculties, or external senses).

Interestingly, Kant hints beyond these aesthetic limitations of taste
when he describes the "Ideal of Beauty" in section 17. In this ideal, so
Kant asserts, the human form can express or at least hint at a moral end,
namely that of human perfection. In such human depictions, then, we
see not only the formal beauty from which we derive sensible pleasure,

but a purposive, intellectual meaning as well. It becomes a nonconceptual yet cognitive way of encountering ourselves in the world. Because of this, Gadamer notes that the "very recognition of the non-conceptuality of taste leads beyond an aesthetics of taste."[53] It is a beauty in which "the ethical [*das Sittliche*] comes to expression."[54] Kant seems to agree when he declares that "judging by an ideal of beauty is not a mere judgment of taste."[55] Nevertheless, Gadamer claims that Kant skirts this revealing insight because, for the purposes of the *Critique of the Judgment* as a whole, he is interested in the pure, contentless beauty of nature. The latter, as "suited to the end of our pleasure," speaks a sort of "language that brings *us* to the intelligible idea of what mankind is to be."[56] Had Kant dealt more deeply with this thematic on the side of art, so Gadamer believes, he would have recognized that art has the advantage of speaking to us far more clearly and directly. Kant had hinted in this direction when speaking of the morally symbolic character of beauty, but he failed to develop this idea further.[57]

Despite the narrowing of taste to the aesthetic realm, then, there remains in Kant's account a strong connection between art and the ethical. It is located in the curious reciprocal development of taste and moral feeling, a mutual cultivation that would seemingly not be able to sever itself from culture or tradition entirely.[58] Here one could point to the character of judgment not only as a transcendental faculty, but as a social task that makes universal demands. While Gadamer does not analyze this circular movement in any detail, he notes that Kant's allusion to the humanities (*humaniora*) as a source of sociability is purely formal, this propaedeutic simply being another requirement for ideal taste.[59] Kant seems interested only in the way in which empirical models help establish the moral feeling that grounds taste, not in their actual content. Moreover, with taste conceived as an ideal, as an unchangeable perfection, it loses all connection to *Bildung,* the cultivated yet continually open ground for tact and taste in the historical human sciences. Gadamer points out that the very idea of a perfect taste "has something nonsensical about it," for it aims at establishing a "uniform taste" through which everyone, formally speaking, would agree what constitutes the quality of a given work of art.[60] Gadamer has in mind here the models of fine art that are abstracted from the genius's work, as the sole ideas capable of being passed on and immortalized. Identifying these eternally significant shapes in art, singling them out as potential experiences of the beautiful, thus constitutes aesthetic abstraction, which uproots the beautiful qualities of art out of their tradition, releases "the work of art from its place and time in history and sequester[s] it in the timeless existence of the museum."[61]

Noting that art historians are just beginning to "return [works] aesthetically to their home,"[62] and seeking to understand just how their ahistorical abstraction has been justified, Gadamer turns to common conceptions of the genius's production of art, as well the nineteenth-century notion of *Erlebniskunst*. For Kant, as we have seen, the reflective judgment's mediating movement evokes, and ultimately satisfies, our desire to see freedom's ideas realized in nature. The genius, inspired by nature, is capable of expressing aesthetic ideas that fulfill this desire, revealing in this invention a certain mysterious source, nature's apparent purposiveness without a purpose. Since the genius's creation is a free, nonconceptual invention, he stands as if unmediated by culture or tradition. Grounded in the formal idea of a common sense, the genius would intend a certain meaning to be communicated, with this then guiding the production of the work. Finally, with this intention fulfilled, the work would stand completed for observation, awaiting reception of the communicated meaning.

As Gadamer indicates, this model of artistic creation presupposes a "reciprocal creativity and profound understanding [. . .] on the part of the artist's fellow-geniuses."[63] It assumes the ability on the part of the observer to experience (*erleben*), in a way analogous to reproducing the work, the aesthetic consciousness and its inspirational source. This *Erlebniskunst* conception of art appreciation, furthermore, presumes the completeness of the artist's creation, as well as the existence of a univocal binding meaning contained in the work. Gadamer takes this abstract stance toward art to be "an illusion,"[64] noting that all art criticism actually refutes the possibility of this view, since it makes no effort or pretense to understand works of art in this binding way. In this regard, any aesthetic theory that seeks to understand much *about* the artwork possesses only a secondary relationship to the work of art, a position intended to be undermined or superseded by that of philosophical hermeneutics.

Historical Effect and the Truth of Art

Richard Velkley, underlining a certain commonality in Gadamer's and Kant's aesthetic remarks, notes that they both want to "preserve a suprahuman dimension of the beautiful on the basis of a turning away from theoretical metaphysics."[65] While for Kant this preservation entails connecting the beautiful (through nature) with freedom, Gadamer would locate the suprahuman in "the whole ocean of the beautiful," the transmission of tradition itself.[66] Thus, what Gadamer has criticized as the abstractive aspects of the Enlightenment's emancipatory stance entail that "'aesthetic consciousness' and 'historical consciousness' represent only alienated forms of our true historical being."[67] In other words, while the pure work of art removes itself from sociality and finitude in aesthetic consciousness, a hermeneutically adequate relationship to art must take historicity and facticity into account: "We must adopt a standpoint in relation to art and the beautiful that does not pretend to immediacy but corresponds to the historical nature of the human condition."[68] The truth of art and the truth of historical experience are thus mutually involved and indeed congruent.

Due to this connection to historical effect, the hermeneutic encounter with art, so Gadamer asserts, must treat encounters with art as experiences of a different sort – as "occurrences of meaning [*Sinngeschehen*]."[69] They are accordingly *Erfahrungen* entailing knowledge rather than mere *Erlebnisse*. This is where Gadamer intends to take over Kant's important insight into the nonconceptuality of imagination, and extend it into the realm of truth. Turning against the abstraction initiated by Kant, Gadamer therefore asserts an "aesthetic non-differentiation," the "inner entanglement of the formal and the substantial in the experience of art."[70] Instead of assuming the work to contain a fixed – if formal and incommunicable – meaning, a hermeneutic perspective understands the work in every encounter as a substantive, social, and "unfinished event."[71]

[nihilism / deference]

Gadamer is well aware of the twofold danger of such a declaration. *
On the one side lies the pitfall of a hermeneutic nihilism, which would *The charges for*
recognize the social relevance of the artwork but, on the basis of its his- *post-*
toricity and taste's inherent variability, would deny the work any last- *modanism*
ing or binding meaning. Gadamer aims to avoid this relativist risk by *Conservatism.*
accounting for our belonging to a work's effect, and by elaborating the
mode of its claim upon us. Thus, though we never possess a complete understanding of a work, we are also not free from its effect. Herein lies the
other side of the danger, however. The risk is that of being too deferential
to the artwork and, by extension, to any claim made upon us by experience. This romanticist accusation stems from Gadamer's formulations
of art-experience as immersive play and "ecstatic self-forgetfulness,"[72]
and accordingly underlines the apparent lack of critical awareness in
this stance. It would be a "movement of subjection" that abrogates any
capacity for reflection.[73]

While both of these challenges extend irrationalist accusations toward Gadamer's overall sense of historical effect, the latter charge in
particular would seriously endanger Gadamer's claim that hermeneutics,
as an ongoing dialogue, remains aligned with the Enlightenment ideal
of rational discourse. It would entail "that his notion of tradition moves
too closely to the sublime self-forgetfulness that characterizes the experience of art."[74] This is a variation of the charge of traditionalism that we
encountered in chapter 1, and is presumably what Oskar Becker had in
mind when he accused Gadamer of "religious faith in history [*Geschichtsgläubigkeit*]."[75] Contrary to this claim, I wish to argue that Gadamer
steers clear of the romanticist association and that his connections with
Enlightenment thematics represent more than just "aspirations" that
he fails to live up to.[76] Making this case will ultimately extend beyond
a discussion of art. For now, however, it is a matter of clarifying how
Gadamer's conception of the experience of art is not deferential, and
therefore does not infect the concept of historical effect with an inherent
subjectivism, religiosity, or anti-Enlightenment irrationalism.

In this regard, it is helpful to take Gadamer's 1974 essay, "The Relevance of the Beautiful," into account. Here Gadamer elaborates and
clarifies his earlier description, in *Truth and Method*, of the play (*Spiel*)

that is involved in the experience of art. He notes that every work of art opens a space for this play, and draws the audience in through a sensible intelligibility. By the latter, Gadamer means that perception itself has inherent meaning-content, and takes this to be the actual phenomenon of the understanding's free play with the imagination that Kant had in mind with the judgment of taste. It is not a matter of simply conjoining the sensible and intelligible, however; the issue is instead that we must think through, following Kant, what an experience of art might involve that is defined neither by the empirical nor by the concept.[77] This entails that the work confronts one with a task of intuition (*Anschauung*), of building it up (*Aufbauen*) and reading it as one would a text.[78] Here Gadamer underlines that this reading "is always an accomplishment of reflection, a spiritual accomplishment [*geistige Leistung*], whether I occupy myself with handed-down formations of typical artistic creation or am challenged by modern creations. The accomplishment of (meaning-) accretion [*Aufbauleistung*] that belongs to the play of reflection lies in the work itself as a demand."[79] From this, it is no leap to grasp what Gadamer states about the symbolic character of art-experience. As symbol, that which the artwork presents is not a reference to an external and preexisting sense. Rather, the meaning is precisely there in the work and demands to be heard.[80] It is our task as interpreters, however, to learn how to hear and understand this meaning, but since the reading and hearing of meaning requires cultivation (and not just the sort that inculcates terms and concepts for understanding artworks conceptually or historically), it is best accomplished in a community that concerns itself with such knowledge. The parsing of the "unknown vocabularies" presented by every work demands the development of a "communicative commonality."[81]

Even with these descriptions of reflective engagement and communal discourse, the conception of the experience of art as a task reveals the core issue of the irrationalist claims against Gadamer. The obligatoriness (*Verbindlichkeit*) with which he takes artworks, especially classical works, to be imbued represents for his critics a lamentable abrogation of critical reason, a "subordination" that "shatters the concept of a dialogical mutuality."[82] At issue, apparently, is the authority with which works make their claims upon us. To respond to this, several points bear addressing. First, it should be clear that, while an artwork may certainly reflect the community it is a part of, the hermeneutical involvement with its truth is not simply a task imposed from the outside, stemming from religious, social, or political pressures. Neither, however, does an artwork's claim reside in a timeless, inherent value. Instead, it arises from the artwork itself, as a work that addresses one by virtue of existing in the present. This address is one of understanding; it places a demand on us when it presents the work's meaning as something to be understood.

Second, contrary to misreadings of Gadamer, this demand is not something that forcefully subsumes us and robs us of agency or voice. An artwork might indeed assail us, envelop us, or make us uncomfortable. It might stand before us an eminent text, imbued with significance or validity (*Geltung*) by a long history of being understood and withstanding critique. In all of these cases, we become aware, via the broader horizon of historical transmission as such, of our situation of belonging to the work's effect. The fact that our consciousness is "subordinate" to or "stands under" (*untersteht*) this effect[83] does not mean that we relinquish our reflective capacities or the dialogical ability to respond. In fact, it is quite the opposite. The encounter with the work demands our critical response, and the work lives on only through the response, not in spite of it. The "constantly self-renewing contemporaneousness,"[84] the ongoing validity of a work in the present, is not achieved without its linguistic operation, and this is both reflectively and intersubjectively dialogical.

With these points, one can see Gadamer working intently against a romanticist notion of involvement with the artwork. The emphasis on reflection and responsive interpretation, and the inclusion of these within a discursive context oriented by a *sensus communis* in the humanist sense, bespeaks an engaged experience that is far from submissive. Furthermore, the purported infective influence of Gadamer's conception of artistic truth upon historical effect is, if anything, actually quite the reverse. The beauty of meaning in art, even in the classical, is one that we always understand differently, and this "engages the historicity of our existence."[85] Art thus speaks to us from our ontological ground of history and tradition. In experiencing, knowing, and understanding beauty, therefore, we are understanding from out of our historical situation, and coming to know this situation for what it is: a situation of ongoing effect. Thus, it is not the case that Gadamer's conception of the truth of art contaminates his notion of the truth-claims of tradition. Rather, the experience of art uncovers the ontological fact of our situatedness in historical transmission as such: "The task of bringing the contemporary and that lapidary residue of the past together is a good elucidation of what tradition always is."[86]

Through this connection with our historicity, the experiential encounter with art is thus both a task and an opportunity. The demand it places, on the one hand, is for us to engage interpretively with its meaning, to listen and potentially understand something that pertains to us and our world. In this latter aspect, on the other hand, lies the opportunity. Since an experience of hermeneutic truth inherently engages our historicity, it challenges us to develop our sense of this aspect of our being, to hone our historical sensitivities such that we might interact with works all the more thoroughly and reflectively. One could think of this as a kind of formative circularity, the being-at-work of *Bildung,* in which the task of using our judgment serves both to induce our reflective awareness of it and to enhance it. Put succinctly in a way that returns us to phrasings from earlier chapters: hermeneutic encounters draw on the ontological fact of historical effect, and both require and potentially strengthen our consciousness of this historical effect.

One purpose of Gadamer's discussion of art and taste, then, is just to arrive at this insight concerning judgment and cultivation, effect and consciousness. By showing that aesthetic experience arises out of the natural and ongoing practice of understanding, it identifies this experience as knowledge and returns it to an intersubjective and historical context. In this way, it directs us far away from Kant's conception of art, and indeed points our attention to the knowledge involved in the humanist ideals. Yet Gadamer's discussion inevitably also pushes us further into Kantian issues of reflection and critique. While the understanding achieved in the hermeneutic encounter with the work of art is not strictly equatable with the reflection involved in the consciousness of historical effect, their partial congruence nevertheless provides a clue as to what this reflection entails. Gadamer's involvement with the *Critique of Judgment* is thus a way both of retrieving a notion of hermeneutic truth from within Kantian aesthetics and of facing the broader thematic of rational, emancipatory discourse with which Enlightenment thinking confronts us. It is to this issue that I will now turn.

HERMENEUTICALLY RATIONAL DISCOURSE

By returning us to the question of belonging and effect, the discussion of art and taste raises to prominence again the issue of hermeneutical reflection and its limits, and brings us to the initial, overarching reason for Gadamer's necessary concern with Kant. Though the status of reflection has been a central issue over the course of the previous chapters, I have not yet fully addressed the claim that the consciousness of historical effect amounts to an anti-Enlightenment position of *Geschichtsgläubigkeit*. I have shown that the experience of art, in its belonging to the work, does not bleed irrationalism into an account of social or historical dialogue, but that, conversely, historical transmission and the experience of contemporaneity is the basis for the experience of art. This experience is accordingly an indication of a more pervasive belonging that envelops all understanding. Such belonging would still promote the suspicion, on many readers' parts, that it is irrational, or at the very least entails a situation of prerational belief that demands decisive reflective clarification. It would thus seem to constitute a blind deference to cultural authority, precisely the force that Enlightenment thought had hoped to eradicate. This is, of course, a constellation of traditionalist and perspectivist suspicions that we already encountered in chapter 1. By squarely confronting them again here, I can underline the way in which Gadamer evades them, formulates a notion of ethical dialogue, and thereby positions himself in proximate and fruitful tension with Enlightenment ideals.

The suspicions of blind deference to tradition, Gadamer replies, are founded upon a fundamental misunderstanding both of authority as a social phenomenon and of hermeneutics as a philosophical task. With respect to the latter, Gadamer notes that his philosophical aim is not to limit the practice of understanding to a specific discipline or range of material, thereby confining it within the realm of specific cultural traditions and their claims. While hermeneutics arose historically out of an engagement with certain texts and interpretive problematics, it can today rightly be viewed as universal in scope, as pertaining to "all the contexts that determine and condition the linguisticality of the human experience of the world."[87] Its range derives from the fact that finite and historical understanding is the fundamental character of our existence, and this issues in the role of hermeneutics as a task: its practice "means that we should try to understand everything that can be understood."[88] If this rules out false conceptions of hermeneutics as culturally bound or subservient, the task remains of correcting false conceptions of what understanding can achieve.

Understanding is limited by virtue of its always being situated within a horizon. The immediate horizon of the historical present includes everything that one takes to be familiar, and is largely made up of one's own prejudices and intentions, but is not derived from one's agency alone. Because of this, it often includes things with which one is not entirely familiar, or which one in any case did not actively decide to bring into the situation. That is the fact of alterity or strangeness within the horizon, and one that cannot ever be eradicated. This is the finitude of thrownness, the effect of history. Yet despite banishing a notion of pure agency, this foreign element of the present horizon possesses neither the sheer bindingness of an unconditional force nor the debilitating isolation of perspectivism. To be sure, the ontological situatedness in history conditions available prejudices, but these prejudices are not themselves fixed, nor is the horizon within which they arise. Since the transmission of history is itself an ongoing movement of "one great horizon," any prejudice or understanding on our part is an extension of this movement, and therefore inherently provisional.

To view the situation as such, to recognize the intertwined relationship to historical transmission, is to view one's position as lying between strangeness and familiarity. Taking account of this position's transmissive movement, one comes to recognize it as revisable and open. Reaching this recognition amounts to a reflective awareness of one's situation, a consciousness of historical effect. Yet this consciousness cannot be established autonomously or by way of decision; nor can it be commanded or imposed. After all, how would one know it to be possible, or upon what authority would one choose to acquire it? It is to be gained only through the experience of negativity, by sensing firsthand the circulation between strangeness and familiarity in one's prejudices. In order to achieve any level of reflection, the involvement with historical effect itself is therefore a necessary preliminary task.

Gadamer thus does not deny the possibility of a reflection that emancipates us from an inimical, unconscious embeddedness in tradition. Indeed, his conception of tradition inherently includes this possibility. After all, the provenance and development of reflective consciousness is directly tied to the experience of historical transmission itself. Because of this connection, however, and due to the constantly provisional nature of prejudices, reflection can never extricate itself from tradition. Instead, as a heightened form of historical experience, it represents a thoughtful involvement with transmission. If maintained with attentiveness to its provenance, the consciousness of historical effect is thus a dialogue with openness at its core.

All of this bears crucially on what Gadamer means by the authority of tradition. This authority is just another term for the sheer fact of our horizon being beyond our control. Since the consciousness of historical effect will always be situated, its reflection will always entail "more 'being' [*Sein*] than consciousness [*Bewusstsein*]."[89] Further, as ontologically inescapable, this being cannot be treated as an unwarranted influence to be dissolved. In other words, understanding need not involve seeing through undue prejudices, but might entail taking them over. Even a stance that wished to renew itself on entirely familiar ground, and to preserve nothing of its handed-down prejudices, could not extricate itself from the need to form and engage with new prejudices. No foothold that one can gain with regard to one's situation is definitive; instead this situation always bears the task of renewed involvement with historical effect. Just as Gadamer showed that the encounter with art involves an aesthetic nondifferentiation, so he asserts here that there is really no "opposition and separation between the ongoing, natural 'tradition' and the reflective appropriation of it."[90]

What is thus frequently mistaken for an authoritarian imposition upon reflection, or a blind acceptance of influence, is in Gadamer's view merely the ongoing presence of historical effect itself, and its implicit demand for reflective-dialogical engagement. Gadamer speaks of a work, idea, or event having some bearing in the present because it makes a claim. The truth of this claim, however, it is not the truth of a proposition, but simply the validity of its being contemporaneous. For whatever reason, it is a part of our present horizon, or juts up against that horizon from out of a distance within the greater horizon of transmission itself. It is part of our experience. The force sustaining this work's validity, moreover, does not reside in its claim alone, but in our conjunctive response to it. Just as authority in the usual sense depends on acceptance for its power, so the preservation of an historical effect depends on our recognition, effort, and accomplishment. It depends on our openness to negative experience. Thus, Gadamer's point regarding the authority of the past is that it is taken over reflectively, through some degree of insight.

 As the activity of engaging with the past has a bearing on what one takes to be valid and hermeneutically true, the dialogue with the alterity of history can be considered fallible in a broad sense. That is, depending on whether we are convinced by the past's claims, we might just as well take them over as reject them, and therein lies the freedom of our responsiveness to tradition.[91] Nevertheless, this freedom can be exercised well or poorly, and there is something of an evaluative standard by which to assess its use. At issue is whether one attends adequately enough to tradition's claims, whether one not only listens to the past, but listens with an ear toward and the questionability of one's own claims. Briefly put, it is a matter of negative experience and openness. This standard of openness that consciousness employs in this dialogue does not supervene upon it from elsewhere, however. It is not a timeless standard of correctness, but is a standard of practice that is itself generated from within historical engagement. It attests to the fact that we can succeed or fail as historically reflective beings and that this success or failure is measured according to the recognition and exercise of our finite freedom.

Since the claims of our historical situation derive from the contemporaneousness of effect, everything pertaining to that effect extends to the realm of intersubjectivity as well. The task of listening and the standard of openness are therefore just as much ethical dimensions of consciousness as they are historical. The consciousness of historical effect, then, amounts to more than a solitary engagement with the contents of a personal horizon. It is instead the constant challenge of engaging adequately with the alterity that one experiences and that one can only ever partially or temporarily comprehend. Put differently, it is the task of communicating clearly, of listening deeply, and of living out our freedom as an infinite project.

Based on these aspects, the consciousness of historical effect bears some, though not perfect, resemblance to an Enlightenment project of rational discourse. Far from relinquishing the standards of reason or the freedom of the individual, it accounts for their possibility and indeed requires their exercise if hermeneutical reflection is at all to be considered ethical. Further, rather than denying the possibility of progress, it involves its own peculiar sense of it, as the capacity for ongoing dialogue can certainly be honed and developed. In another peculiar proximity to Kant, Gadamer's account of historical belonging could be said to involve his own critique of judgment, inasmuch as he delimits the capacity of reflection to a constant pursuit of a universal (understanding), enacted as an ethical response to a situation that offers nothing but particulars.

As much as Gadamer's stance approximates an Enlightenment position, it also contains powerful criticisms of the way the Enlightenment project has been conceived over the course of its history. Thus, while Gadamer certainly maintains Kant's ongoing importance for philosophy, and views the *Critique of Judgment* in particular as a "lasting challenge to our thinking,"[92] he sees definite limits in Enlightenment reason and its contemporary instantiations. These pertain chiefly to emancipation, autonomy, and completion. Regarding the first, Gadamer clearly restricts the power of reason to free itself from a given situation. While consciousness "is not deprived of the possibility of critically approaching and interrogating the norms and principles that dominate in a given historical situation,"[93] it nevertheless cannot extricate itself from that situation as such. This amounts to a denial of isolated subjectivity or rational autonomy. Individuals can still be said to possess freedom, and this freedom in fact pervades any social or historical encounter, but the way in which it can be exercised depends greatly on a person's capacity for hermeneutical dialogue and openness. It is therefore not a transcendental power merely needing to be released from empirical chains.

This, then, challenges the "illusion" of an "infinite task" inherent in rational progress.[94] Echoing the sentiment at the core of his critique of Hegel, Gadamer calls into question the notion of taking one's hermeneutic bearing from a "limiting concept of perfect interaction."[95] This concept would amount, after all, to a completely congruent alignment of clear motives and performed action, a banishment of anything foreign from one's historical situation. To be sure, one might couch this concept of perfection in the language of social ideals, but Gadamer notes that even posing such an infinite task is itself already dangerous, as it sets up an expectation that we are not actually capable of fulfilling.[96] Any notion of completion involves this danger, for Gadamer. He therefore pointedly asks "whether a completed enlightenment which would dissolve all human predisposition and societal prejudices is an intelligible claim."[97] By asking this, he is turning the Enlightenment's aversion to dogmatism against itself.

In thus stepping back behind Kant in a crucial way, Gadamer is demonstrating the importance of humanist ideals in the conception of historical existence and the truths that are to be formulated in it. By reconnecting reflection and judgment to the exercise of a finite, situated freedom, Gadamer widens the scope of core Enlightenment concepts onto the expanse of social life from which they were originally derived. Though I have begun to trace here how the consciousness of historical effect embodies humanist ideals and relates to social life as an ethical task, I will treat these relations in more detail in the next chapter.

FIVE

The *Bildung* of Community

HISTORICAL EFFECT AND HUMAN CONDUCT

Over the course of the previous four chapters, I have shown how Gadamer develops an expansive constellation of concepts concerning historical existence. These concepts, drawn from debates spanning two centuries of German thought, account for both an ontological structure of historical-linguistic finitude and an intersubjective task of ongoing reflection and openness. Far from being a concession to historicist perspectivism, the historical belonging at the core of philosophical hermeneutics always entails transmission, dialogical practice, and ongoing experience. Arising from this experience is the central concept of the consciousness of historical effect, which, contrary to popular misreadings, is not a dogmatically imposed or traditionalist outlook, but a form of reflection that acknowledges our finitude and inherently transmissive movement and that takes the shape of dialogical engagement with the tradition. Accordingly, the significance of this consciousness is precisely that it avoids the respective positions of hegemonic appropriation and incommensurability, and amounts instead to a form of sensitivity to difference and alterity.

In recognizing the ineluctable finitude of historical situatedness, the consciousness of historical effect is not a merely ontological perspective in the theoretical sense; in being intrinsically intertwined with the rhetorical and social elements of transmission, it carries with it an immediate ethical dimension. Further, as its task of listening and its standard of openness pertain not only to traditional cultural objects but to foreign horizons and accordingly to alterity as such, its ethical position cannot be narrowly confined to a backward-gazing judgment upon history, nor to romanticist nostalgia for unity with the past. Rather, the reflective capacities involved in the consciousness of historical effect are constantly directed toward human conduct as such, the individual's situation within a broader social horizon, and the normative questions that inherently attend such situatedness. Put differently, the consciousness of historical effect is the furthest possible reflective development of our finite mode of understanding. This is why, with Herder, Gadamer emphasizes that the task of such reflection is not an artificial end derived from any specific tradition or conception of human essence, but constitutes instead the "infinite element" of life, indeed the meaning of "humanity" (*Humanität*) itself.[1]

This emphatic identification returns us to the theme of Gadamer's retrieval of humanist ideals. In situating Gadamer with respect to Enlightenment and romanticist issues, the previous chapter helped prepare this theme and trace out the character of hermeneutical reflection as social reason. There, through Gadamer's critique of aesthetic consciousness, we saw that he takes judgment to be far from a groundless and formal faculty. Rather, by demanding an experiential and nonconceptual engagement with alterity, judgment opens onto a whole of human experience, along with the historical senses of memory and community, and requires an ongoing openness in order to function. Together, these therefore amount to a *praxis* rather than to cognitive-theoretical capacities. Here we see how Gadamer delineates his own concepts in terms of humanist ideals, retrieving the latter through a connection with more recent conceptual developments brought forth through dialogue with the likes of Hegel and Heidegger. This enables Gadamer to formulate the outlines of a social reason that is not methodical or guided by impossible Enlightenment ideals, but is rooted in finitude and approximates something like Aristotle's notion of *phronêsis*.[2]

In chapter 1, I described how Gadamer adopts the process of application entailed by *phronêsis* to the hermeneutical task of historically situated dialogue. I also noted that the consciousness of historical effect bears more than a mere structural kinship to *phronêsis*. Arising from and pertaining to habits within a community, they are both inherently ethical modes of understanding. Yet neither *phronêsis* nor the reflective openness toward historical effect arises automatically or suddenly. They develop out of natural practices and on the basis of everyday experience, and because of this developmental character they can be honed and exercised well or poorly. As human practices, they arise gradually and admit of gradations. *Phronêsis* and the consciousness of historical effect therefore involve all of the difficulties that attend to human cultivation. Their inception obviously cannot be commanded dogmatically nor inculcated through expert training. They are certainly in need of teachers, but the latter can serve at most as role models rather than as instructors of rote behavior.[3] After all, both *phronêsis* and the consciousness of historical effect require actual firsthand experience in order to arise, develop, and become stable. The negativity of experience – its calling into question of one's presuppositions, prejudices, and motives – constitutes the fertile soil from which any reflection regarding past and present, desire and action, can arise. Not only this, but experience constitutes the very element of *phronêsis* and the consciousness of historical effect. They both develop from out of the demands of experience, and in turn become modes of engaging with and more adequately understanding experience.

This presents two significant characteristics of experience in the cultivation of these ethical positions. First, it underscores the necessity of experience being of a certain sort. If one is to cultivate an ethical stance that is both reflective and open, one must come to know the possibilities of action and the limits of one's commitments, as well as one's own tendencies and proclivities. This self-knowledge can develop, however, only by these commitments and tendencies being challenged. Without putting one's stance at actual risk in confrontation with another position, one has no sense of the validity of one's stance, nor of the possible truth of what one faces. One lacks any sense of what is questionable. Secondly, since what is at issue is the honing of an ethical sense or sensitivity, the task of cultivation reveals the need of something other than a haphazard accumulation of various experiences. If one is to become receptive to experience and capable of judging about it, one certainly needs a diverse array of challenges, but one also needs the time and setting to reflect on them and incorporate them into one's overall sense of self.

Beyond its close connection to *phronêsis,* the sensitivity entailed by the consciousness of historical effect can also be located in the humanist senses of tact, memory, and community. Gadamer takes these to contribute to our capacity for engaging in rational ethical discourse, that is, the nonconceptual, intersubjective conversation of *Sittlichkeit*. Further, he points out that these senses have typically arisen in confrontations with the material that forms the core of the historical human sciences, that is, the works of art, literature, philosophy, and religion that have proven to be continually challenging and formative over the course of their transmission. This partially ordered and historical confrontation is itself circumscribed by another central humanist ideal, namely that of *Bildung* or cultivation, and this ideal captures Gadamer's attention as a perfect embodiment of the true experience he seeks.[4] *Bildung* is the formative encounter with texts, ideas, questions, events, and figures that draws out our sense of historicity by challenging our situated stances, and like *phronêsis* bears close resemblance to the consciousness of historical effect.

Currently, this ideal of *Bildung* has all but disappeared from the popular discourse concerning the humanities. One tends to frame education in general in terms of inculcation of facts or, at most, as useful skill development, and this ends up engulfing the humanities as well. The dominant paradigm of "data-driven decision making" demands that any educative process always be accountable to some form of testing, be it through outcome assessment or ongoing measurement.[5] At the scholarly level, this manifests itself in a pervasive emphasis on empirical research and attempts at technological augmentation – as when software is employed to analyze the content of literary texts. There is certainly a strain of discourse that seeks to counteract these trends, but its effectiveness remains debatable. Recent defenses of the humanities, even when delivered by scholars and public intellectuals, have tended to paint far too vague or weak a picture of what a humanistic education entails.[6] Stuck in a defensive position against data-obsessed and budget-driven administrators and politicians, these accounts merely advocate for the continued existence of the humanities as such, and risk characterizing these disciplines as providing mere supplementary social abilities to the sciences, skills that would lend a more humane face to pragmatic or economically minded professions. The humanities are credited with developing critical thinking or logical reasoning skills, which ostensibly allow their possessors to free themselves from the bonds of tradition and authority; engagement with classical texts is said to generate freedom, which of course any democracy should value. Yet the conceptual underpinnings of this process – theoretical or practical – are rarely discussed, leaving only anecdotal descriptions, rather than philosophical defenses, of what a humanistic education entails. Thin accounts such as these thus lack any reference to the ontological grounding of the humanities in historical effect, and accordingly fail to adequately emphasize the pervasive ethical role that this form of cultivation can play.

As mentioned, part of the reason for this omission and failure certainly lies in the defensive position the humanities have been forced to take. Due to higher education's insistence on cosmetic appearance and financial success, the current crisis of the humanities is barely even perceived beyond liberal arts departments, and it is thus an uphill struggle for the issue to even gain recognition. In this regard, works like Nussbaum's are fulfilling a necessary popular role. However, this "silent crisis," while indeed a problem, is rooted in a much deeper crisis that had its climax a century ago and yet that was never adequately resolved. This was the crisis of historicism, which pitted human sciences broadly speaking against the demands of a burgeoning and empirically advantaged scientism, with the latter eventually infecting the human sciences through its formalism and paving the way for such phenomena as impact figures in scholarly publishing and the reduction of philosophy to ten basic problems.[7]

Heidegger, through his approach of *Destruktion,* was one of the first thinkers to have broken through the entrenchments of that earlier crisis by referring to the very ontological-historical conditions that make any science possible.[8] In chapter 2, I showed how Gadamer takes up Heidegger's early impetus in this regard and directs it toward a humanistic engagement with the tradition. Gadamer's claim at the outset of *Truth and Method* and sustained over the course of his career is that, despite their nineteenth-century crisis in method, and their current crisis in confidence, support, and identity, the humanities remain connected to the ideal of cultivation – and thereby to the shaping of human conduct in general – by virtue of the fact that they have their source in the experience of historical effect. In fact, the experience of historical effect and the consciousness of it would be unimaginable without some traditional practice of reading and interpreting texts. It is through the engagement with this effect in its diverse historical guises that the humanities generate properly hermeneutical experiences, raise our historicity to awareness, and thus possess their formative and transformative capacity. That is, the humanities call forth understanding and challenge it in such a way that it becomes critically reflective yet receptive to further experience. In short, they present and fulfill the task of historical belonging; as disciplines of *Bildung,* they cultivate the ethical comportment of openness. By ceaselessly requiring application and its accompanying sensitivities, the humanities are, for Gadamer, the only adequate hermeneutical training through which a widespread critical consciousness can possibly arise. It is thus through engagement with and reflection upon the hermeneutical core of historical belonging that the humanities can come to constitute communities. In what follows, I will elaborate and defend this claim.

THE INTERTWINED HISTORICAL
CORE OF THE HUMANITIES

To say that the humanities represent the *only* path to a reflective consciousness seems too strong a claim for Gadamer to possibly make, and one might hesitate to agree for several reasons. First, Gadamer's focus on the humanities would seem to deny the hermeneutical relevance of the natural sciences, whereas it is precisely these sciences that have seen a burgeoning interest in questions of interpretation, language, and history. Second, given his assertion of the universality of hermeneutics, the narrowing of attention to any one discipline or range thereof seems highly arbitrary. After all, as Gadamer himself underscores, hermeneutics is broader than any discipline or the "arena of the *Geisteswissenschaften*"; it "reaches into all the contexts that determine and condition the linguisticality of the human experience of the world."[9] Thus, in order to reflect upon historical and linguistic situatedness, one evidently need not limit oneself to the human sciences in general, or the humanities in particular. The phenomena with which Gadamer is concerned are broader than any given area of study, and therefore cannot be aligned with any definite practice apart from human understanding as a whole.

In response to the first hesitation, Gadamer points out that while the natural sciences do indeed belong to – and more recently engage with – our historical-linguistic determinacies, they will always fall short of full hermeneutical reflection in the sense accounted for by philosophical hermeneutics. This is because human history is its "own whole" apart from natural history, bearing concerns and aims that fall outside the purview of objective verification and prediction.[10] To employ a Kantian distinction, this whole constitutes the realm of freedom rather than nature. This is the realm in which we continually (re)attempt to formulate our ultimate ends and situate our cultural progress. The *praxis* of life and responsibility does not admit of expert evidence or definitive proof, demanding instead an ethical approach that seeks mutual recognition and validity. Here Gadamer views the humanities as needing to overcome their subordination to the methods of natural science – and the latter as indeed needing to recognize its hermeneutical aspects. Yet one might argue that, just as positivism is no longer the dominant counterposition to hermeneutical truth in general, the target of methodology at which Gadamer takes aim here is no longer the substantive threat to the humanities. Instead, they face a deeper and more existential threat that stems from a fundamental misunderstanding of our historical nature. Facing this danger requires clarifying our ontology. By engaging with human tradition as more than a mere object of investigation, but instead as the very element of our existence, the humanities play the crucial role of addressing our normative commonalities and thereby contributing to our grasp of possibilities. They do so by being themselves of the same, singular order as the events of concrete action.

This helps address the second hesitation. For rather than constituting a narrowing of focus, Gadamer's preeminent concern for the humanities stems precisely from their character of reflecting the whole of human life, always being reshaped and reconfigured as is life itself. Thus, the issue behind Gadamer's seemingly exclusive disciplinary focus is not that other areas of life lack hermeneutical character. The point is that, if we are on the whole concerned with the social rationality of hermeneutical reflection, it can be cultivated only through the experience that engenders it. This experience, moreover, stems from engagement with the interrogative texture and intersubjective character of our historical-linguistic belonging; and even if this texture and character has faded from prominence in the historical human sciences, they above all are most capable of bringing it back to importance. Yet in order to raise this capacity and prompt this retrieval, the humanities of the present day are in drastic need of conceptual grounding and self-understanding, and Gadamer takes it as his task to at least make inroads in this endeavor.[11] The key to this clarification consists in retrieving the historical core of *Bildung,* the formative experience that embodies the character of the humanities for Gadamer.

This should not give the impression, however, that Gadamer is merely engaged in resuscitation of a past pedagogical tradition or of its canonical content. For those readers already inclined to relegate Gadamer to romanticist irrationalism, his espousal of the *Bildung*-ideal would appear to confirm an uncritical commitment to a specific bourgeois culture. However, Gadamer is not advocating the revival of a particular historical ideal, and in fact criticizes the romanticist attempts to sustain or rebuild a unified historical narrative at all costs. He instead takes *Bildung,* this core idea of the historical human sciences, to provide an insight into universal conditions of understanding that always already exist. Viewed from the present, that also means that what Gadamer considers under the guise of these disciplines is more than just a Western educational context; the humanities are part of a "civilizational multiplicity," a "history full of questions" that will continue to challenge us.[12] In this way, these human sciences, like a work of art spanning centuries, are an "unfinished event" that reveals on a large scale what human truth can be.[13] By generating an experience of how truth occurs historically, the humanities offer instruction in the fact and the process of continual historical understanding, and present the task of an ethical comportment of openness that best sustains this understanding. Far more than simply accumulating historiographical detail, they present ontological insight combined with a normative task. They mediate a "truth in which one must *try to share.*"[14]

In one sense, this sharing always already occurs, regardless of our attempts at reflecting upon it; the transmissive movement of history takes place whether we are aware of it or not. In another sense, however, it is not a shared experience until it is raised to the level of a reflective dialogue and maintains the experiential openness of this conversation. The humanities thus "have their own logic,"[15] preserving experience in a different way than natural science does. They do so in an explicitly historical fashion, with reference to and reflection upon experience itself. That is, they engender and expressly employ the consciousness of historical effect that I have investigated over the course of the previous four chapters. The *Bildung* that Gadamer locates within the humanities, then, is not a specific historical bourgeois ideal, but a potential for formation and transformation in general. It is "a truly historical concept, whose historical character of preservation [*Aufbewahrung*] is precisely the key point for understanding the human sciences."[16] Describing the key characteristics of this preservation or shared truth will allow me to elaborate how the consciousness of historical effect arises in the humanities, and to subsequently treat how this cultivation results in a form of community.

To begin with, regarding the overall notion of preservation, it should be clear from our prior analyses that the task of the humanities is not just to naively appropriate tradition. To be sure, their "path of truth" is "[t]o listen to tradition and to stand in it,"[17] but this attentive belonging, as we have seen from descriptions of historical effect, is anything but submissive. The point is not to apprentice oneself to and absorb a set canon or fixed array of ideas. From the broadest angle, it is not necessarily even about maintaining the relevance of specific great works and their teachings. Rather, what is preserved in the humanities lies in the effect one engages with through any historical encounter. The works and ideas of history are important not simply for the factual matter of their content, but for the comportment they reveal toward questions of human concern. To be sure, the content cannot be separated from this comportment, but that is precisely why preservation involves an encounter rather than a summary of key points. The works themselves are delineated opportunities for an experience of historical effect; they are "sites of dialogical engagement," and thereby offer a demonstrative account of the various potential attitudes toward historical effect.[18]

Thus, just as it is not the specific contents of poetry that matter in revealing what Gadamer calls the infinitely speculative nature of language, but indeed the poetic possibilities within language itself, it is also not primarily a matter of gleaning formulable historical lessons when encountering tradition as such. The objects of *Bildung* cannot be used up or disposed; they do not constitute momentary and sequential parts of a greater whole that could be formulated. To be sure, the history of ideas presents us with an array of thought-paths of which some lead in more promising directions than others. Nevertheless, it cannot be prescribed in advance which encounter will take us further, or what our future directions will consist in. Instead, through engagement with specific works, one is faced with the open ontological basis of tradition's transmission, the ongoing historical effect with which one is irrevocably intertwined.

Recognizing this intertwining of self and tradition – the reciprocally conditioned and mutually dependent relation between the subject in history and the subject matter of history – constitutes a further dimension of what *Bildung* preserves. The recognition amounts to the development of a hermeneutical receptivity, an ability to hear the sites of dialogical engagement as questions or claims stemming from the subject-matter of tradition. While on the one hand this involves a philosophical insight into one's ontology, the confrontation between past claims and one's contemporary horizon inevitably poses an ethical task of adequate engagement. As the claims represent a strong form of negativity, this experience can be an extremely difficult challenge to meet. Coming upon an idea that challenges one's position often leads to an impulsive reaction of immediate dismissal, especially if it can be ascribed to the unenlightened mentality of a bygone age. Yet the proper engagement of recognizing this claim does not require actually taking this idea over; one might instead find one's own position strengthened through the dialogue with it. Conversely, it might also reveal that one's own position is unwarranted or at least unreflected. One of the most crucial insights that this experience can engender, then, is that one side of the relation need not be right or universally valid; through the interplay of horizons, one can find both one's own prejudices and the claims of tradition to be unconvincing. One has then laid bare the historical space of interpretation itself, which is a space of questionability as well as one of finite freedom.[19]

This helps underscore that the preservation in question is not a one-sided determination of the present by the past, nor is it the gradual absorption of the past into the present. As we have already had occasion to see with regard to historicist positions in chapter 1 and Enlightenment aims in chapter 4, the entire framing of historical reflection as being about escape from undue influences fails to properly grasp our situation and task. Any notion of leaping out of tradition's influence and beginning anew is therefore problematic and illusory. What is needed instead is a hermeneutical stance, an ethical commitment to finitude that maintains a position beyond the disjunctive attitude of "self *or* tradition," and sustains a capacity for engaging over and over again with tradition's effect of questionability. This sustaining movement is precisely what preservation in the humanities means. It is not unlike the twofold infinity and openness elaborated in chapter 3, through which one recognizes both the unsurveyable ground of one's historical position and the endless task of mediating between strangeness and familiarity. As such an operation of mediation, one could also describe it as a form of translation: not a matter of simply transferring a past idea into the present, it is also a matter of moving toward this idea from one's own position and without relinquishing this position.[20] In historical encounters, through the fusion of horizons, we learn to translate ourselves and thereby to understand differently. Since this process is never complete, and since it bears the forward and backward mobility that underlies the interplay of horizons, it can be aligned with the movement of history itself.[21]

The task of *Bildung,* then, is to recognize the present possibilities generated by the intertwined relation of self and tradition, that is, to grasp the situatedness in tradition both as an effective encounter and as an ongoing dialogue. This involves attention, active reflection, and participation. The fact that *Bildung* takes place within the element of constant historical movement, furthermore, means that one's conversational belonging is conditioned by the decisive aspects of distance and contingency. Experientially, an initial distance will always be necessary to provide some inceptive impulse. After all, horizons cannot jut up against one another unless they at least seem to exist in themselves: "Tradition, which consists in part in handing down self-evident traditional material, must have become questionable before it can become explicitly conscious that appropriating tradition is a hermeneutic task."[22] To induce the alterity necessary for such questionability is thus itself a task for *Bildung,* and this helps explain the continued use of certain materials over others.[23] Such intensification of difference creates a space of questionability, a distance within which intertwining is first uncovered and interpretation flourishes. Once generated, however, this distance performs its effectiveness all on its own. That is, once the task becomes manifest of delivering-over or translating the past across a distance, it is a matter of responsive comportment. The distance of questionability reveals the contingency of specific traditions and ideas, resulting in an experience of negativity that cannot be procured within the bounds of one's present horizon. The decisive point is how one reacts to this contingency.

While one is never able to escape experience as such, one can, of course, always close oneself off and deny the full force of experience. Alternatively, one can delude oneself in thinking that one's experience is complete, that no further claims can have an effect. The unique capacity of the humanities, however, lies in challenging these stances and, keeping the space of questionability open, making them less meaningful and desirable than the task of actual reflective engagement. This occurs when, through differential encounters in the space of interpretation, one develops a consciousness of one's intertwined relation to tradition.

This consciousness – which is congruent with the consciousness of historical effect – involves taking one's perspective as part of the greater movement of transmission and fostering an openness to what this movement has to communicate. Yet, as just elaborated, this development is not imposed upon tradition as an external point of view upon it; the consciousness arises from engagement with, and belonging to, the movement itself. Within the activity of *Bildung,* history accordingly comes to possess the same maieutic capacity as that contained on a smaller scale in Platonic dialogues. We are drawn along into the activity of questioning, and through *aporiae* and attempts at understanding we arrive at something like *anamnesis,* the recollection of our situatedness in a greater historical transmission. Yet just as Platonic dialogues end up generating the awareness of ignorance, so an engagement with tradition reveals an opacity in this situatedness, and throws open the question of our identity. Through involvement with the past, we indeed recognize that we have no fixed and essential nature, but it is for precisely this reason that we need tradition. Apart from the reflective engagement with our historicity, there simply is nothing to which human existence can be firmly attached. We *are* the experience of historical effect.

The ongoing dialogue of tradition, reinvigorated and preserved in the *Bildung* of the humanities, is an extended and reflective form of this experience. The core of the humanities, their object of concern and the source of their cultivation, is thus the substance of history in which we always already find ourselves, and which we in fact are. The challenge that they issue is to remain constantly on the way to self-knowledge by continually engaging with this substance.

THE EXPERIENCE OF HISTORICAL ENGAGEMENT

Given that the humanities are thus not capable of teleological completion, and are not mere means to an external end, it is difficult to speak of results when describing such an education. Nevertheless, Gadamer points out that *Bildung* refers both to the process of cultivation and to the outcome of having-been-formed,[24] and we have seen how one such outcome involves the commitment to ongoing preservation. I have elucidated this preservation as a reflective stance that acknowledges our belonging to the movement of tradition, but that also sees the inherent transformative possibilities in this belonging. Preservation therefore means sustaining the relation that suspends a distinct dichotomy of self and tradition, instead taking them together as the element of experience. By taking part explicitly in this experience and sustaining it, *Bildung* really produces nothing more than experience – or the state of having-become-experienced, which amounts to an openness to further experience. *Bildung* is thus finite and hermeneutically negative, but just herein lie its substantial formative capacities.

The first such capacity, and the most fundamental, is that of revealing who or what we are. In uncovering our situatedness within the broader movement of history, the historical-hermeneutical core of *Bildung* clarifies that we are formed by dialogical engagements, and are thus more closely identified with practices than with an essential human nature. This recognition amounts to an insight into finitude, and when taken over explicitly involves a reflective dwelling amid the transitory horizons of experience. It entails the transformative double realization both that one's situation is given but open to continual revision and that the future consists of indeterminate new challenges for thought. This insight into hermeneutically finite subjectivity indeed poses serious tasks, such as maintaining the awareness of one's in-between nature and stemming the temptation toward fixity or sedimentation. These are actually challenges of discernment or prudence, of knowing one's acquired experiences as capable of generating adequate responses to future experience.

A second crucial capacity assists in this discernment. Broadly conceived, it is the awareness of depending on something larger than oneself, be it the ongoing movement of tradition or the linguisticality of specific discourses and practices. Both of these aspects join to make up the actual texture of our human communities.[25] From a negative perspective, the awareness of these aspects helps relinquish or at least temper the constant desire to establish firm grounds or methods concerning one's situated involvement; one is less tempted by reason's illusions of individual control if one can trust in a broader process. It is in this relinquishment and embrace of uncertainty that one can locate a positive movement toward a notion of communal engagement. The awareness of dependence, a form of *sensus communis* borne out of historical engagement, indeed entails a receptivity for alterity but also involves an active acknowledgment of the importance of social ties. The hermeneutic comportment brought about by *Bildung* includes the realization that one's identity – one's having-been and one's projective possibility – is connected to the horizons and historical effect of others. Herein lies the humanities' powerful antidote to relativism, elaborating in its place the inherent good of intersubjective exchange.

To be sure, this good does not carry the normative force of a rule or an a priori value, nor does it include a readily formulable standard by which to assess human interaction as a source of experience. Because of its uncertain ground and seemingly nihilistic conclusions, the historicity at the core of the humanities makes the latter extremely susceptible to influences of fashionability and power. Nevertheless, these influences are precisely what the humanities develop a sense for and guard against. By demonstrating intersubjective and historical exchange to be a practice rather than a methodical procedure, the humanities stem the general instrumentalization of human action, effecting a reversal of *technê* toward *phronêsis* that is precisely to help us live in a world where "there are no rules."[26] By emphasizing transmission and the differential space of interpretation, they also counteract a tendency within the sciences to normalize language and concepts, and thus hone one's judgment of particulars. Rather than being oriented toward a fixed, ideal conception of human essence or morality, the humanities continually pose the challenge of generating and questioning our own aims and standards.

Through these aspects, *Bildung* can be seen to engender the capacity for critical reflection traced out in the previous chapter. Far more than a pedagogical device or theoretical approach to be applied in an educational setting, it is bound up with our existence as historical-linguistic beings and promotes a conscious engagement with that existence. Further, *Bildung* is neither a regime or ideology of its own nor an instrumental social virtue that merely enables the smoother functioning of an existing regime. The experience at the heart of the humanities, the result of being-experienced to which they are conducive, is thus a form of freedom. It is a freedom that is cognizant of its finitude, but equally aware of its capacity to appropriate its situation differently and thereby shape the future of humanity.

GADAMER'S ENACTMENT OF BILDUNG

Despite this immense significance of the humanities for critical thought and social reason, Gadamer himself showed extreme reticence about any prescriptive statements concerning education. He refused to advocate for any specific form of *Bildung,* and saw that getting the historical human sciences to discover their core identity is not purely an administrative task. No matter how freely one shapes an educational framework, it cannot of itself bring about the insights described here. These insights are, by and large, a human issue, always linked to the interior life of students and the external pressures they are under. Thus Gadamer was, on the whole, quite skeptical of a critical consciousness ever arising from *Bildung,* noting that any education, no matter how hermeneutical, always arrives "too late" to exercise its truly cultivating task.[27] This is quite likely another point he has absorbed from Aristotle: whether a student is attentive enough in a lecture course on ethics, and experienced enough to understand its significance, depends almost entirely on how she has been raised.[28] Gadamer's analogous position would seem to claim that our familial experience prior to academic *Bildung* greatly determines – and potentially undermines – the latter's effectiveness. Yet this claim, if taken too far, would seem to advocate a quietism concerning education, and relegate philosophical hermeneutics to a merely descriptive role in matters of cultivation; indeed, Gadamer underscores that his philosophy shows what *does* occur in understanding, not what *should* occur.[29] Yet given his insistence on the interconnection of theory and practice, and given everything I have elaborated here concerning the ethical implications of his core concept of historical effect, it remains significant that the humanities – more so than any other single field of human activity – can engender the form of reflection that properly engages our historical nature. Gadamer is well aware of this significance, and does not believe it impossible for the humanities to survive and succeed, but ultimately considers theirs a "barely solvable task" of recognizing the "new and the fruitful" in historical engagement.[30]

A crucial requirement for this success is the development of historical sensitivity and the ability to recognize good or classical examples. What is surprising about Gadamer's reticence and tone here is the fact that he himself embodies this sensitivity and finesse for exemplars. His was a lifetime of new and fruitful involvement with historical effect, and of attentive yet critical listening to the claims of tradition. The central three chapters of the present investigation attest to this interpretive capacity; Gadamer leaves a distance and questionability in place throughout his conversations with other thinkers. Perhaps taking a cue from his early experience as a student of Heidegger's, Gadamer pursues a similar aim to the once "hidden king": that of making history come alive.[31] Given this aim, one might therefore even say that Gadamer's philosophical hermeneutics *performs* the justification of its core concepts as much as it offers a theoretical defense of them. He may not offer a decisively prescriptive account of hermeneutics' educational capacity, but his stance is far more than observationally descriptive. The account and resuscitation of humanist ideals, announced at the outset of *Truth and Method*, is a matter not of mere historiographical research or objective proof of their validity, but of a present enactment that performatively reveals their pertinence. Historical understanding is shown to be central to social life not through a detached argument, but through Gadamer's own undergoing of *Bildung* by the tradition he engages with. The consciousness of historical effect thereby ceases to be just a concept with strong theoretical entailments, but instead becomes a guiding principle of conduct. The concept is universal and cognitive in that it underlies all understanding, but Gadamer exemplifies a grasp of its productive and normative dimensions as well, taking to heart the task of a continual and questionable dialogue.

Through this conjunction of the structure and task of historical reflection, the joining of *praxis* and a deep conceptual grasp of our ontology, Gadamer's philosophical hermeneutics offers a crucial contribution to the strengthening of the humanities. It shows how an engagement with the claims of tradition induces philosophical insights, and how these glimpses into our ontology, in turn, bear immediately upon the ethical practices of everyday life. By virtue of these efforts, Gadamer is able "to correct false thinking about what they [the human sciences and the conduct of life] are."[32] This correction itself, no matter how cogent, cannot stand as a fixed solution; there remains the ongoing task of understanding and applying it. The success of the humanities, and of Gadamer's contribution to them, depends largely on how we take up the work of tradition, how we continue the transmission of historical effect through conversation.

Conclusion

I BEGAN THE PRESENT WORK BY TREATING THE PHENOMENON
of a moralizing historiography that fixates the past into a permanent and
univocal lesson. Contemporary reactions register an intuitive problem
with this tendency; the past does not mean the same from one generation
to another. However, it is far more challenging to precisely account for
the falsity of univocity: one needs an alternative account of how the past
continually achieves a different significance, of how history's meaning
is not complete but fluid. This must, at the same time, avoid the pitfall of
emptying all meaning from history. It is a question, therefore, of identity
and movement, of self and tradition. The intervening five chapters have
tried, on the basis of Gadamer's concept of historical effect, to elaborate
this alternative account of historical meaning, and have thereby hope-
fully provided ample evidence against historical fixation by correcting
the false conception of historicity that underlies it. While Gadamer
never formulated a concise, direct rebuttal of historical sedimentation,
his stance as a whole is deeply attuned to this issue, and a synthesis of his
works can therefore offer a conceptual framework to reveal and critique
its dangers.

Broadly speaking, Gadamer's philosophical hermeneutics challenge
any approach that limits truth to methodically achieved results. This
goes for the linguistic normalization of phenomena that occurs in the
social sciences, as well as for the general tendency to relegate anything
beyond scientific method to the realm of the subjective. Following a
long tradition of thought, Gadamer points out that there are structures
conditioning subjectivity, and that by investigating these, we can arrive at conditions of an understanding that, while always temporary and

revisable, is no less true than the facts of science. In chapter 1, I honed in on these historical conditions of understanding, the opaque conceptual realm from which most misunderstandings of historical meaning arise. These misunderstandings (of purported elevation or immediacy in history) typically fail to acknowledge both our situatedness within tradition and the necessity of continual mediation with that situation. Since these latter concepts are themselves prone to misunderstanding, however, I elaborated how Gadamer employs the notion of an interplay between self and tradition to avoid the charges of traditionalism on the one hand and incommensurabilism on the other. This intertwined relation, it turns out, does not prioritize one term over the other, nor is it a process that can conceivably be contained or come to an end: the relation is equatable with the transmission of tradition itself, with the ongoing nature of historical effect.

Here I noted a strange ambiguity: although historical effect constitutes an ontological condition as opposed to a choice, one can nevertheless engage with it in various ways. The relation between self and tradition can be exercised with more or less reflectivity, making the genesis and degree of this reflectivity into essential areas of interest. When Gadamer accounts for our consciousness of historical effect, he makes clear that this awareness does not extricate itself from the chiasmic relation to tradition. There is thus no possible total reflection of the effect. Instead, the fullest self-understanding granted by historically effected consciousness amounts to an insight into the constantly shifting nature of one's horizon within the overall movement of tradition. It involves seeing tradition as a space of questionability. While this is fundamentally an insight into the historicity of our existence, it also brings with it a practical demand of remaining open for further experience; it involves at once both an ontological structure and an ethical task. In subsequent chapters, I took the unpacking of this ambiguity as my chief aim, noting its inherent themes of sociality, freedom, and reflection.

In chapter 2, I began developing these themes through an elucidation of Gadamer's relation to Heidegger on the topic of historical belonging. Gadamer adopts his teacher's ideas of historicity and finitude, yet ends up formulating quite different conclusions concerning historical occurrence and situatedness. Through this difference, I also began to delineate how, in his relation to Heidegger, Gadamer combines a conceptual account and performative enactment of the freedom within tradition. Gadamer thereby immediately shows what it means "to belong to the historical effect of a significant thinker."[1]

To present this effect from Heidegger's side, I began by tracing the notion of *Destruktion,* which expresses the possible renewal of the questionability of traditional, sedimented concepts through a movement of enactment, but at the same time also requires reflection upon the self's own enacted structure as a basis for this retrieval. It thus involves a dual aim of fluidity and transparency, and with these raises the task of an ongoing repetition of meaning. The authenticity of this repetition, its recognition of thrownness and enactment of finite freedom, becomes the measure of the adequate appropriation of history. Yet this appropriation itself occurs with the broader movement of time itself, so the question of tradition ushers in the deeper problem of how to account for temporality as such. Heidegger takes previous accounts of this to be unsatisfactory, and identifies the entire history of philosophy with an obliviousness concerning the event-like nature of temporality. It is this event to which the tradition itself belongs, and to which a new form of thinking must attune itself. Such thinking bears the task of belonging so exclusively to the event that prior historical determinations – including those of language – lose their force, yet of nevertheless seeking this belonging as a current historical position.

Inspired both by Heidegger's conceptions of enactment and thrownness, and by his reliance on Aristotelian ideas, Gadamer in his own way undertakes an investigation of how historical understanding develops concretely. Although he is concerned to draw out and bolster ontological and protreptic themes from Heidegger, there are considerable differences in how philosophical hermeneutics conceives of the ongoing task of historical belonging. The differences pertain to both language and historicity. At the core of each of these lie the tasks of repetition and retrieval, situations in which Gadamer chooses to underscore the possibility of continuity and openness over Heidegger's emphasis on severance and dismantling. Gadamer does not think that a distance from tradition, a new form of thought or language, is actually necessary or possible, and instead advocates an attentive and dialogical approach to tradition's transmission. For him it is an inherently interrogative and intersubjective task that still maintains the core of finite freedom that Heidegger had uncovered in *Being and Time*.

Gadamer turns to Hegel for an elaboration of this freedom, and chapter 3 accounted for the grounds and results of this engagement. The reasons for Hegel's attractiveness on this topic stem from his exacting account of the negativity of human experience and from his insights into the historicity and intersubjectivity of thought. He underscores mediation, interwovenness, and mutual participation as fundamental aspects of historical existence, and thereby helps bolster Gadamer's conception of dialogue within the consciousness of historical effect. To this extent Hegel's ideas do not supplant, but instead complement, Heidegger's. Nevertheless, to arrive at this influence requires a similar internal critique as occurred with Heidegger, in which Gadamer transposes or translates Hegel's systematic ideas of infinity and dialectic into a framework that, while still infinite in crucial respects, is more open to human historicity.

One aspect of this opening involves the resuscitation of limits of reflection from within Hegel's *Science of Logic* and *Phenomenology*. Regarding the latter, Gadamer draws on the substance of experiential mediation as an intersubjective realm, pointing to the process of reconciliation that can never be completed by any particular subject. In the realm of objective spirit, this takes the shape of morality, where the good must always be established and where the success of this endeavor cannot be methodically assured. Even at the level of absolute knowing, Hegel acknowledges its identity with history itself, making the latter into the finite texture of consciousness.

Yet to Gadamer an absolute knowledge of historicity is an impossible idea; here I began to trace his growing distance from Hegel, namely in the denial of full reconciliation between self and tradition. Contrary to Hegel's suppositions, consciousness in Gadamer's view cannot retrieve its origins and full identity. There is an infinity of possibility both at the developing, futural end of subjectivity and at its root-point of historical belonging. I presented this critical aspect again in light of Hegel's philosophy of history, which accounts only for a residual, futural infinity that remains after the past has been mediated and subsumed. Based on the fact that consciousness always remains intertwined with historical effect, Gadamer denies the possibility of ever grasping our historical situatedness with this level of finality, clarity, or determinacy. Gadamer's opening of Hegel's thought is thus not merely an infinitization of a metaphysical-consumptive outlook. Despite Hegel's insights into open-ended dialectical movement, Gadamer emphatically stresses the need to admit of an openness in another direction, an experience that "exceeds the omnipotence of reflection."[2]

To show that this experience nevertheless allows for freedom within history, that it does not involve a relinquishment of critical capacities in the face of authority, chapter 4 pursued this issue of reflection into Enlightenment thematics. In broad agreement with Kant on the notion of an emancipatory consciousness, Gadamer notes the capacity and task of hermeneutical thought to free us from the unquestioned authority of sedimented ideas. Further, in line with Kant's warning about reason overstepping its bounds, Gadamer continues his emphasis on the limits of reflection, yet eventually also brings these limits to bear on Kant's thought itself. I accordingly showed Gadamer to be more indebted to Enlightenment ideas than is commonly believed, but also highly critical of their trajectory and implications.

A crucial problem with the Enlightenment's trajectory is that it paves over a conception of truth that accounts for historical belonging and its ethical ramifications. This conception, revolving around earlier humanist ideals of tact, taste, cultivation, memory, judgment, and a communal sense, was gradually relegated from public life to subjective feeling through a discourse greatly influenced by Kant's third *Critique*. By reducing the capacity of taste to a formal feeling, and by separating the experience of art from the realm of intersubjective and experiential truth, the *Critique of Judgment* initiates a movement of aesthetic abstraction that eventually uproots humanist ideals from their historical and ethical setting. Further, with taste conceived as a fixed ideal, it loses all connection to *Bildung*, the cultivated yet continually open space of experience at the center of the humanities.

Gadamer urges us instead to view the experience of art as a substantive, historical, and "unfinished event,"[3] and this is where we encountered the strongest criticism of Gadamer's position. Many take him to espouse a romanticist irrationalism that blindly submits to the authority of tradition. Far from entailing such a subjugation, however, Gadamer's stance lays bare our historicity and its concomitant intersubjective task; to grasp the "unknown vocabularies" presented by every work indeed requires the development of a "communicative commonality,"[4] a cultivation of taste as a communal sense. The suspicions of deference to tradition, then, are founded upon a fundamental misunderstanding both of authority as a social phenomenon and of hermeneutics as a philosophical task. What is thus mistaken for an authoritarian imposition is in Gadamer's view merely the ongoing presence of historical effect itself, with its intense questionability and implicit demand for reflective-dialogical engagement.

In reconnecting reflection and judgment to the exercise of a historically situated freedom, Gadamer thus widens the scope of Enlightenment concepts back onto the expanse of ethical life from which they were originally derived. I thus showed, through various conceptual frameworks and conversations with significant thinkers, how he connects the consciousness of historical effect to the practical conduct of a human life and to the humanist ideals that once addressed that conduct. While maintaining no illusions of complete reflection, he imbues this consciousness with the tasks of attentive understanding and critical openness, identifying it directly with Aristotle's virtue of *phronêsis*.

In the fifth and final chapter, I underscored the ways in which Gadamer takes the practice of *Bildung* to fulfill an intermediary role between historical understanding and human conduct by cultivating a critical hermeneutical consciousness that reflects and addresses the concerns of practical life as such. The structured encounter with texts and ideas, central to the practice of the humanities, generates an experience of the historicity of understanding. What is generative here is not the specific content of the works that would purportedly stand on its own apart from our engagement. Rather, as themselves sites of questionability and questioning, these objects uncover what it means to be enmeshed in tradition, namely to be dialogically engaged. They constitute a conversation that, if one attends to it, will address one and draw one in.

The receptivity to this address is one initial result of a hermeneutical *Bildung.* Yet along with this receptivity comes the capacity for seeing the interpretive space of history as such. By grasping the ontology of this space, in recognizing that neither self nor tradition stands alone and needs be correct in a fixed sense, but that they will instead continually connect in different ways, one acquires the ability to translate across this differential space and remain open to its continual development. This, in turn, engenders the sort of freedom and openness required for the adequate engagement with any alterity. It communicates the inherent good of exchange, while supplying the capacities through which to navigate it. The *Bildung* of the humanities thus ideally amounts to a kind of hermeneutical training.

Unfortunately, the current discourse surrounding the humanities utterly fails to address the historical-hermeneutical core of their identity, and therefore also tends to overlook their ethical potential. Rather than looking to their ontological foundations in a time of crisis, the humanities defend themselves either by donning the costumes of science or by explicitly fleeing the domain of truth. They thereby become sedimented into the issues of *Problemgeschichte* and canonization or dissolve into the perennial waves of cultural interest. While Gadamer himself does not offer a simple antidote to these developments, his account of historical understanding and its rootedness in *Bildung* provides a solid defense of the humanities as an ethical practice. In his own philosophical conduct, moreover, Gadamer gives us a lived example of what attentive and productive listening entail. We would do well to share in his experience, as one does with a *phronimos*.

Notes

Introduction

1. Bernard Schlink, "The Presence of the Past," accessed September 8, 2013, http://worldofideas.wbur.org/2009/02/15/the-presence-of-the-past.

2. For recent philosophical forays in this direction, see *The Ethics of History*, ed. David Carr, Thomas R. Flynn, and Rudolf A. Makkreel (Evanston, Illinois: Northwestern University Press, 2004); *Tradition und Kontingenz*, ed. Alfred Schäfer and Michael Wimmer (Münster: Waxmann, 2004); *The Past's Present: Essays on the Historicity of Philosophical Thinking*, ed. Maria Sá Cavalcante Schuback and Hans Ruin (Huddinge, Sweden: Södertörn, 2005); Emil Angehrn, *Wege des Verstehens: Hermeneutik und Geschichtsdenken* (Würzburg: Königshausen & Neumann, 2008); *Rethinking Time: Essays on History, Memory, and Representation*, ed. Hans Ruin and Andrus Ers (Huddinge, Sweden: Södertörn, 2011).

3. Gadamer, *TM*, 309.

4. Gadamer, *TM*, 297.

5. Gadamer, *TM*, 346.

6. Gadamer, *TM*, xxiii.

7. Alasdair MacIntyre explicitly draws this line of thinking out of Gadamer's works; see "On Not Having the Last Word: Thoughts on Our Debts to Gadamer," in *GC*, 158.

8. Gadamer, *TM*, xxv.

9. The term *Geisteswissenschaften* does not have a clear equivalent in the English language or in Anglo-American academic history. Like many, and as Gadamer himself occasionally does, I will use 'historical human sciences' and 'humanities' to mean roughly the same.

10. Gadamer, "Hermeneutik und Historismus," *GW* 2, 394.

11. Gadamer makes this eminently clear in his account of the debate with Emilio Betti in "Hermeneutik und Historismus," *GW* 2, 392–395.

12. Gadamer, *TM*, 355.

13. Gadamer, *TM*, 15.

14. Gadamer, *TM*, 355.

15. See Gadamer, "Der Mensch und seine Hand im heutigen Zivilisationsprozeß," *Lob der Theorie* (Frankfurt am Main: Suhrkamp, 1983), 139–148.

16. In this regard, I hold that Gadamer provides just the sort of solution to Habermasian critiques that Robert Piercey takes Ricoeur to attempt but ultimately fail at. If Ricoeur's 'dubious distinction' of traditionality, traditions, and tradition does not arrive at the necessary subtle understanding of historical effect because his "purely general account of how *one* participates in tradition, in the abstract, is a pipe dream," then Gadamer can address this precisely by way of his demonstrative account. See Robert Piercey, "Ricoeur's Account of Tradition and the Gadamer-Habermas Debate," *Human Studies* 27 (2004): 259–280, here 277.

17. Although the relation between Gadamer's theory of historical effect and Merleau-Ponty's notion of the chiasmic structure of being remains to be fully ascertained, there is an overview of the possibility in Ralf Elm, "Schenkung, Entzug, und die Kunst schöpferischen Fragens," in K A 30, 151–176.

18. Gadamer, CP, 29. The term is Riccardo Dottori's.

19. Gadamer, "Reflections on my Philosophical Journey," in PG, 37. See also Gadamer, H D, 104.

20. Gadamer, TM, 342.

21. Gadamer, "Kant 'Kritik der reinen Vernunft' nach 200 Jahren," G W 4, 348.

22. Gadamer, TM, 41.

23. For an elucidation of Gadamer's reading of the third *Critique* in these terms, see Kristin Gjesdal, "Reading Kant Hermeneutically: Gadamer and the *Critique of Judgment*," *Kant-Studien* 98, 3 (2007): 351–371.

24. Gjesdal, "Reading Kant Hermeneutically," 19.

25. In the field of education, see Deborah Kerdemann, "Exposure and Expertise: Philosophy for Teacher Education," *Philosophy of Education* (2001): 100–103; in political science, see Michael T. Gibbons, "Hermeneutics, Political Inquiry and Practical Reason: An Evolving Challenge to Political Science," *American Political Science Review* 100, 4 (2006): 563–571; in social work, see Michael Whan, "On the Nature of Practice," *British Journal of Social Work* 16 (1986): 243–250; in sociology, see Susan Hekman, *Hermeneutics and the Sociology of Knowledge* (Notre Dame, Indiana: University of Notre Dame Press, 1986); in the area of medicine, see Fredrik Svenaeus, "Hermeneutics of Medicine in the Wake of Gadamer: The Issue of Phronêsis," *Theoretical Medicine* 24 (2003): 407–431; in popular media, see Barry Schwartz, *Practical Wisdom: The Right Way to Do the Right Thing* (New York: Riverhead, 2010).

1. From Structure to Task

A portion of this chapter previously appeared in my article "Waves and Horizons: Literary Response in the Space of Questionability," *International Yearbook for Hermeneutics* 13 (2014): 144–159. I am grateful to Mohr Siebeck (Tübingen) for permission to reprint the material here.

1. Gadamer, "Hermeneutik und Historismus," G W 2, 394. Emphasis in original.

2. It also, as I will develop in chapter 5, "poses the question concerning the 'possibility' of the human sciences [*Geisteswissenschaften*]"; Gadamer, "Hermeneutik und Historismus," G W 2, 394.

3. Gadamer, TM, 460.

4. One need only point to the culmination of *Truth and Method* with its ontological shift "guided by language" (381), as well as the many essays concerning language that make up GW 2, the collection of supplements to *Truth and Method*.

5. Gadamer, "Die Universalität des hermeneutischen Problems," GW 2, 228.

6. Jean Grondin, *Einführung in die philosophische Hermeneutik* (Darmstadt: Wissenschaftliche Buchgesellschaft, 1991), 147; cited in Hans-Helmuth Gander, "Erhebung der Geschichtlichkeit des Verstehens zum hermeneutischen Prinzip," in KA 30, 120. On the centrality of historical effect in Gadamer, see also Dieter Teichert, *Verstehen und Wirkungsgeschichte* (Bonn: Bouvier, 2000), 22.

7. Damir Barbaric makes a convincing case that the theme of occurrence is the truly uniting thread of *Truth and Method*, as well as the most significant point of unity with Heidegger. See "Geschehen als Übergang," in HW, 63–83.

8. Gadamer, *TM*, 293.

9. Ibid., xxxiv.

10. For a partial assessment of these effects, see Bruce Krajewski, ed., *Gadamer's Repercussions: Reconsidering Philosophical Hermeneutics* (Berkeley: University of California Press, 2004).

11. Gadamer, *TM*, 266.

12. For an excellent treatment of the conceptual development of historical consciousness, see Charles R. Bambach, *Heidegger, Dilthey, and the Crisis of Historicism* (Ithaca, N.Y.: Cornell University Press, 1995). For a thorough account of the ways that historical thematics were intertwined at the outset of the twentieth century, see Jeffrey Barash, *Martin Heidegger and the Problem of Historical Meaning* (Boston: Martinus Nijhoff, 1988), 17–89. With regard to Gadamer's position over against these early-twentieth-century developments, see Manfred Brelage, "Die Geschichtlichkeit der Philosophie und die Philosophiegeschichte," *Zeitschrift für philosophische Forschung* 16, no. 3 (1962): 375–405.

13. The following works are indispensable for presenting various angles of Gadamer's relation to prior thinkers and themes: on the topic of history, see Georgia Warnke, *Gadamer: Hermeneutics, Tradition, and Reason* (Stanford, Calif.: Stanford University Press, 1987), and Ingrid Scheibler, *Gadamer: Between Heidegger and Habermas* (New York: Rowman and Littlefield, 2000); on the topic of German Idealism and the art of hermeneutics, see Angelika Rauch, *The Hieroglyph of Tradition: Freud, Benjamin, Gadamer, Novalis, Kant* (Cranbury, N.J.: Associated University Presses, 2000), and Kristin Gjesdal, *Gadamer and the Legacy of German Idealism* (New York: Cambridge University Press, 2009); on Heidegger, Hegel, and Hölderlin, see Rod Coltman, *The Language of Hermeneutics: Gadamer and Heidegger in Dialogue* (Albany: State University of New York Press, 1998); on ancient influences, see Gerald Bruns, *Hermeneutics Ancient and Modern* (New Haven, Conn.: Yale University Press, 1995).

14. Historicism is notorious for being defined in a multitude of ways, almost all polemical. Whether or not the views that Gadamer attributes to historicism here would describe themselves as such remains debatable. These concerns, however, lie beyond the purview of the present analysis. For a survey of the many senses this term had come to embody by the twentieth century, see Friedrich Meinecke, *Die Entstehung des Histo-*

rismus (Munich: Oldenbourg, 1936). In *Heidegger, Dilthey, and the Crisis of Historicism*, Bambach elucidates the shifts in historicist positions over the course of the nineteenth century.

15. Bambach, *Heidegger, Dilthey, and the Crisis of Historicism*, 60.

16. Gadamer, *TM*, 377.

17. Nicolai Hartmann, "Zur Methode der Philosophiegeschichte," *Kant-Studien* 15, no. 4 (1910): 459–485. Reprinted in *Kleinere Schriften* 3 (Berlin: de Gruyter, 1958), 1–22. I will cite the latter version in what follows.

18. Gadamer, *TM*, 13.

19. Ibid., 5.

20. Ibid., 8–10.

21. See Heinrich Rickert, *Die Probleme der Geschichtsphilosophie* (Heidelberg: Winter, 1924), 70: "The concrete meaning that is found in the real objects, as well as the historical principle of selection, lies not in the sphere of real *being* but in that of *value*, and it is from here that the connection between the individual value-related method and the meaningful material of history must be understood." Emphasis in original.

22. Friedrich Nietzsche, *Vom Nutzen und Nachteil der Historie für das Leben*, in *Sämtliche Werke: Kritische Studienausgabe*, ed. Giorgio Colli and Mazzino Montinari (New York: de Gruyter, 1980), 1:254; hereinafter cited as KSA. See also Barash, *Martin Heidegger and the Problem of Historical Meaning*, 81; Gadamer, "Die Universalität des hermeneutischen Problems," GW 2, 221; *TM*, 304.

23. Gadamer, *TM*, 276.

24. See Gadamer, "Die Kontinuität der Geschichte und der Augenblick der Existenz," GW 2, 144.

25. See Gadamer, "Selbstdarstellung Hans-Georg Gadamer," GW 2, 494.

26. Gadamer is extremely fond of this example, though one could generate countless others. See Gadamer, "Selbstdarstellung Hans-Georg Gadamer," GW 2, 484; see also Gadamer, *BP*, 25–26. As an alternative to the historiography of *Problemgeschichte*, Gadamer proposes a conceptual history (*Begriffsgeschichte*) that attends to the specific linguistic and conceptual usages in the time under investigation, as well as their current significance. On this idea, see Gadamer, "Begriffsgeschichte als Philosophie," GW 2, 77–91. See also Jean Grondin, "The Neo-Kantian Heritage in Gadamer," in *Neo-Kantianism in Contemporary Philosophy*, ed. Rudolf A. Makkreel and Sebastian Luft (Bloomington: Indiana University Press, 2010), 102–104. Grondin argues that Gadamer's criticism of *Problemgeschichte* is too harsh, that the latter does in fact account for the present situation of the subject, and that it is closer to Gadamer's position of *Begriffsgeschichte* than Gadamer, in his purported allegiance to Heidegger, would like to believe.

27. In outlining these arguments here, I am responding in a preliminary way to Sebastian Luft's suggestion that "it would be a worthy enterprise to reconstruct Gadamer's effective history [*Wirkungsgeschichte*] as critical rejection or productive reception of *Problemgeschichte*"; see Sebastian Luft, *Subjectivity and Lifeworld in Transcendental Phenomenology* (Evanston, Ill.: Northwestern University Press, 2011), 415n7. On the topic of questions and questioning in Gadamer, see Thomas Schwarz Wentzer, "Toward a Phenomenology of Questioning: Gadamer on Questions and Questioning," in HAC, 243–266; Thomas Schwarz Wenzer, "Das Diskrimen der Frage," in HW, 219–240; Robert

Schnepf, "Der hermeneutische Vorrang der Frage: Die Logik der Fragen und das Prob-
lem der Ontologie," in *Gadamer Verstehen/Understanding Gadamer,* ed. Mirko Wischke
and Michael Hofer (Darmstadt: Wissenschaftliche Buchgesellschaft, 2003), 302–323;
Elm, "Schenkung, Entzug, und die Kunst schöpferischen Fragens," 151–176; Carl Page,
"Historicist Finitude and Philosophical Hermeneutics," *The Philosophy of Hans-Georg
Gadamer,* ed. Lewis Edwin Hahn (Chicago: Open Court, 1997), pp. 369–384, esp. 373;
Jerome Veith, "Waves and Horizons: Literary Response in the Space of Questionability,"
in *International Yearbook for Hermeneutics* 13 (2014): 144–159.

28. Taking these issues into account, MacIntyre distinguishes between relativism
and perspectivism, noting that "[t]he relativist challenge rests upon a denial that rational debate and rational choice among rival traditions is possible; [and that] the perspectivist challenge puts in question the possibility of making truth-claims from within any
one tradition"; Alasdair MacIntyre, *Whose Justice? Which Rationality?* (Notre Dame,
Ind.: University of Notre Dame Press, 1988), 352.

29. Accusations of traditionalism from the side of incommensurabilism can be found
in Robert Bernasconi, "'You Do Not Know What I Am Talking About': Alterity and the
Hermeneutical Ideal," in *SR,* 178–195; and John Caputo, "Gadamer's Closet Essentialism:
A Derridean Critique," in *Dialogue and Deconstruction: The Gadamer-Derrida Encounter,*
ed. Diane P. Michelfelder and Richard E. Palmer (Albany: State University of New York
Press, 1989), 258–264. Earlier charges of traditionalism can be found in Manfred Frank,
Das individuelle Allgemeine (Frankfurt am Main: Suhrkamp, 1985), Jürgen Habermas,
On the Logic of the Social Sciences, trans. Ciaran Cronin (Cambridge: MIT Press, 1988),
and Hans-Herbert Kögler, *The Power of Dialogue* (Cambridge: MIT Press, 1996); a more
recent charge stems from Kristin Gjesdal, "Between Enlightenment and Romanticism:
Some Problems and Challenges in Gadamer's Hermeneutics," *Journal of the History of
Philosophy* 46, no. 2 (2008): 285–306. Gadamer's alleged relativism is frequently used as
a basis for accusations of incommensurabilism. In describing a hermeneutic community
of interpretations, Robert T. Valgenti elaborates ways to defend hermeneutics against
such accusations of incessant conflict; see "The Tradition of Tradition in Philosophical
Hermeneutics," in *Consequences of Hermeneutics: Fifty Years After Gadamer's* Truth and
Method, ed. Jeff Malpas and Santiago Zabala (Evanston, Ill.: Northwestern University
Press, 2010), 66–80.

30. For an excellent recent elucidation of this position, see Gary Brent Madison, "On
the Importance of Getting Things Straight," *Phaenex* 1, no. 1 (2006): 257.

31. The Gadamer-Habermas debate was initially taken to rest on tensions between
reason and authority (see Habermas, *Logic of the Social Sciences,* 170: "Gadamer's prejudice in favor of the legitimacy of prejudices [. . .] validated by tradition is in conflict
with the power of reflection"). Robert Piercey has convincingly shown, via Ricoeur's
Time and Narrative, that the debate "rests on an insufficiently subtle understanding of
what tradition is"; see "Ricoeur's Account of Tradition and the Gadamer-Habermas Debate," 271.

32. At this point, a terminological note is in order. Henceforth, the terms "tradition,"
"transmission," and "handing-down" refer to what Gadamer calls *Überlieferung,* the
passing-along involved in historicity as such. When these terms are to denote the narrower cultural-historical phenomena that Gadamer labels with the German term *Tradi-*

tion, I will qualify them with adjectives such as "cultural," "individual," or "specific." This distinction will become more apparent as the analysis proceeds.

33. Gadamer, *TM,* 304.

34. Ibid., 270.

35. See Günter Figal, "Kulturkritik, Aufklärung, hermeneutische Kehre," in *Der Sinn des Verstehens: Beiträge zur hermeneutischen Philosophie* (Stuttgart: Reclam, 1996), 88.

36. Because of his acknowledgment of these influences, some have sought to align Gadamer with the psychoanalytic tradition. See Angelika Rauch-Rapaport, "Gadamer Needs Lacan and Lacan Needs Gadamer," *Journal of the British Society for Phenomenology* 34, no. 3 (2003): 309–326.

37. See Hans-Helmuth Gander, "Between Strangeness and Familiarity: Towards Gadamer's Conception of Effective History," *Research in Phenomenology* 34 (2004): 121–122.

38. See Madison, "On the Importance of Getting Things Straight," 264.

39. See James Risser, "Shared Life," *Symposium* 6, no. 2 (2002): 167–180.

40. See Saulius Geniusas, "On the Oneness of the Hermeneutical Horizon(s)," *PhaenEx* 1, no. 1 (2006): 240.

41. Gadamer, *TM,* 305.

42. Ibid., 306. My emphasis.

43. See ibid., 304.

44. The most articulation Gadamer gives the one horizon of tradition is that he equates it with language: "Tradition, however, is not simply an event that one comes to realize through experience and learns to master, but it is language, i.e., it speaks by itself like a thou" (*TM,* 358). Here we see the inseparability of the two moments that make up our finite condition.

45. Risser, "Interpreting Tradition," 301.

46. See Elm, "Schenkung, Entzug, und die Kunst schöpferischen Fragens," 151–176. The notion of an intertwining at the ontological-historical level can be traced back to Dilthey, who spoke of an "interwoven texture of world and self"; *Gesammelte Schriften* (Göttingen: Vandenhoeck & Ruprecht, 1970), 19:167. For a recent account of Gadamer's relation to Dilthey on the topic of history, see Anders Odenstedt, "History as Conversation Versus History as Science: Gadamer and Dilthey," in *HAC,* 481–504.

47. Gadamer, *TM,* 300.

48. In this term that is central to his philosophy and to our investigation here, Gadamer is making use of the German ambiguity of *Wirkung.* As the result of an *Ursache,* a *Wirkung* can be an effect. Yet in its adjectival application, *wirkend* amounts to "being in effect" or "still acting as a cause." Thus, *Wirkungsgeschichte* is frequently rendered as "effective history" – history as an ongoing cause. In *The Beginning of Philosophy,* Gadamer elaborates this sense of historical beginning, noting that it does not possess the distinctness or immediacy of an empirical *archê,* but is instead inaccessible and indeterminate, yet absolutely intrinsic to human finitude. See Gadamer, *BP,* 20–22. It is highly likely that Gadamer gleaned the notion of the past as an ongoing effect from Dilthey's concept of *Wirkungszusammenhang,* which entails that "[i]n time, life exists in the relation of parts to a whole, that is, as a context – there"; Dilthey, *Gesammelte Schriften,* 7:229.

49. See esp. Gadamer, "Wort und Bild – 'so wahr, so seiend,'" GW 8, 373.

50. Gadamer, *TM,* 293.

51. For accounts of how Gadamer's concept of play factors into his notion of historicity, see Flemming Lebech, "The Concept of the Subject in the Philosophical Hermeneutics of Hans-Georg Gadamer," *International Journal of Philosophical Studies* 14, no. 2 (2006): 221–236; Valgenti, "The Tradition of Tradition in Philosophical Hermeneutics," esp. 71.

52. Gadamer, TM, 314.

53. Ibid., 281.

54. Ibid., 328. See Günter Figal and Hans-Helmuth Gander, "Vorwort," in DH, 8.

55. Gadamer, TM, 282.

56. Ibid., 281.

57. I will raise the issue of this affirmation and preservation once again in chapter 4 when discussing the possibility of emancipatory reflection.

58. For a thorough account of Gadamer's sense of infinity within finitude, see Damir Barbaric, "Die Grenze zum Unsagbaren: Sprache als Horizont einer hermeneutischen Ontologie," in KA 30, 199–218.

59. See Elm, "Schenkung und Entzug," 166–167.

60. Gadamer, TM, xxxiv.

61. Ibid., 341; see also ibid., 301.

62. See Elm, "Schenkung und Entzug," 151; see also John McDowell, "Gadamer and Davidson on Understanding and Relativism," in GC, 178.

63. Gadamer, TM, xxxiv.

64. Ibid. Leo Strauss criticizes the apparent contradiction in a universal claim of finitude; see "Correspondence Concerning *Wahrheit und Methode:* Leo Strauss and Hans-Georg Gadamer," *Independent Journal of Philosophy* 2 (1978): 7.

65. See Gadamer, "Hermeneutics as Practical Philosophy," in RAS, 88–112.

66. Gadamer, TM, 307.

67. Ibid., 340.

68. Gadamer, BP, 19.

69. See Jerome Veith, "Concerned with Oneself as One Person: Self-Knowledge in *Phronêsis,*" *Epoché* 18, no. 1 (2013): 17–27.

70. Eventually, Gadamer will want to stress more than just structural similarities between Aristotle's ethics and hermeneutics. It is beyond the scope of the present work, however, to elaborate the full importance of *phronêsis* for Gadamer's corpus. Fortunately, and appropriate to this centrality, there is extensive literature on the subject: Gary Brent Madison, "The Theory of Practice/The Practice of Theory," in *The Politics of Postmodernity: Essays in Applied Hermeneutics* (Dordrecht: Kluwer, 2001), 137–162; Walter Brogan, "Gadamer's Praise of Theory: Aristotle's Friend and the Reciprocity between Theory and Practice," *Research in Phenomenology* 32 (2002): 141–155; Gerald Bruns, "The Hermeneutical Anarchist: *Phronêsis,* Rhetoric, and the Experience of Art," in GC, 45–76; Lawrence K. Schmidt, ed., *The Specter of Relativism: Truth, Dialogue, and Phronêsis in Philosophical Hermeneutics* (Evanston, Ill.: Northwestern University Press, 1995); James Risser, "*Phronêsis* as Kairological Event," *Epoché* 7, no. 1 (2002): 107–119; Paul Schuchman, "Aristotle's *Phronêsis* and Gadamer's Hermeneutics," *Philosophy Today* 23, no. 1 (1979): 41–50; Richard J. Bernstein, "From Hermeneutics to Praxis," *Review of Metaphysics* 35 (1982): 823–845; MacIntyre, "On Not Having the Last Word," in GC; Frie-

dericke Rese, "*Phronêsis* als Modell der Hermeneutik: Die hermeneutische Aktualität des Aristoteles," in K A 30, 127–150; Christopher P. Smith, "*Phronêsis*, the Individual, and the Community: Divergent Appropriations of Aristotle's Ethical Discernment in Heidegger's and Gadamer's Hermeneutics," in *Gadamer Verstehen/Understanding Gadamer*, ed. Mirko Wischke (Darmstadt: Wissenschaftliche Buchgesellschaft, 2003), 169–185.

71. Geniusas, "On the Oneness of the Hermeneutical Horizon(s)," 245.

72. See Aristotle, *Nicomachean Ethics* I, 3, 1095a10.

73. Gadamer, *TM*, 299.

74. Ibid., 357.

75. Ibid., 361.

76. See Geniusas, "On the Oneness of the Hermeneutical Horizon(s)," 246.

77. See Gadamer, *TM*, 346, 357.

78. Ibid., 353.

79. Ibid., 341.

80. See Elm, "Schenkung und Entzug," 163. The twentieth century is, of course, replete with other accounts that challenge the linear and positivist conception of science, not least those of Bachelard, Husserl, Cassirer, Heidegger, and Foucault; for a survey account of these challenges, see Hans-Jörg Rheinberger, *On Historicizing Epistemology: An Essay*, trans. David Fernbach (Stanford, Calif.: Stanford University Press, 2010), esp. 35–49. For a further discussion of how hermeneutics relates to natural science, see Joseph Rouse, *Knowledge and Power: Toward a Political Philosophy of Science* (Ithaca, N.Y.: Cornell University Press, 1987).

81. Gadamer, *TM*, 346.

82. Ibid., 355. Gadamer's complex relation to Hegel, which demands its own analysis, will form the subject-matter of chapter 3.

83. See Gadamer, *TM*, 301; see also Elm, "Schenkung und Entzug," 167.

84. Gadamer, "Rhetorik, Hermeneutik und Ideologiekritik," G W 2, 247.

85. Gadamer, *TM*, 310.

86. Ibid., xxi.

87. Ibid., 301.

88. See esp. ibid., 346–356. Gadamer here relies on the famous image of the retreating army from Aristotle's *Posterior Analytics* (II, 19). For a thorough discussion of Gadamer's reliance on Aristotle, see Rese, "*Phronêsis* als Modell der Hermeneutik," 127–149. For a presentation of this issue in Aristotle's works themselves, see Friedericke Rese, *Praxis und Logos bei Aristoteles* (Tübingen: Mohr Siebeck, 2003). For a critical evaluation of Gadamer's position over against Aristotelian philosophy, see Carl Page, *Philosophical Historicism and the Betrayal of First Philosophy* (University Park: Pennsylvania State University Press, 1995).

89. It is noteworthy that Gadamer precedes Derrida not only in the adoption of chiasmic structures and the notion of *différance* in general (see Elm, "Schenkung und Entzug," 168), but on the specific insight into the movement of deferral that lies at the heart of scientific progress. Derrida comes to formulate the latter's historicity with the claim that the "absolute is passage." Jacques Derrida, *Edmund Husserl's Origin of Geometry: An Introduction*, trans. John P. Leavey (Lincoln: University of Nebraska Press, 1978), 149.

90. See MacIntyre, "On Not Having the Last Word," in GC, 167.

91. Gadamer, TM, 309.

92. Ibid., 301.

93. Gadamer discusses this distinction on several occasions: see "Hermeneutics as Practical Philosophy," in RAS, 102; "Zur Problematik des Selbstverständnisses: Ein hermeneutischer Beitrag zur Frage der Entmythologisierung," GW 2, 121–132; "Die Marburger Theologie," GW 3, 197–208, esp. 203. For an elucidation of the role that this distinction plays in the Gadamer-Derrida encounter, see Donatella Di Cesare, "Stars and Constellations: The Difference Between Gadamer and Derrida," *Research in Phenomenology* 34, no. 1 (2004): 83.

94. Di Cesare, "Stars and Constellations," 83. Emphasis in original.

95. Gadamer, TM, 309.

96. Ibid., 341.

97. See Gander, "Erhebung der Geschichtlichkeit des Verstehens zum hermeneutischen Prinzip," 109.

98. See Gadamer, TM, 297.

99. See ibid., 375–377.

100. Gadamer takes this as a rebuttal both of Betti's separation of the descriptive from the juridical, and of Betti's subsequent concern that philosophical hermeneutics, as merely descriptive, is not methodical enough. See "Hermeneutik und Historismus," GW 2, 392–395.

101. See Gadamer, TM, 301.

102. Ibid., 367.

103. See Elm, "Schenkung und Entzug," 169–175.

104. See Gadamer, TM, 374–375. There has been a recent (re)turn to this approach in historiography, instantiated particularly well by the work of Robert N. Bellah, *Religion in Human Evolution: From the Paleolithic to the Axial Age* (Cambridge, Mass.: Harvard University Press, 2011).

105. See Gadamer, TM, 361.

106. See Damir Barbaric, "Hörendes Denken," in DH, 46. On the topic of freedom in Gadamer, see Morten Sørensen Thaning, "Freiheit und Verantwortung bei Heidegger und Gadamer," in *Frei sein, frei handeln: Freiheit zwischen theoretischer und praktischer Philosophie*, ed. Diego D'Angelo, Sylvaine Gourdain, Tobias Keiling, and Nikola Mirkovic (Freiburg: Alber, 2013), 29–57.

107. See Gadamer, TM, 279. Herein lies the core of Gadamer's response to Habermas, who initially saw in listening and openness an irrational subordination to a specific tradition's authority; see Jürgen Habermas, "Zu Gadamers *Wahrheit und Methode*," and "Der Universalitätsanspruch der Hermeneutik," in *Hermeneutik und Ideologiekritik* (Frankfurt: Suhrkamp, 1971). For Gadamer's responses, see "Rhetorik, Hermeneutik und Ideologiekritik: Metakritische Erörterungen zu Wahrheit und Methode," GW 2, 232–250, and "Replik zu Hermeneutik und Ideologiekritik," GW 2, 251–275. Habermas has more recently shifted his view toward acknowledging an irrevocable tension between reason and history; see *Between Facts and Norms*, trans. William Regh (Cambridge, Mass.: MIT Press, 1996).

108. See MacIntyre, "On Not Having the Last Word," GC, 157–172. It remains the constant task not just of philosophical hermeneutics, but of any philosophical endeavor, to elaborate what such standards may be.

109. Gadamer accounted for this nexus under the heading of "poetic dwelling," which is meant to convey the task-like nature of living within historical and linguistic questionability. For an account of this concept; see James Risser, "Poetic Dwelling in Gadamer's Hermeneutics," *Philosophy Today* 38, no. 4 (1994): 369–379. The alignment of tradition with conversation entails that "we speak to one another in becoming who we are," and Gadamer takes the literary work to serve as a spur to this dialogue; James Risser, *Hermeneutics and the Voice of the Other: Re-reading Gadamer's Philosophical Hermeneutics* (Albany: State University of New York Press, 1997), 187.

110. See Gadamer, "Die Marburger Theologie," GW 3, 208.

111. See Gadamer, TM, 311n240.

112. See Gadamer, "On the Scope and Function of Hermeneutical Reflection," in *Philosophical Hermeneutics*, trans. and ed. David Linge (Berkeley: University of California Press, 1976), 18–43; "Über die Planung der Zukunft," GW 2, 155–173; "Die Unfähigkeit zum Gespräch," GW 2, 207–218; "Was ist Praxis? Die Bedingungen gesellschaftlicher Vernunft," GW 4, 216–228; "Die Idee der praktischen Philosophie," GW 10, 238–246.

113. See Geniusas, "On the Oneness of the Hermeneutical Horizon(s)," 231–236.

114. See Madison, "On the Importance of Getting Things Straight," 258.

115. Gadamer, TM, 295, emphasis in original.

116. Geniusas, "On the Oneness of the Hermeneutical Horizon(s)," 241.

117. Even Richard Kearney, whose position is actually fairly close to Gadamer's own, makes this accusation; see Richard Kearney, "Between Oneself and Another: Paul Ricoeur's Diacritical Hermeneutics," in *Between Suspicion and Sympathy: Paul Ricoeur's Unstable Equilibrium*, ed. Andrzej Wiercinski (Toronto: Hermeneutic Press, 2003), 149–161. For a thorough rebuttal of this critique, see Geniusas "On the Oneness of the Hermeneutical Horizon(s)."

118. Gadamer, TM, 304.

119. Dennis J. Schmidt, "Einige Betrachtungen zur Sprache und Freiheit," in DH, 70.

120. Geniusas, "On the Oneness of the Hermeneutical Horizon(s)," 250.

121. Gadamer, TM, 281.

122. Geniusas, "On the Oneness of the Hermeneutical Horizon(s)," 246.

2. Historical Belonging as Finite Freedom

A portion of this chapter was previously published as "*Destruktion* and Repetition: Freedom and Historical Belonging in Heidegger," in *Heideggers Marburger Zeit: Themen, Argumente, Konstellationen*, ed. Tobias Keiling (Frankfurt am Main: Klostermann, 2013), 305–318. I am grateful to the publisher for permission to reprint the material here.

1. Some notable forays into this area include Robert Bernasconi, "Bridging the Abyss: Heidegger and Gadamer," *Research in Phenomenology* 16 (1986): 1–24; Barbaric, "Geschehen als Übergang," 63–83; James Risser, "Interpreting Tradition," *Journal of the British Society for Phenomenology* 34, no. 3 (2003): 297–308; Jean Grondin, *Von Heidegger zu Gadamer: Unterwegs zur Hermeneutik* (Darmstadt: Wissenschaftliche Buchgesellschaft, 2001); James Risser, HVO. On the general relation of these two thinkers, see

Figal and Gander, DH; Richard E. Palmer, "Two Contrasting Heideggerian Elements in Gadamer's Philosophical Hermeneutics," in *Consequences of Hermeneutics: Fifty Years after Gadamer's* Truth and Method, ed. Jeff Malpas and Santiago Zabala (Evanston, Ill.: Northwestern University Press, 2010), 121–131.

2. See Gadamer, TM, 254–271.

3. See GW 3, 87–101 and 175–430.

4. Günter Figal and Hans-Helmuth Gander, "Vorwort," in DH, 8.

5. Strangely enough, aside from pointing out the intertwining of the theoretical and practical in general, Gadamer rarely drew attention to this feature of his own thought. Habermas, however, underscores it heavily in his speech on the occasion of Gadamer's acceptance of the Hegel Prize in 1979. See Jürgen Habermas, "Urbanisierung der Heideggerschen Provinz," in Hans-Georg Gadamer and Jürgen Habermas, *Das Erbe Hegels: Zwei Reden aus Anlaß des Hegel-Preises* (Frankfurt am Main: Suhrkamp, 1979), 9–31.

6. Gadamer, TM, 259; translation modified. See also "Die deutsche Philosophie zwischen den beiden Weltkriegen," GW 10, 366: "Understanding is not something that Dasein occasionally does when it encounters meaningful things; rather, understanding is that which defines Dasein as Dasein. The human is a being that desires to understand and that must understand itself." Finally, see Gadamer, TM, 259, and Istvan M. Feher, "Verstehen bei Heidegger und Gadamer," in DH, 89–115.

7. For an excellent and thorough study of the unity of Heidegger's thought on the topic of history, see Barash, *Martin Heidegger and the Problem of Historical Meaning*. Coltman provides a detailed reading of Heidegger and Gadamer's intricate proximity, with an emphasis on linguistic rather than historical structure, in *Language of Hermeneutics*.

8. Indeed, Gadamer holds that "Heidegger's *Kehre* is an attempt and a series of attempts to elude the problems of historicism"; Gadamer, Letter to Charles Bambach (February 26, 1990), cited in Bambach, *Heidegger, Dilthey, and the Crisis of Historicism,* 260. Bambach's book presents a convincing case in support of this claim.

9. Barash points out that Adorno, for instance, takes this position in claiming that Heidegger's concept of historicity "places history at rest in the unhistorical"; see Theodor W. Adorno, *Negative Dialektik* (Frankfurt am Main: Suhrkamp, 1975), 135. Habermas, moreover, sees Gadamer as having paved pathways by which to rescue Heidegger from his "self-chosen isolation"; see Habermas, "Urbanisierung," 14. For an account of how Heidegger's contemporaries came to regard him in this way, see Peter E. Gordon, *Continental Divide: Heidegger, Cassirer, Davos* (Cambridge, Mass.: Harvard University Press, 2010).

10. For a recent study concerning the role of history in Husserl's thought, see Andrea Staiti, *Geistigkeit, Leben und geschichtliche Welt in der Transzendentalphänomenologie Husserls* (Würzburg: Ergon, 2010).

11. See Gadamer, "Die religiöse Dimension," GW 3, 315. For a concise account of Heidegger's theological roots, see Barash, *Martin Heidegger and the Problem of Historical Meaning,* 165–191, and Bambach, *Heidegger, Dilthey, and the Crisis of Historicism,* 187–203.

12. For secondary sources on this development, see John van Buren, *Young Heidegger: Rumor of the Hidden King* (Bloomington: Indiana University Press, 1994), as well as

Theodore Kisiel and John van Buren, eds., *Reading Heidegger from the Start: Essays in His Earliest Thought* (Albany: State University of New York, 1994).

13. See Werner Marx, *Heidegger und die Tradition* (Hamburg: Meiner, 1980).

14. Martin Heidegger, "Das Realitätsproblem in der modernen Philosophie," GA 1.

15. Barash, *Martin Heidegger and the Problem of Historical Meaning*, 99.

16. Heidegger, "Die Lehre vom Urteil im Psychologismus," GA 1, 3–132.

17. The text on which Heidegger commented in his *Habilitation* was later found to be written by Scotus's follower Thomas of Erfurt. See Rüdiger Safranski, *Ein Meister aus Deutschland: Heidegger und seine Zeit* (Munich: Carl Hanser, 1994), 80.

18. Ibid., 66.

19. Heidegger, "Die Kategorien- und Bedeutungslehre des Duns Scotus," GA 1, 352.

20. Ibid.

21. Heidegger made this point even more emphatically in his 1915 *Habilitationsvortrag* on "The Concept of Time in the Science of History." There, he emphasized that historical understanding deals with particularities, and is concerned not simply with the sequence of facts and quantitative distinctions, but with their inner coherence (*Zusammenhang*) and qualitative characteristics. There are no general laws under which such an investigation can fall. Martin Heidegger, "Der Zeitbegriff in der Geschichtswissenschaft," GA 1, 413–433; "The Concept of Time in the Science of History," trans. Harry S. Taylor and Hans Uffelmann, *Journal of the British Society for Phenomenology* 9 (1978): 3–10.

22. Martin Heidegger, "Die Kategorien- und Bedeutungslehre des Duns Scotus," GA 1, 278.

23. While most view Heidegger's extensive use of life-concepts at the end of the *Habilitationsschrift* as a sign of Dilthey's influence, Barash sees it as the mark of Heidegger's theological mentor of the Tübingen school, Carl Braig. See Barash, *Martin Heidegger and the Problem of Historical Meaning*, 123.

24. Martin Heidegger, Letter to Engelbert Krebs (January 9, 1919), cited in Hugo Ott, *Martin Heidegger: Unterwegs zu seiner Biographie* (Frankfurt am Main: Campus, 1992), 106–107.

25. Heidegger, *Phänomenologie des religiösen Lebens*, GA 60.

26. Martin Heidegger, "Anmerkungen zu Karl Jaspers "Psychologie der Weltanschauungen," GA 9, 3.

27. Hannah Arendt, "Martin Heidegger Is Eighty Years Old," in *Letters 1925–1975: Hannah Arendt and Martin Heidegger*, ed. Ursula Ludz, trans. Andrew Shields (New York: Harcourt, 2004), 151. Originally published as "Martin Heidegger ist achzig Jahre alt." *Merkur* 258, no. 10 (October 1969): 893–902.

28. Heidegger in these early years saw this dimension exemplified in Christianity and the vigilant, wakeful life called for by the letters of Paul in the New Testament.

29. Heidegger, "Anmerkungen," GA 9, 32.

30. Responsibility will surface again in *Being and Time*'s notion of authenticity, where it amounts to Dasein's consciousness of its possibility-to-be, and where some have attempted to locate a proto-ethics in Heidegger. See Thomas Rentsch. "Zeitlichkeit und Alltäglichkeit," in KA 25, 202n6.

31. In Heidegger's view, recognizing the connection between historical experience and conscience also reveals the meaning-source (*Sinnquelle*) from which objective-historical knowledge (especially in the historical human sciences) originates. See Heidegger, "Anmerkungen," GA 9, 33.

32. Ibid., 34.

33. Safranski, *Ein Meister aus Deutschland,* 111.

34. Heidegger, "Anmerkungen," GA 9, 34.

35. Heidegger elaborates this aspect of the phrase in his 1923 lecture *Ontology – The Hermeneutics of Facticity,* trans. John van Buren (Bloomington: Indiana University Press, 1999), 11–16.

36. Heidegger, "Anzeige der hermeneutischen Situation," GA 62, 346. For a recent English translation, see Heidegger, "Indication of the Hermeneutical Situation," in *The Heidegger Reader,* ed. Günter Figal and trans. Jerome Veith (Bloomington: Indiana University Press, 2009), 38–61. In what follows, I will cite this English version along with the German (D/E).

37. Heidegger, "Anzeige der hermeneutischen Situation," GA 62, 347/39.

38. Ibid., 347n4/39n4.

39. Ibid., 347/39.

40. Ibid., 348/40. In his later thought, Heidegger will speak in similar ways about language, noting that it is not so much a finalized "outcome" (*Ergebnis*) of human activity as it is an ongoing "event" (*Ereignis*) of Being; see Martin Heidegger, "Der Weg zur Sprache," GA 12, 247.

41. Heidegger, "Anzeige der hermeneutischen Situation," GA 62, 350/41. One would be justified in noting a certain influence of Kierkegaard's concept of repetition in this aspect of Heidegger's thought. See Risser, HVO, 33–40.

42. Heidegger, "Anzeige der hermeneutischen Situation," GA 62, 349n7/41n8.

43. Ibid., 349–50/41, emphasis in original.

44. Ibid., 368/55, emphasis in original.

45. Ibid., 369/56.

46. Ibid., 368/56.

47. Ibid., 369/56.

48. Ibid., 358/47–48.

49. Martin Heidegger, *Being and Time,* trans. John Macquarrie and Edward Robinson (San Francisco: Harper & Row, 1962), 31. Hereinafter cited as SZ, followed by the German pagination of the Niemeyer edition and an indication of which English translation was cited.

50. Heidegger, SZ, 2 (Macquarrie and Robinson). Regarding these opening moves of *Being and Time,* see John Sallis, "Where Does *Being and Time* Begin?," in *Delimitations: Phenomenology and the End of Metaphysics,* 2nd expanded ed. (Bloomington: Indiana University Press, 1995), 98–118, and Jean Grondin, "Die Wiedererweckung der Seinsfrage auf dem Weg einer phänomenologisch-hermeneutischen Destruktion," in KA 25, 1–27.

51. Heidegger, SZ, 22 (Macquarrie and Robinson), emphasis in original.

52. Ibid., 10. Translation modified.

53. See Heidegger, *SZ*, 21. On Heidegger's diagnostic approach to history, see Robert Piercey, *The Uses of the Past from Heidegger to Rorty* (New York: Cambridge University Press, 2009), 127–163.

54. Heidegger, *SZ*, 7 (Macquarrie and Robinson).

55. See Heidegger, *SZ*, 15. This explains the ambivalence in *Being and Time's* approach, its apparent thematic elevation and simultaneous descent into specificity. It is an ontological shift on both sides of an equation: Just as the thematic focus of *Destruktion* shifts to the question of Being, so the identification between method and object that I already noted at the root of this approach moves beyond the textually sedimented, primordial experiences of phenomena to one being (ourselves) as the locus of this question. This ontological shift in the identification also underscores that there is no mere linear grounding of the question of Being in Dasein. One equally and conversely arrives at the question of Being as one's "ground" if one pursues in detail the activity of Dasein. After all, Dasein has questioning, apprehending, and understanding as part of its Being, and to inquire about the ground of these possibilities is to ask about that meaning of Being that first allows for beings to be disclosed to understanding. See also John Sallis, "The Origins of Heidegger's Thought," in *Delimitations*, 91–92.

56. See Heidegger, *SZ*, 371. Even in supplying this short background, I am of course limiting the scope to only a small portion of what Heidegger says about temporality as the unifying condition of Dasein's being-in-the-world, and evading the immense (yet fertile) problematics issued in by Heidegger's establishment of this unity and conditionality in §§67–71 of *Being and Time*. These problematics, which include everything from sociality and culture to natality and embodiment, are not unrelated to my thematic interest, but extend far beyond the reach of the present work. In the latter half of this chapter, I will have the opportunity to return to some of these ideas from Gadamer's angle. For an analysis of these sections and a presentation of the many possible questions they open up, see Rentsch, "Zeitlichkeit und Alltäglichkeit," 199–228.

57. Thomas Sheehan and Corinne Painter, "Choosing One's Fate: A Re-reading of *Sein und Zeit* §74," *Research in Phenomenology* 28 (1999): 71, emphasis in original.

58. Rentsch ("Zeitlichkeit und Alltäglichkeit," 201) points out the possibility, on the basis of Heidegger's own statements, of gradations between authenticity and inauthenticity.

59. Heidegger, *SZ*, 373 (Macquarrie and Robinson), emphasis in original. "Occurrence" is Stambaugh's translation of *Geschehen*, whereas Macquarrie and Robinson employ the less than useful term "historizing."

60. Heidegger, *SZ*, 375 (Macquarrie and Robinson), emphasis in original.

61. Sheehan and Painter, "Choosing One's Fate," 73.

62. Heidegger, *SZ*, 223 (Macquarrie and Robinson), emphasis in original. See Gadamer, "Die Grenzen der historischen Vernunft," in *GW* 10, 178.

63. Heidegger, *SZ*, 383. "Alreadiness" is the translation that Sheehan and Painter use for *Gewesenheit*, "Choosing One's Fate," 72. Nietzsche makes a similar ontological claim at the outset of his *Second Untimely Meditation*, stating "that human existence is just an uninterrupted having-been [*Gewesensein*]." See Nietzsche, *Vom Nutzen und Nachtheil der Historie für das Leben*, *KSA* 1, 249.

64. Sheehan and Painter, "Choosing One's Fate," 73.

65. See Heidegger, *sz*, 383. For a detailed analysis of the various layers of Heidegger's thought here regarding temporality, history, and heritage, see Hans-Helmuth Gander, "Existentialontologie und Geschichtlichkeit," in K A 25, 237.

66. See Heidegger, *sz*, 384.

67. Ibid.

68. Sheehan and Painter ("Choosing One's Fate," 74) make a strong case for translating *Überlieferung* as "freeing-up," and note the Latin root of *liberare* in *Überlieferung*.

69. Heidegger, *sz*, 384.

70. Stambaugh renders it as "retrieve," perhaps to emphasize the active character of the appropriation.

71. Heidegger, *sz*, 386.

72. Sheehan and Painter, "Choosing One's Fate," 68.

73. Ibid.

74. Risser, "Interpreting Tradition," 303.

75. It would also help bring out the proto-ethical dimension of Heidegger's thinking. If, in order to authentically exist, one must resolutely attend to Being as it shows itself, then this task entails a responsibility toward particularity, both in the world and in others. See Charles E. Scott, "The Question of Ethics in Heidegger's Account of Authenticity," in *Heidegger Toward the Turn: Essays on the Work of the 1930s*, ed. James Risser (Albany: State University of New York Press, 1999), 211–224. On the topic of responsibility in Heidegger, see Thaning, "Freiheit und Verantwortung bei Heidegger und Gadamer."

76. See Heidegger, *sz*, 384.

77. See Gander, "Existentialontologie und Geschichtlichkeit," 242. Gadamer sees Heidegger's conception of *Mitsein* as a "concession" rather than an essential part of his elaborations, and takes it to be a particularly "weak idea of the other." This, even though the notion of thrownness contains the inkling of an alterity that could be developed further (and that Gadamer in fact picks up on). See Gadamer, *CP*, 23.

78. Many have pointed out Heidegger's indebtedness to Dilthey for this concept, though Heidegger clearly means something deeper than an ideal social meaning. See Barash, *Martin Heidegger and the Problem of Historical Meaning*, 207.

79. Ricoeur underscores the difficulty in assessing how one is to "move from the history of every individual to the history of all." See Paul Ricoeur, *Die erzählte Zeit*, vol. 3 of *Zeit und Erzählung* (Munich: Fink, 2007), 119. Heidegger's conception of the role of poetry, broadly construed, is central to understanding this move; see Martin Heidegger, "Der Ursprung des Kunstwerks," G A 5, 1–74. Translated by Albert Hofstadter as "The Origin of the Work of Art," in B W, 143–212. See also David Espinet and Tobias Keiling, eds., *Heideggers "Urpsrung des Kunstwerks": Ein kooperativer Kommentar* (Frankfurt am Main: Klostermann, 2011); Robert Bernasconi, "Race and Earth in Heidegger's Thinking during the Late 1930s," *Southern Journal of Philosophy* 48, no. 1 (2010): 49–66.

80. Martin Heidegger, *What Is Called Thinking?*, trans. J. Glenn Gray (New York: HarperCollins, 1968), 68.

81. See Günter Figal, *Martin Heidegger: Phänomenologie der Freiheit* (Frankfurt am Main: Athenäum, 1988), 23.

82. On Heidegger's notion of the "unthought," see Piercey, *The Uses of the Past from Heidegger to Rorty*, 136n24.

83. For a thorough examination of the reasons for *Being and Time*'s incompleteness, and for a detailed account of the immediate subsequent development of Heidegger's thought, see Theodore Kisiel, "Das Versagen von *Sein und Zeit:* 1927–1930," in K A 25, 253–279. The rest of Heidegger's career can be seen as a struggle to transform his and our relation to language and its essence. See "Preface: Letter to Fr. Richardson," in William J. Richardson, *Heidegger: Through Phenomenology to Thought* (The Hague: Martinus Nijhoff, 1963), xxiii.

84. Heidegger, S Z, 328 (Macquarrie and Robinson), emphasis in original. *Sich zeitigen* can also simply mean "to bring oneself about."

85. Heidegger, *Besinnung,* G A 66, 413–414.

86. Heidegger, *Metaphysische Anfangsgründe der Logik im Ausgang von Leibniz,* G A 26, 270.

87. Heidegger, *Die Grundprobleme der Phänomenologie,* G A 24, 429.

88. Heidegger, *Metaphysische Anfangsgründe der Logik,* G A 26, 268.

89. In a more detailed investigation, any analysis of the *Contributions* should be supplemented with the aphoristic 1938–39 volume *Die Geschichte des Seyns.* See Martin Heidegger, G A 69.

90. See Gadamer, "Martin Heidegger 75 Jahre," G W 3, 192. Regarding Heidegger's "turn" and the various readings of it, see Risser, *Heidegger toward the Turn.*

91. Heidegger, *Beiträge zur Philosophie (Vom Ereignis),* G A 65, 11.

92. For a detailed elaboration of this concept in the *Contributions,* see Alejandro Vallega, "'Beyng-Historical Thinking' in Heidegger's *Contributions to Philosophy,*" in *Companion to Heidegger's* Contributions to Philosophy, ed. Charles E. Scott et al. (Bloomington: Indiana University Press, 2001), 48–65.

93. Heidegger, *Nietzsche: der europäische Nihilismus* (Pfullingen: Günther Neske, 1989), 25; Heidegger, *Nietzsche,* vol. 3, trans. Frank A. Capuzzi, David Farrell Krell, and Joan Staumbaugh, ed. David Farrell Krell (San Francisco: Harper San Francisco, 1987), 5.

94. Heidegger, *Beiträge,* G A 65, 33.

95. See ibid., 14–23. Though the attunement of wonder (that there is anything at all) is identified here as one of the traits of the "first beginning," Heidegger deals with astonishment as crucial to the new constellation. This notion had already been present explicitly in the lecture course *Introduction to Metaphysics,* and more implicitly in the development of *Being and Time.* On the latter, see Sallis, "Where Does *Being and Time* Begin?," 98–100.

96. Based on this latter term alone, however, one could surmise that art plays a role in the transformation; see Heidegger, "Der Ursprung des Kunstwerkes," G A 5, 54. As Julian Young observes, "since the root of the problem of modernity is metaphysics, the principle by which Heidegger selects the exceptional artists he considers to be genuinely significant is the overcoming of metaphysics. The art which is important to our 'needy' times is art which provides an antidote to metaphysics"; Julian Young, *Heidegger's Philosophy of Art* (Cambridge: Cambridge University Press, 2001), 124. See also Dominique Janicaud, "The 'Overcoming' of Metaphysics in the Hölderlin Lectures," in *Reading Heidegger: Commemorations,* ed. John Sallis (Bloomington: Indiana University Press, 1993), 383–391.

97. Vallega, "'Beyng-Historical Thinking,'" 57.

98. Heidegger (*Die Geschichte des Seyns*, GA 69, 170) labels this "the beyng-historical genitive (not *genitivus 'objectus'* and *'subjectus'*)." For more on the middle voice in Heidegger, see Charles Scott, *The Language of Difference* (Atlantic Highlands, N.J.: Humanities Press, 1987), 67–87, and John Llewelyn, *The Middle Voice of Ecological Conscience* (New York: St. Martin's, 1991).

99. Heidegger, "Time and Being," in *On Time and Being*, trans. Joan Stambaugh (New York: Harper & Row, 1972), 7. The original version of this volume was published as *Zur Sache des Denkens* (Tübingen: Niemeyer, 1969).

100. Heidegger, "Time and Being," 5.

101. Ibid., 9.

102. Ibid.

103. Ibid.

104. Ibid., 13–14.

105. Ibid., 14.

106. Ibid., 16. Heidegger's adoption of the term "time-space" denotes his increasing distance from earlier talk of history, Dasein, and historicity. It also aligns with his contemporaneous turn to spatiality and givenness. See Martin Heidegger, "Art and Space," in HR, 305–309.

107. Heidegger, "Time and Being," 23.

108. See ibid., 24.

109. Heidegger, "Summary of a Seminar on the Lecture 'Time and Being,'" in *On Time and Being*, 41. Translation modified.

110. See ibid., 50. Despite phrasings that seem to indicate the possibility of a permanent twisting-free from metaphysics (e.g., the "leap" described in the *Contributions*), Heidegger comes to realize the untenability of this approach. He then proceeds to speak of a "being-twisted-up" (*Verwindung*) in metaphysics rather than of its overcoming (*Überwindung*). For Heidegger's correspondence confirming these notions, see Hans-Georg Gadamer, "Nachwort," in *Das Erbe Hegels*, 82n13 and 84n15; the English version is the "Afterword" to "The Heritage of Hegel," in RAS, 53–63. On *Verwindung*, see also Gianni Vattimo, "Nihilism and the Postmodern in Philosophy," in *The End of Modernity* (Baltimore: Johns Hopkins University Press, 1988), 164–181, and Bernasconi, "Bridging the Abyss," 15.

111. Heidegger, "Summary of a Seminar on the Lecture 'Time and Being,'" 35.

112. See Heidegger, "The End of Philosophy and the Task of Thinking," in *On Time and Being*, 55–73.

113. See Heidegger, "On the Essence of Truth," trans. John Sallis, in BW, 115–138.

114. Heidegger, "The End of Philosophy and the Task of Thinking," 60.

115. Heidegger, "Summary of a Seminar on the Lecture 'Time and Being,'" 26.

116. On this "political multivocity," see Fred Dallmayr, *The Other Heidegger* (Ithaca, N.Y.: Cornell University Press, 1993), 6.

117. See Barbaric, "Hörendes Denken," 38n6; Habermas, "Urbanisierung"; see also Feher, "Verstehen bei Heidegger und Gadamer," 111.

118. Coltman gives an insightful discussion of these developments in *The Language of Hermeneutics*, 9–23.

119. Gadamer, *TM*, 322.

120. Gadamer, *Philosophical Apprenticeships,* trans. Robert R. Sullivan (Cambridge, Mass.: MIT Press, 1987), 47. See also "Martin Heidegger 75 Jahre," GW 3, 263.

121. See Gadamer, "Heidegger's theologische Jugendschift," in Martin Heidegger, *Phänomenologische Interpretationen zu Aristoteles,* ed. Günther Neumann (Stuttgart: Reclam, 2003), 76–86, here 84.

122. See Feher, "Verstehen bei Heidegger und Gadamer," 111.

123. Gadamer, *TM*, 256.

124. Ibid., 259.

125. See Heidegger, "Der Satz der Identität," in *Identität und Differenz,* GA 11, 5–18; translated as "The Principle of Identity," in HR, 284–294.

126. Gadamer, *TM*, 262.

127. Ibid., 264.

128. Ibid., 262. See also *TM*, 277–285.

129. Gadamer, "Selbstdarstellung Hans-Georg Gadamer," GW 2, 495–496. See also "The Problem of Self-Understanding," in *PH,* 50.

130. Gadamer, "Gibt es auf Erden ein Maß?," GW 3, 346.

131. Gadamer, "Heidegger's theologische Jugendschift," 84.

132. This led Heidegger to attribute his "turn" not to his own shift in perspective, but to the matter at hand, to Being in its self-disclosure and simultaneous concealment. See Heidegger, "Preface: Letter to Fr. Richardson," xxiii.

133. Heidegger, *Hölderlin's Hymnen Germanien und Der Rhein,* GA 39, 70. For an excellent recent exposition of Heidegger's conception of language, see Michael Steinmann, *Die Offenheit des Sinns. Untersuchungen zu Sprache und Logik bei Martin Heidegger* (Tübingen: Mohr Siebeck, 2008).

134. Gadamer interprets poetry in Heidegger as a double projection akin to the thrown projection of *Being and Time.* One projection, language in the broad sense, has always already occurred, and the second simply extends this into specific languages; see Gadamer, "Die Wahrheit des Kunstwerks," GW 3, 261.

135. Coltman, *The Language of Hermeneutics,* 71.

136. Ibid., 72.

137. On the significance of poetic language for the "other beginning," see Jerome Veith, "Dichten, Denken, Sagen: Wirkungen des Kunstwerkaufsatzes im späteren Sprachdenken Heideggers," in *Heideggers 'Ursprung des Kunstwerks': Ein kooperativer Kommentar,* ed. David Espinet and Tobias Keiling (Frankfurt am Main: Vittorio Klostermann, 2011), 234–240.

138. See Gadamer, GW 3, 193, 227, 233, 261, 283, 329. For an excellent account of Gadamer's critical stance toward Heidegger on these themes, see Stefano Marino, "Gadamer on Heidegger: Is the History of Being 'Just' Another Philosophy of History?," *Journal of the British Society for Phenomenology* 41, no. 3 (2010): 287–303.

139. Gadamer in fact stresses and deeply empathizes with this aspect of Heidegger's thought throughout *Heideggers Wege;* see GW 3, 190, 194, 268, 281, 326. See also the "Nachwort" to *Das Erbe Hegels.*

140. See Gadamer, *TM,* xxxvii.

141. This is how Habermas comes to view Gadamer's relation to Heidegger; see Bernasconi, "Bridging the Abyss," 1–5.

142. Gadamer, GW 3, 300.

143. Ibid., 225.

144. Iain Thompson, "Ontotheology? Understanding Heidegger's *Destruktion* of Metaphysics," in *Heidegger Reexamined,* ed. Hubert Dreyfus and Mark Wrathall (New York: Routledge, 2002), 2:109.

145. This is why Heidegger's reading of Plato exemplifies a "continuous challenge" for Gadamer; see Robert J. Dostal, "Gadamer's Continuous Challenge: Heidegger's Plato Interpretation," in *The Philosophy of Hans-Georg Gadamer,* ed. Lewis Edwin Hahn (Chicago: Open Court, 1997), 289–307.

146. This stance also factored into the encounter between Gadamer and Derrida. See Sallis, *Delimitations,* 220.

147. Gadamer, Letter to Leo Strauss (April 5, 1961), "Correspondence Concerning *Wahrheit und Methode,*" 8.

148. Gadamer, "Nachwort," in *Das Erbe Hegels,* 72, 77n9.

149. Coltman, *The Language of Hermeneutics,* 120.

150. Gadamer, "Die Geschichte der Philosophie," GW 3, 302. See also Coltman, *The Language of Hermeneutics,* xi.

151. Heidegger, "Die Bedeutungs- und Kategorienlehre des Duns Scotus," GA 1, 278.

152. Heidegger, "Die Anzeige der hermeneutischen Situation," GA 62, 348/40.

153. See Gadamer, "Sein Geist Gott," GW 3, 331.

154. "A Conversation with Hans-Georg Gadamer," *Journal of the British Society for Phenomenology* 2 (1995), 123.

155. Gadamer stresses that he is not simply after a *Seinserinnerung* in contrast to Heidegger's *Seinsvergessenheit;* "Selbstdarstellung Hans-Georg Gadamer," GW 2, 502. See also Gadamer, "Die Sprache der Metaphysik," GW 3, 236.

156. Gadamer, "Gibt es auf Erden ein Maß?," GW 3, 348.

157. Coltman, *The Language of Hermeneutics,* 96.

158. Coltman, *The Language of Hermeneutics,* 95.

159. Gadamer, "Text und Interpretation," GW 2, 332.

160. Risser, HVO, 14. See also Coltman, *The Language of Hermeneutics,* 2. Dottori refers to this as Gadamer's "ethical turn" in *CP,* 29.

161. Heidegger, SZ, 447. See Gadamer, "Der Weg in die Kehre," GW 3, 282. See also Feher, "Verstehen bei Heidegger und Gadamer," 108–109, and Risser, "Interpreting Tradition," 304–305.

162. Bernasconi, "Bridging the Abyss," 22.

163. See Figal, *Phänomenologie der Freiheit,* 334–401.

164. See Gadamer, "Die Wahrheit des Kunstwerks," GW 3, 250. On the ethical problematics of Heidegger's decisionism, see Thaning, "Freiheit und Verantwortung bei Heidegger und Gadamer," 32–41.

165. Gadamer, "Heidegger's theologische Jugendschift," 81.

166. Ibid., 85.

167. Heidegger, "Brief über den Humanismus," GA 9, 356.

168. Dennis J. Schmidt makes a strong case for this perspective in "Einige Betrachtungen zu Sprache und Freiheit aus einem hermeneutischen Blickwinkel," 59–72.

169. See Barbaric, "Hörendes Denken," 38n6; Feher, "Verstehen bei Heidegger und Gadamer," 111.

170. Grondin, "The Neo-Kantian Heritage in Gadamer," 102.

3. The Infinity of the Dialogue

1. See Gadamer, "Selbstdarstellung Hans-Georg Gadamer," GW 2, 505. For excellent analyses of this triad of thinkers and their interrelation, see Bernasconi, "Bridging the Abyss," and Riccardo Dottori, *Die Reflexion des Wirklichen: Zwischen Hegels absoluter Dialektik und der Philosophie der Endlichkeit von M. Heidegger und H. G. Gadamer* (Tübingen: Mohr Siebeck, 2006).

2. Gadamer, "Hegel und Heidegger," GW 3, 87.

3. See Gadamer, "Hegel und der geschichtliche Geist," GW 4, 384–394, here 385. For a thorough discussion of Hegel's hermeneutic relevance, see Paul Redding, *Hegel's Hermeneutics* (Ithaca, N.Y.: Cornell University Press, 1996).

4. Gadamer underscores that his preoccupation with Hegel arose, in fact, out of his prior elucidation of ethical dimensions in Plato's dialectic. See Gadamer, *CP,* 29.

5. See esp. Gadamer, TM, 353–355.

6. Gadamer, "The Heritage of Hegel," in RAS, 53.

7. Ibid., 50.

8. Gadamer, *CP,* 27.

9. Coltman, *The Language of Hermeneutics,* 6.

10. Hegel describes this concept of infinite progress as "bad infinity" (*schlechte Unendlichkeit*), as it grasps only one aspect of the infinite, namely that which is opposed to finitude; see Hegel, SL, 137. For a brief analysis of Hegel's conception of bad infinity, see Jean-Luc Nancy, *Hegel: The Restlessness of the Negative,* trans. Jason Smith and Steven Miller (Minneapolis: University of Minnesota Press, 2002), esp. 12, 23. For more sustained discussions, see Wayne M. Martin, "In Defense of Bad Infinity: A Fichtean Response to Hegel's *Differenzschrift,*" *Bulletin of the Hegel Society of Great Britain* 55/56 (2007): 168–187; Stephen Houlgate, *The Opening of Hegel's Logic: From Being to Infinity* (West Lafayette, Ind.: Purdue University Press, 2006). Further afield, see William Desmond, "Between Finitude and Infinity: On Hegel's Sublationary Infinitism," in *Hegel and the Infinite: Religion, Politics, and Dialectic,* ed. Slavoj Zizek, Clayton Crockett, and Creston Davis (New York: Columbia University Press, 2011), 115–140.

11. See John Caputo, *Radical Hermeneutics: Repetition, Deconstruction, and the Hermeneutic Project* (Bloomington: Indiana University Press, 1987), 108–115; *More Radical Hermeneutics* (Bloomington: Indiana University Press, 2000); "Firing the Steel of Hermeneutics: Hegelianized Hermeneutics Versus Radical Hermeneutics," in *Hegel, History, and Interpretation,* ed. Shaun Gallagher (Albany: State University of New York Press, 1997), 59–70.

12. Gadamer, TM, 346.

13. Ibid., xxxiv. See James Risser, "In the Shadow of Hegel: Infinite Dialogue in Gadamer's Hermeneutics," *Research in Phenomenology* 32 (2002): 86–102.

14. Gadamer, *TM*, 341.

15. Ibid., 342.

16. See Gadamer, "Die Idee der hegelschen Logik," GW 3, 72–74.

17. Martin Heidegger, "Hegels Begriff der Erfahrung," GA 5, 169. Cited in *TM*, 354.

18. See Hegel, *PS*, 50–51. Hereinafter I will refer to the *Phenomenology of Spirit* by using paragraph numbers from the Miller translation (M).

19. See Hegel, *PS*, M81–87. In this way, Gadamer sees Hegel in proximity to the *logon didonai* of Plato; see "Verkehrte Welt," GW 3, 29.

20. Nancy, *The Restlessness of the Negative*, 4.

21. Hegel, *PS*, M33; translation modified. See Gadamer, "Hegel und die antike Dialektik," GW 3, 5–6.

22. Gadamer, "Hegel's Philosophy and Its Aftereffects," RAS, 35. Hegel treats the concept most extensively at *PS*, M780, M782–785, M787, M793–794.

23. For an excellent discussion of the Hegelian difficulties and post-Hegelian tasks concerning this concept, see Richard J. Bernstein, "Reconciliation/Rupture," in *The New Constellation: The Ethical-Political Horizons of Modernity/Postmodernity* (Cambridge, Mass.: MIT Press, 1992), 293–322.

24. Gadamer, "Hegel's Philosophy and Its Aftereffects," RAS, 36.

25. See Jean Hyppolite, "Anmerkungen zur Vorrede der Phänomenologie des Geistes und zum Thema: das Absolute ist Subjekt," in *Materialien zu Hegels* Phänomenologie des Geistes, ed. Hans Friedrich Fulda and Dieter Henrich (Frankfurt am Main: Suhrkamp, 1973), 51.

26. Hegel, *PR*, 8.

27. Gadamer, *TM*, 355.

28. See ibid., 350–351.

29. Ibid., 357.

30. Elm, "Schenkung, Entzug, und die Kunst schöpferischen Fragens," KA 30, 169.

31. Robert Pippin, "Gadamer's Hegel," in *The Cambridge Companion to Gadamer*, ed. Robert Dostal (Cambridge: Cambridge University Press, 2002), 227.

32. John Russon, *Reading Hegel's* Phenomenology (Bloomington: Indiana University Press, 2004), 133.

33. Hegel, *PS*, M597. Emphases in original.

34. Ibid., M442.

35. Ibid., M480.

36. Ibid., M488.

37. Ibid., M529.

38. Ibid., M634.

39. Ibid., M640.

40. Russon, *Reading Hegel's* Phenomenology, 144.

41. See Hegel, *PS*, M646–649.

42. Martin De Nys, "The Substance of Knowing Is History: Absolute Knowing and History in Hegel's *Phenomenology*." *Proceedings of the American Catholic Philosophical Association* 68 (1994): 139.

43. Gadamer, "Hegel und der geschichtliche Geist," GW 4, 386.

44. On this conceptual move, see Merold Westphal, *Hegel, Freedom, and Modernity* (Albany: State University of New York Press, 1992), 95–96. See also Gadamer, "Hegel's Philosophy and Its Aftereffects," RAS, 29–30.

45. Gadamer, "Hegel's Philosophy and Its Aftereffects," RAS, 31. See also "On the Philosophic Element in the Sciences and the Scientific Character of Philosophy," RAS, 14–15.

46. Pippin, "Gadamer's Hegel," 229n7 and 239.

47. See Gadamer, "Philosophical Foundations," PH, 128.

48. Westphal, *Hegel, Freedom, and Modernity*, 96.

49. G. W. F. Hegel, *Die Vernunft in der Geschichte* (Hamburg: Hoffmeister, 1955), 30.

50. Gadamer, GW 1, 169/TM, 163. My translation.

51. Westphal, *Hegel, Freedom, and Modernity*, 106.

52. Gadamer, GW 1, 494/TM, 490. See James Risser, "The Lateness of Arrival in the Event of Understanding," in *Internationales Jahrbuch für Hermeneutik* 10 (2011): 30.

53. Russon gives a clear account of how the two works run "in tandem": beginning with immediacy, observing the latter's own dialectic, and concluding that "the nature of being is intersubjectivity." See *Reading Hegel's* Phenomenology, 224–228.

54. See Gadamer, "Die Idee der hegelschen Logik," GW 3, 74.

55. See Westphal, *Hegel, Freedom, and Modernity*, 95. For a further discussion of the sort of necessity at work in Hegel's dialectic, see Robert Pippin, "You Cannot Get There from Here: Transition Problems in Hegel's *Phenomenology of Spirit*," in *The Cambridge Companion to Hegel*, ed. Frederick Beiser (New York: Cambridge University Press, 1993), 52–85.

56. See Stephen Houlgate, *Freedom, Truth, and History: An Introduction to Hegel's Philosophy* (New York: Routledge, 1991), 65.

57. Russon, *Reading Hegel's* Phenomenology, 228.

58. See Gadamer, "Die Idee der hegelschen Logik," GW 3, 71.

59. See Gadamer, "Hegel und die antike Dialektik," GW 3, 27.

60. Coltman, *The Language of Hermeneutics*, 109.

61. Gadamer, "Die Idee der hegelschen Logik," GW 3, 80.

62. See Risser, "Infinite Dialogue," 92. For a detailed analysis of Gadamer's argument regarding language and logic in his Hegel essays, see Dottori, *Die Reflexion des Wirklichen*, 525–550.

63. Gadamer, TM, 301.

64. Gadamer, "Die Idee der hegelschen Logik," GW 3, 83; see also "Dialektik und Sophistik im siebenten platonischen Brief," GW 6, 115.

65. See Gadamer, "Die Idee der hegelschen Logik," GW 3, 83. See also Hyppolite, "Anmerkungen zur Vorrede," 46.

66. Gadamer, "Die Idee der hegelschen Logik," GW 3, 86.

67. For a thorough presentation of these points, see Coltman, *The Language of Hermeneutics*, 101–113.

68. See Heidegger, SZ, 408 and 378.

69. See Aristotle's comparison of poetry and history in the *Poetics* (1451a38–b7). History, he claims, is less philosophical, indeed is not knowledge at all, because it deals

merely with particulars, and does therefore not bear significantly upon everyone. On this point, see Michael Davis, *Wonderlust: Ruminations on Liberal Education* (South Bend, Ind.: St. Augustine's Press, 2006), 25–31, and *Aristotle's Poetics* (Lanham, Md.: Rowman and Littlefield, 1992), 57.

70. See George Dennis O'Brien, *Hegel on Reason and History: A Contemporary Interpretation* (Chicago: University of Chicago Press, 1975), 13–14. As an example of this procedure, see Umberto Eco's essay "Dreaming of the Middle Ages," in which he points out and critiques various ways of narratively construing that time period. In *Travels in Hyperreality,* trans. William Weaver (New York: Harcourt, Brace, Jovanovich, 1986), 61–72.

71. O'Brien, *Hegel on Reason and History,* 13.

72. Hegel, PR, §343, 258.

73. Ibid., 10.

74. Ibid., 10.

75. Immanuel Kant, CPR, B596.

76. Ibid., B675, emphasis in original.

77. Hegel, PR, 4.

78. Donald J. Maletz, "History in Hegel's *Philosophy of Right,*" *Review of Politics* 45, no. 2 (1983): 214.

79. Hegel, PR, 3. This sense of freedom is expressed in a song, popular in liberal circles in the early 1800s, which Hegel would surely have heard during his tenure at Heidelberg: "Die Gedanken Sind Frei." A sample verse from the song runs: "And locking me up in the darkest of dungeons / Would be just another futile effort / For my thoughts tear the bars / And walls in two: Thoughts are free!"

80. Hegel, PR, 3–4.

81. Ibid., 13.

82. Ibid., 3.

83. Ibid., 3, 13–18, as well as §§212–214. For an account of this critique in the broader context of Hegel's historical thought, see Frederick Beiser, "Hegel's Historicism," in *The Cambridge Companion to Hegel,* ed. Frederick Beiser (New York: Cambridge University Press, 1993), 270–299.

84. Hegel, PR, 14.

85. Ibid., 9.

86. Johann Wolfgang Goethe, *Goethes Werke* (Stuttgart: Cotta, 1833), 47:101. The reference is in §13 of the Introduction, PR, 27. The last two stanzas of the sonnet run: "Thus it also is with all formative endeavor: / Seeking the fulfillment of pure elevation, / Unbound spirits will strive, to no avail. // He who wants great things must pull himself together: / The master first shows himself in limitation, / And only the law can give us freedom."

87. Hegel, IPH, 12.

88. Ibid., 13. See Herman Van Erp, "The End of History and Hegel's Conception of Modernity," *Ideas y Valores* 107 (1998): 6.

89. Hegel, IPH, 9. For Hegel's treatment of the methods of history, see Hegel, IPH, 3–11, and RH, trans. Robert S. Hartman (New York: Macmillan Publishing, 1953), 3–10.

90. Hegel, RH, 9.

91. This is echoed in Heidegger's distinction in *Being and Time* (SZ, 380) between external classification of objects as historical (as occurs with museum artifacts and heirlooms) and their actual inner world-historicality.

92. On this notion of internal history, see Herbert Butterfield, *The Origins of Modern Science* (New York: Free Press, 1957); Edmund Husserl, *The Crisis of the European Sciences and Transcendental Phenomenology*, trans. David Carr (Evanston, Ill.: Northwestern University Press, 1970); Derrida, *Edmund Husserl's Origin of Geometry*.

93. Hegel, PR, §341, 258.

94. See ibid., §343, 258.

95. Ibid., §342, 258.

96. See Stephen Houlgate, "World History as the Progress of Consciousness: An Interpretation of Hegel's Philosophy of History," *Owl of Minerva* 22, no. 1 (1990): 69–80.

97. Hegel, PR, §4, 18.

98. Ibid., §360, 263.

99. Ibid., §330, 254; see also §§322–324 and §345.

100. Ibid., §340, 257.

101. Ibid., §333, 255.

102. Ibid., §339, 257. Translation modified.

103. Maletz, "History in Hegel's *Philosophy of Right*," 221.

104. Hegel, IPH, 18. See Rolf Ahlers, "History and Philosophy as Theodicy: On *World History as the World's Judgment*," *Idealistic Studies* 30, no. 3 (2000): 159–172.

105. Maletz, "History in Hegel's *Philosophy of Right*," 222.

106. Hegel, PR, §360, 263.

107. Ibid., §214, 166.

108. Richard Dien Winfield, "The Theory and Practice of the History of Freedom: On the Right of History in Hegel's *Philosophy of Right*," in *History and System: Hegel's Philosophy of History*, ed. Robert L. Perkins (Albany: State University of New York Press, 1984), 143.

109. Gadamer, "The Heritage of Hegel," RAS, 38.

110. See Houlgate, *Freedom, Truth, and History*, 26; see also Nancy, *The Restlessness of the Negative*, 8.

111. Francis Fukuyama, "The End of History?," *National Interest* 16 (1989): 17.

112. See Beiser, "Hegel's Historicism," 294.

113. Gadamer, "The Heritage of Hegel," RAS, 37. See also "On the Philosophic Element in the Sciences and the Scientific Character of Philosophy," ibid., 9.

114. Ibid., 51.

115. Ibid., 51.

116. See Theodore George, "What Is the Future of the Past? Gadamer and Hegel on Truth, Art and the Ruptures of Tradition," *Journal of the British Society for Phenomenology* 40, no. 1 (2009): 8.

117. Houlgate, *Freedom, Truth, and History*, 34.

118. See Gadamer, "Das Alte und das Neue," GW 4, 160.

119. Gadamer, TM, 302.

120. See Pippin, "Gadamer's Hegel," 229.

121. Gadamer, *TM*, 355.

122. Ibid., 342.

123. Risser, "Infinite Dialogue," 86.

124. Gadamer, "Über leere und erfüllte Zeit," GW 4, 150–151.

125. Gadamer, "Kant und die hermeneutische Wendung," GW 3, 221.

126. Gadamer, "Selbstdarstellung Hans-Georg Gadamer," GW 2, 505.

127. Ibid., 506.

128. See Gadamer, *TM*, 356–362.

129. See Gadamer, *Hans-Georg Gadamer im Gespräch,* ed. Carsten Dutt (Heidelberg: Universitätsverlag C. Winter, 1993), 32.

130. Bernstein, "Reconciliation/Rupture," 313, emphasis in original.

131. George, "What Is the Future of the Past?," 4.

132. Gadamer, "Die Stellung der Poesie in der Hegelschen Ästhetik und die Frage des Vergangenheitscharakters der Kunst," GW 8, 229–230.

133. See Pippin, "Gadamer's Hegel," 237.

4. New Critical Consciousness

1. Dennis J. Schmidt follows a similar course of thought in "Einige Betrachtungen zu Sprache und Freiheit aus einem hermeneutischen Blickwinkel," 61. For the passage in Heidegger, see "Brief über den Humanismus," GA 9, 356.

2. Gadamer, *TM*, xxv.

3. Gadamer, "Kant und die hermeneutische Wendung," GW 3, 221.

4. Gadamer, *TM*, xxx.

5. Ibid., xxiv and xxxi.

6. Though beyond the purview of the present investigation, it remains to be assessed to what extent Kant, in turn, could be considered proto-hermeneutical in his notions concerning interpretation. On this subject, see Rudolf A. Makkreel, "Gadamer and the Problem of How to Relate Kant and Hegel to Hermeneutics," *Laval théologique et philosophique* 53, no. 1 (1997): 151–166; *Imagination and Interpretation in Kant: The Hermeneutic Import of the Critique of Judgment* (Chicago: University of Chicago Press, 1990).

7. Dennis J. Schmidt, "Aesthetics and Subjectivity," in KA 30, 30.

8. Kant, *CPR*, A xi.

9. Gadamer, "Reply to David Detmer," in *The Philosophy of Hans-Georg Gadamer,* ed. Lewis Edwin Hahn, Library of Living Philosophers 24 (Chicago: Open Court, 1997), 286.

10. Gadamer, *TM*, 22.

11. Ibid., 99.

12. Ibid., 85.

13. Schmidt, "Aesthetics and Subjectivity," KA 30, 31.

14. Immanuel Kant, *CJ,* 13/174. Page numbers indicate English and *Akademie* editions, respectively (E/Ak.).

15. Ibid., 13/174.

16. Ibid., 15/176, emphasis in original.

17. Ibid., 46/205.

18. For a thorough investigation of this form, and of Kant's cognitive or "para-epistemic" intentions in the *Critique of Judgment,* see Rodolphe Gasché, *The Idea of Form: Rethinking Kant's Aesthetics* (Stanford, Calif.: Stanford University Press, 2003).

19. Kant, *CJ,* 30/190.

20. Ibid., 58–59/215, emphasis in original.

21. Ibid., 60/216.

22. Ibid., 62/217–218, emphasis in original. Translation modified.

23. Ibid., 64/219.

24. Ibid., 88/238.

25. Ibid., 63/219.

26. Ibid., 160/293.

27. Ibid., 87/238 and 160/293.

28. Ibid., 160/294.

29. Ibid., 162/296.

30. Ibid., 90/240.

31. Manfred Kuehn, *Scottish Common Sense in Germany, 1768–1800* (Kingston: McGill-Queen's University Press, 1987), 201.

32. Kant, *CJ,* 232/356.

33. Ibid., 232/356.

34. Ibid., 79/232.

35. Ibid., 80/233.

36. Ibid., 79/232, emphasis in original.

37. Ibid., 146/283.

38. Ibid., 146/283, emphasis in original.

39. At *CJ,* 186–187/318, Kant uses the distinction between following and imitating again, this time in reference to those wishing to learn from the genius.

40. Kant, *CJ,* 168/301.

41. Ibid., 167/300, emphasis added.

42. Ibid., 164/297.

43. Ibid., 230/354.

44. Ibid., 46/205n10, emphasis in original.

45. See ibid., 169/302: "In order for us to be able to take a direct *interest* in the beautiful as such, it must be nature, or we must consider it so." Kant is obviously making room for the possibility of the genius here.

46. Ibid., 167/300, emphasis in original.

47. Ibid., 174/307, emphasis in original.

48. Ibid., 186/317.

49. Ibid., 186/318, emphasis in original.

50. Ibid., 177–178/310.

51. Gadamer, *TM,* 5.

52. Ibid., 41.

53. Ibid., 49.

54. Gadamer, "Anschauung und Anschaulichkeit," *GW* 8, 198.

55. Kant, *CJ,* 84/236.

56. Gadamer, *TM*, 51. Emphasis in original.

57. Dennis Schmidt has taken up the subtle pervasiveness of this thematic, pointing out the inherent connection between nature, language, and freedom in the third *Critique;* see "Einige Betrachtungen zu Sprache und Freiheit," 59–72; see also "On the Idiom of Truth and the Movement of Life: Some Remarks on the Task of Hermeneutics," *Internationales Jahrbuch für Hermeneutik* 10 (2011): 41–53.

58. See Allen Hance, "The Hermeneutic Significance of the *Sensus Communis.*" *International Philosophical Quarterly* 37, no. 2 (1997): 133–148.

59. See Gadamer, *TM*, 44, and Kant, *CJ*, 231/355.

60. Gadamer, "Zur Fragwürdigkeit des ästhetischen Bewusstseins," GW 8, 10.

61. Ibid., 11.

62. Ibid., 11.

63. Ibid., 12.

64. Ibid., 13.

65. Richard L. Velkley, "Gadamer and Kant: The Critique of Modern Aesthetic Consciousness in *Truth and Method,*" *Interpretation* 9 (1981): 358.

66. Gadamer, *TM*, 39.

67. Gadamer, "Reflections on my Philosophical Journey," in *The Philosophy of Hans-Georg Gadamer,* 27.

68. Gadamer, *TM*, 97.

69. Gadamer, "Zur Fragwürdigkeit des ästhetischen Bewusstseins," 17.

70. Gadamer, "Anschauung und Anschaulichkeit," GW 8, 204–205. See also *TM*, 117.

71. Gadamer, *TM*, 99.

72. Ibid., 128.

73. Gjesdal, "Between Enlightenment and Romanticism," 304.

74. Ibid., 286.

75. Gadamer, "Anschauung und Anschaulichkeit," GW 8, 204.

76. Gjesdal, "Between Enlightenment and Romanticism," 286.

77. This clarification is Gadamer's explicit aim in "Anschauung und Anschaulichkeit," GW 8, esp. 190–192.

78. Ibid., 193.

79. Gadamer, "Die Aktualität des Schönen," GW 8, 118.

80. Ibid., 127.

81. Gadamer, "Die Aktualität des Schönen," GW 8, 138.

82. Gjesdal, "Between Enlightenment and Romanticism," 304.

83. Gadamer, *TM*, 288.

84. Gadamer, "On the Scope and Function of Hermeneutical Reflection," *PH*, 19.

85. Gadamer, "Zur Fragwürdigkeit des ästhetischen Bewusstseins," 16.

86. Gadamer, "Die Aktualität des Schönen," GW 8, 139. On this connection between the truth of art and the significance of the tradition for Gadamer, see Robert J. Dostal, "Gadamer's Platonism: His Recovery of Mimesis and Anamnesis," in *Consequences of Hermeneutics: Fifty Years after Gadamer's Truth and Method,* ed. Jeff Malpas and Santiago Zabala (Evanston, Ill.: Northwestern University Press, 2010), 45–65.

87. Gadamer, "On the Scope and Function of Hermeneutical Reflection," *PH*, 19.

88. Ibid., 31.

89. Gadamer, "Rhetorik, Hermeneutik und Ideologiekritik," GW 2, 247.

90. Gadamer, "On the Scope and Function of Hermeneutical Reflection," PH, 28.

91. Because of this, the involvement with tradition is just as much a matter of logic and argumentation as it is a matter of rhetoric and the recognition of what is fitting. See James Risser, "Hermeneutics of the Possible: On Finitude and Truth in Philosophical Hermeneutics," in SR, 111–128, esp. 127.

92. Gadamer, "Kants *Kritik der reinen Vernunft* nach 200 Jahren: 'Von hier und heute geht eine neue Epoche der Weltgeschichte aus,'" GW 4, 348.

93. Gjesdal, "Between Enlightenment and Romanticism," 299.

94. Gadamer, "Die Grenzen der historischen Vernunft," GW 10, 177.

95. Gadamer, "On the Scope and Function of Hermeneutical Reflection," PH, 30.

96. Gadamer uses Habermas's own example, that of psychotherapy, to illustrate this issue. See "On the Scope and Function of Hermeneutical Reflection," PH, 40–42.

97. Gadamer, "Reply to David Detmer," 287.

5. The *Bildung* of Community

In developing the ideas in this chapter, I was particularly influenced by Nicholas Davey's book *Unquiet Understanding: Gadamer's Philosophical Hermeneutics* (Albany: State University of New York Press, 2006) and John Arthos's paper "Subtilitas Applicandi: Addressing the Crisis of the Humanities with Hermeneutics," presented at the 5th annual meeting of the North American Society for Philosophical Hermeneutics, Seattle University, September 16–18, 2010.

1. Gadamer, "Herder und die geschichtliche Welt," GW 4, 329–330.

2. For a recent account of how Gadamer's hermeneutical approach relates to human conduct and "discursive identity," see John Arthos, *Speaking Hermeneutically: Understanding in the Conduct of a Life* (Columbia: University of South Carolina Press, 2011). For a thorough investigation of the ethical roots and aims of hermeneutics, see P. Christopher Smith, *Hermeneutics and Finitude: Toward a Theory of Ethical Understanding* (New York: Fordham University Press, 1991).

3. See Gadamer, "Die Grenzen des Experten," in Gadamer, *Das Erbe Europas* (Frankfurt: Suhrkamp, 1989), 136–157; translated as "The Limitations of the Expert," in *Hans-Georg Gadamer on Education, Poetry, and History: Applied Hermeneutics,* ed. Dieter Misgeld and Graeme Nicholson, trans. Lawrence Schmidt and Monica Reuss (Albany: State University of New York Press, 1992), 181–192.

4. One could also translate the term as "formation" or "shaping." For an excellent account of the concept's history, see W. H. Bruford, *The German Tradition of Self-Cultivation: "Bildung" from Humboldt to Thomas Mann* (New York: Cambridge University Press, 1975); for more recent analyses of contemporary relevance, see Lars Løvlie, Klaus Peter Mortensen, and Sven Erik Nordenbo, eds., *Educating Humanity: Bildung in Postmodernity* (Malden, Mass.: Blackwell, 2003); for a good exposition of *Bildung* as a core concept to hermeneutics, see Davey, *Unquiet Understanding,* 37–108. See Shaun Gallagher, *Hermeneutics and Education* (Albany: State University of New York Press, 1992) for an account of how Gadamer's employment of this concept distinguishes him from other recent philosophers of education.

5. Julie Marsh, John Paine, and Laura Hamilton, *Making Sense of Data-Driven Decision-Making in Education: Evidence from Recent RAND Research* (Santa Monica, Calif.: RAND, 2006).

6. See Martha C. Nussbaum, *Not for Profit: Why Democracy Needs the Humanities* (Princeton, N.J.: Princeton University Press, 2010); Donald Phillip Verene, *The Art of Humane Education* (Ithaca, N.Y.: Cornell University Press, 2002).

7. The educational theorist Dennis Shirley, accounting for the dearth of qualitative concepts guiding American higher education, points to the "unholy trinity of historical amnesia, educational reductionism, and spiritual displacement" as determining today's pedagogical climate. Without a sense of the provenance of our crisis, it is easy to resort to pragmatic solutions that only adapt to a present system rather than critiquing it; without a deeper foundation than economic concerns, exchange value on the global market becomes the only feasible measure of success. See Dennis Shirley, "American Perspectives on German Educational Theory and Research: A Closer Look at Both the American Educational Context and the German Didaktik Tradition," in *Allgemeine Didaktik und Lehr-Lernforschung: Kontroversen und Entwicklungsperspektiven einer Wissenschaft von Unterricht,* ed. Karl-Heinz Arnold, Sigrid Blömeke, Rudolf Messner, and Jörg Schlömerkemper (Bad Heilbrunn: Klinkhardt, 2009), 195–209, here 196. Bolstering Shirley's points, Eva Brann brilliantly traces the origins of contemporary American educational dilemmas in *Paradoxes of Education in a Republic* (Chicago: University of Chicago Press, 1979).

8. For an excellent account of this development, see Bambach, *Heidegger, Dilthey, and the Crisis of Historicism.*

9. Gadamer, "On the Scope and Function of Hermeneutical Reflection," PH, 19.

10. Gadamer, "Geschichte des Universums und Geschichtlichkeit des Menschen," GW 10, 211.

11. See Gadamer, TM, 6.

12. Gadamer, "The Future of the European Humanities," in *Hans-Georg Gadamer on Education, Poetry, and History: Applied Hermeneutics,* 200.

13. Gadamer, TM, 99.

14. Ibid., xxiii, emphasis in original.

15. Ibid., 4. On this point, see Arnd Kerkhecker, "Bedeutung der humanistischen Tradition für die Geisteswissenschaften," in KA 30, 9–27, esp. 15.

16. Gadamer, TM, 12. Translation modified.

17. Gadamer, "Wahrheit in den Geisteswissenschaften," GW 2, 40.

18. Davey, *Unquiet Understanding,* 50.

19. The reading of literature is an exemplary case of this experience, which Gadamer calls the "hermeneutic priority of the question"; see TM, 362. For an excellent account of literature's role in generating questions, see Wolfgang Iser, *Der Akt des Lesens: Theorie Ästhetischer Wirkung* (Munich: Fink, 1976); translated as *The Act of Reading: A Theory of Aesthetic Response* (Baltimore: Johns Hopkins University Press, 1978). For a more theoretical account of how texts involve readers by way of problems, see Michel Meyer, "The Interrogative Theory of Meaning and Reference," in *Questions and Questioning,* ed. Michel Meyer (New York: Walter de Gruyter, 1988), 121–143. For an application of Gadamer's idea of questionability to a specific text, see Veith, "Waves and Horizons."

20. On these hermeneutic aspects of translation, see Gadamer, *TM,* 384–389.

21. See Heidegger, *Der Satz vom Grund,* GA 10, 29–30.

22. Gadamer, *TM,* xxxiii.

23. The vast trove of works and ideas that we take to be classical in the hermeneutic sense thus contains claims, ideas, and questions that confront us strangely and continually provoke thoughtful responses. With regard to this notion of the classical, then, it is crucial to grasp that these works are preserved not for the purported objective truth of their teachings as such, but for their dialogical capacity or questionability.

24. See Gadamer, *TM,* 11.

25. A recent case for this contribution of the humanities is made, with debatable success, in Hubert Dreyfus and Sean Dorrance Kelly, *All Things Shining: Reading the Western Classics to Find Meaning in a Secular Age* (New York: Simon and Schuster, 2010). See also Gadamer, "Wahrheit in den Geisteswissenschaften," GW 2, 42.

26. Gadamer, "Hermeneutics as a Theoretical and Practical Task," RAS, 121.

27. Ernest Fortin, "Gadamer on Strauss: An Interview," *Interpretation* 12, no. 1 (1984): 8.

28. See Aristotle, *Nicomachean Ethics* I, 3, 1094b28–1095a12.

29. See Gadamer, "Hermeneutik und Historismus," GW 2, 394.

30. Gadamer, "Wahrheit in den Geisteswissenschaften," GW 2, 41.

31. Arendt, "Heidegger ist achzig Jahre alt," 894.

32. Gadamer, *TM,* xxiii.

Conclusion

1. Günter Figal and Hans-Helmuth Gander, "Vorwort," in DH, 8.

2. Gadamer, *TM,* 342.

3. Ibid., 99.

4. Gadamer, "Die Aktualität des Schönen," GW 8, 138.

Bibliography

Adorno, Theodor. *Negative Dialektik*. Frankfurt am Main: Suhrkamp, 1975.

Ahlers, Rolf. "History and Philosophy as Theodicy: On *World History as the World's Judgment*." *Idealistic Studies* 30, no. 3 (2000): 159–172.

Angehrn, Emil. *Wege des Verstehens: Hermeneutik und Geschichtsdenken*. Würzburg: Königshausen & Neumann, 2008.

Arendt, Hannah. "Martin Heidegger ist achzig Jahre alt." *Merkur* 258, no. 10 (October 1969): 893–902.

——. "Martin Heidegger Is Eighty Years Old." In *Letters 1925–1975: Hannah Arendt and Martin Heidegger*, ed. Ursula Ludz, trans. Andrew Shields, 148–162. New York: Harcourt, 2004.

Aristotle. *Nicomachean Ethics*. Trans. Joe Sachs. Newburyport, Mass.: Focus Publishing, 2002.

——. *Poetics*. Trans. Joe Sachs. Newburyport, Mass.: Focus Publishing, 2005.

Arthos, John. *Speaking Hermeneutically: Understanding in the Conduct of a Life*. Columbia: University of South Carolina Press, 2011.

——. "Subtilitas Applicandi: Addressing the Crisis of the Humanities with Hermeneutics." Paper presented at the 5th annual meeting of the North American Society for Philosophical Hermeneutics, Seattle University, September 16–18, 2010.

Bambach, Charles R. *Heidegger, Dilthey, and the Crisis of Historicism*. Ithaca, N.Y.: Cornell University Press, 1995.

Barash, Jeffrey. *Martin Heidegger and the Problem of Historical Meaning*. Boston: Martinus Nijhoff, 1988.

Barbaric, Damir. "Geschehen als Übergang." In *Hermeneutische Wege: Hans-Georg Gadamer zum Hundertsten*, ed. Günter Figal, Jean Grondin, and Dennis J. Schmidt, 63–83. Tübingen: Mohr Siebeck, 2000.

——. "Die Grenze zum Unsagbaren: Sprache als Horizont einer hermeneutischen Ontologie." In *Hans-Georg Gadamer: Wahrheit und Methode*, ed. Günter Figal, 199–218. Klassiker Auslegen 30. Berlin: Akademie Verlag, 2007.

——. "Hörendes Denken." In *Dimensionen des Hermeneutischen*, ed. Günter Figal and Hans-Helmuth Gander, 37–57. Frankfurt am Main: Klostermann, 2005.

Baur, Michael. "Hegel and Aquinas on Self-Knowledge and Historicity." *Proceedings of the American Catholic Philosophical Association* 68 (1994): 125–133.

Baur, Michael, and John Russon, eds. *Hegel and the Tradition: Essays in Honor of H. S. Harris.* Toronto: University of Toronto Press, 1997.

Beiser, Frederick, ed. *The Cambridge Companion to Hegel.* New York: Cambridge University Press, 1993.

———. "Hegel's Historicism." In *The Cambridge Companion to Hegel,* ed. Frederick Beiser, 270–300. New York: Cambridge University Press, 1993.

Bellah, Robert N. *Religion in Human Evolution: From the Paleolithic to the Axial Age.* Cambridge, Mass.: Harvard University Press, 2011.

Benjamin, Walter. *Kairos: Schriften zur Philosophie.* Frankfurt am Main: Suhrkamp, 2007.

Bernasconi, Robert. "Bridging the Abyss: Heidegger and Gadamer." *Research in Phenomenology* 16 (1986): 1–24.

———. "Race and Earth in Heidegger's Thinking during the Late 1930s." *Southern Journal of Philosophy* 48, no. 1 (2010): 49–66.

———. "'You Do Not Know What I Am Talking About': Alterity and the Hermeneutical Ideal." In *The Specter of Relativism: Truth, Dialogue, and Phronêsis in Philosophical Hermeneutics,* ed. Lawrence K. Schmidt, 178–195. Evanston, Ill.: Northwestern University Press, 1995.

Bernstein, Richard J. "From Hermeneutics to Praxis." *Review of Metaphysics* 35 (1982): 823–845.

———. *The New Constellation: The Ethical-Political Horizons of Modernity/Postmodernity.* Cambridge, Mass.: MIT Press, 1992.

Bloom, Allan. *The Closing of the American Mind.* New York: Simon & Schuster, 1988.

Brann, Eva. *Paradoxes of Education in a Republic.* Chicago: University of Chicago Press, 1979.

Brelage, Manfred. "Die Geschichtlichkeit der Philosophie und die Philosophiegeschichte." *Zeitschrift für philosophische Forschung* 16, no. 3 (1962): 375–405.

Brogan, Walter. "Gadamer's Praise of Theory: Aristotle's Friend and the Reciprocity between Theory and Practice." *Research in Phenomenology* 32 (2002): 141–155.

Bruford, W. H. *The German Tradition of Self-Cultivation: "Bildung" from Humboldt to Thomas Mann.* New York: Cambridge University Press, 1975.

Bruns, Gerald. "The Hermeneutical Anarchist: *Phronêsis,* Rhetoric, and the Experience of Art." In *Gadamer's Century,* ed. Jeff Malpas, Ulrich Arnswald, and Jens Kertscher, 45–76. Cambridge, Mass.: MIT Press, 2002.

———. *Hermeneutics Ancient and Modern.* New Haven, Conn.: Yale University Press, 1995.

Butterfield, Herbert. *The Origins of Modern Science.* New York: Free Press, 1957.

Caputo, John. "Firing the Steel of Hermeneutics: Hegelianized Hermeneutics versus Radical Hermeneutics." In *Hegel, History, and Interpretation,* ed. Shaun Gallagher, 59–70. Albany: State University of New York Press, 1997.

———. "Gadamer's Closet Essentialism: A Derridean Critique." In *Dialogue and Deconstruction: The Gadamer-Derrida Encounter,* ed. Diane P. Michelfelder and Richard E. Palmer, 258–264. Albany: State University of New York Press, 1989.

———. *More Radical Hermeneutics.* Bloomington: Indiana University Press, 2000.

———. *Radical Hermeneutics: Repetition, Deconstruction, and the Hermeneutic Project.* Bloomington: Indiana University Press, 1987.

Carr, David. "Modernity, Post-Modernity and the Philosophy of History." *Proceedings of the American Catholic Philosophical Association* 68 (1994): 45–57.

———. *Time, Narrative, and History.* Bloomington: Indiana University Press, 1986.

Carr, David, Thomas R. Flynn, and Rudolf A. Makkreel, eds. *The Ethics of History.* Evanston, Ill.: Northwestern University Press, 2004.

Cavalcante Schuback, Marcia Sá, and Hans Ruin, eds. *The Past's Presence: Essays on the Historicity of Philosophical Thinking.* Huddinge, Sweden: Södertörn, 2005.

Cleary, John, and Padraig Hogan. "The Reciprocal Character of Self-Education: Introductory Comments on Hans-Georg Gadamer's Address 'Education Is Self-Education.'" *Journal of Philosophy of Education* 35, no. 4 (2001): 520–527.

Cohen, Ted, and Paul Guyer, eds. *Essays in Kant's Aesthetics.* Chicago: University of Chicago Press, 1982.

Collingwood, R. G. *The Idea of History.* New York: Oxford University Press, 1974.

Coltman, Rod. *The Language of Hermeneutics: Gadamer and Heidegger in Dialogue.* Albany: State University of New York Press, 1998.

Dallmayr, Fred. *The Other Heidegger.* Ithaca, N.Y.: Cornell University Press, 1993.

Danto, Arthur C. *Analytical Philosophy of History.* New York: Cambridge University Press, 1965.

Davey, Nicholas. *Unquiet Understanding: Gadamer's Philosophical Hermeneutics.* Albany: State University of New York Press, 2006.

Davis, Michael. *Aristotle's Poetics.* Lanham, Md.: Rowman and Littlefield, 1992.

———. "First Things First: History and the Liberal Arts." In *Wonderlust: Ruminations on Liberal Education,* 25–31. South Bend, Ind.: St. Augustine's Press, 2006.

Deleuze, Gilles. *Kant's Critical Philosophy: The Doctrine of the Faculties.* Trans. Hugh Tomlinson and Barbara Habberjam. Minneapolis: University of Minnesota Press, 1984.

Denker, Alfred, and Michael Vater, eds. *Hegel's Phenomenology of Spirit: New Critical Essays.* Amherst, N.Y.: Humanity Books, 2003.

De Nys, Martin. "The Substance of Knowing Is History: Absolute Knowing and History in Hegel's *Phenomenology.*" *Proceedings of the American Catholic Philosophical Association* 68 (1994): 135–144.

Derrida, Jacques. *Edmund Husserl's Origin of Geometry: An Introduction.* Trans. John P. Leavey. Lincoln: University of Nebraska Press, 1978.

———. *Of Spirit: Heidegger and the Question.* Chicago: University of Chicago Press, 1989.

Desmond, William. "Between Finitude and Infinity: On Hegel's Sublationary Infinitism." In *Hegel and the Infinite: Religion, Politics, and Dialectic,* ed. Slavoj Zizek, Clayton Crockett, and Creston Davis, 115–140. New York: Columbia University Press, 2011.

Di Cesare, Donatella. "Stars and Constellations: The Difference between Gadamer and Derrida." *Research in Phenomenology* 34, no. 1 (2004): 73–102.

Dilthey, Wilhelm. *Gesammelte Schriften.* Göttingen: Vandenhoeck & Ruprecht, 1970.

Dostal, Robert J., ed. *The Cambridge Companion to Gadamer.* New York: Cambridge University Press, 2002.

———. "Gadamerian Hermeneutics and Irony: Between Strauss and Derrida." *Research in Phenomenology* 38 (2008): 247–269.

———. "Gadamer's Continuous Challenge: Heidegger's Plato Interpretation." In *The Philosophy of Hans-Georg Gadamer*, ed. Lewis Edwin Hahn, 289–307. Chicago: Open Court, 1997.

———. "Gadamer's Platonism: His Recovery of Mimesis and Anamnesis." In *Consequences of Hermeneutics: Fifty Years after Gadamer's* Truth and Method, ed. Jeff Malpas and Santiago Zabala, 45–65. Evanston, Ill.: Northwestern University Press, 2010.

Dottori, Riccardo. *Die Reflexion des Wirklichen: Zwischen Hegels absoluter Dialektik und der Philosophie der Endlichkeit von M. Heidegger und H. G. Gadamer*. Tübingen: Mohr Siebeck, 2006.

Dreyfus, Hubert, and Sean Dorrance Kelly. *All Things Shining: Reading the Western Classics to Find Meaning in a Secular Age*. New York: Simon and Schuster, 2010.

Dux, Günter. *Die Zeit in der Geschichte: Ihre Entwicklungslogik vom Mythos zur Weltzeit*. Frankfurt am Main: Suhrkamp, 1989.

Dux, Günter, and Ulrich Wenzel, eds. *Der Prozeß der Geistesgeschichte: Studien zur ontogenetischen und historischen Entwicklung des Geistes*. Frankfurt am Main: Suhrkamp, 1994.

Eco, Umberto. *Travels in Hyperreality*. Trans. William Weaver. New York: Harcourt, Brace, Jovanovich, 1986.

Elm, Ralf. "Schenkung, Entzug, und die Kunst schöpferischen Fragens: Zum Phänomen der Geschichtlichkeit des Verstehens in Gadamers 'Analyse des wirkungsgeschichtlichen Bewusstseins.'" In *Hans-Georg Gadamer: Wahrheit und Methode*, ed. Günter Figal, 151–176. Klassiker Auslegen 30. Berlin: Akademie Verlag, 2007.

Espinet, David, and Tobias Keiling, eds. *Heideggers "Ursprung des Kunstwerks": Ein kooperativer Kommentar*. Frankfurt am Main: Klostermann, 2011.

Fackenheim, Emil. *Metaphysics and Historicity*. Milwaukee: Marquette University Press, 1961.

Faulconer, James, and Richard N. Williams. "Temporality in Human Action: An Alternative to Positivism and Historicism." *American Psychologist* 40, no. 11 (1985): 1179–1188.

Feher, Istvan M. "Verstehen bei Heidegger und Gadamer." In *Dimensionen des Hermeneutischen*, ed. Günter Figal and Hans-Helmuth Gander, 89–115. Frankfurt am Main: Klostermann, 2005.

Fenves, Peter D. *A Peculiar Fate: Metaphysics and World-History in Kant*. Ithaca, N.Y.: Cornell University Press, 1991.

Figal, Günter, ed. *Begegnungen mit Hans-Georg Gadamer*. Stuttgart: Reclam, 2000.

———. "The Doing of the Thing Itself: Gadamer's Hermeneutic Ontology of Language." In *The Cambridge Companion to Gadamer*, ed. Robert J. Dostal, 102–125. New York: Cambridge University Press, 2002.

———. *Erscheinungsdinge: Ästhetik als Phänomenologie*. Tübingen: Mohr Siebeck, 2010.

———, ed. *Hans-Georg Gadamer: Wahrheit und Methode*. Klassiker Auslegen 30. Berlin: Akademie Verlag, 2007.

———. *Martin Heidegger: Phänomenologie der Freiheit*. Frankfurt am Main: Athenäum, 1988.

———. *Der Sinn des Verstehens: Beiträge zur hermeneutischen Philosophie*. Stuttgart: Reclam, 1996.

———. *Verstehensfragen: Studien zur phänomenologisch-hermeneutischen Philosophie.* Tübingen: Mohr Siebeck, 2009.

———. *"Wahrheit und Methode zur Einführung."* In *Hans-Georg Gadamer: Wahrheit und Methode,* ed. Günter Figal, 1–7. Klassiker Auslegen 30. Berlin: Akademie Verlag, 2007.

Figal, Günter, and Hans-Helmuth Gander, eds. *Dimensionen des Hermeneutischen: Heidegger und Gadamer.* Frankfurt am Main: Vittorio Klostermann, 2005.

———. "Vorwort." In *Dimensionen des Hermeneutischen: Heidegger und Gadamer,* ed. Günter Figal and Hans-Helmuth Gander, 7–9. Frankfurt am Main: Mohr Siebeck, 2005.

Figal, Günter, Jean Grondin, and Dennis J. Schmidt, eds. *Hermeneutische Wege: Hans-Georg Gadamer zum Hundertsten.* Tübingen: Mohr Siebeck, 2000.

Flynn, Thomas. "The Future Perfect and the Perfect Future: History and Its Reasons." *Proceedings of the American Catholic Philosophical Association* 68 (1994): 3–15.

Fortin, Ernest. "Gadamer on Strauss: An Interview." *Interpretation* 12, no. 1 (1984): 1–13.

Foucault, Michel. *Die Ordnung der Dinge: Eine Archäologie der Humanwissenschaften.* Trans. Ulrich Köppen. Frankfurt am Main: Suhrkamp, 1971.

Frank, Manfred. *Das individuelle Allgemeine.* Frankfurt am Main: Suhrkamp, 1985.

Fukuyama, Francis. "The End of History?" *National Interest* 16 (1989): 3–18.

Fulda, Hans Friedrich. "Philosophiegeschichte als Selbsterkenntnis der Vernunft: Warum und wie wir die Philosophiegeschichte studieren sollten." *Abhandlungen der Akademie der Wissenschaften in Göttingen* 231 (1999): 17–38.

Fulda, Hans Friedrich, and Dieter Henrich, eds. *Materialien zu Hegels* Phänomenologie des Geistes. Frankfurt am Main: Suhrkamp, 1973.

Gadamer, Hans-Georg. *The Beginning of Philosophy.* Trans. Rod Coltman. New York: Continuum, 2000.

———. *A Century of Philosophy: Hans-Georg Gadamer in Conversation with Riccardo Dottori.* Trans. Rod Coltman with Sigrid Koepke. New York: Continuum, 2003.

———. "A Conversation with Hans-Georg Gadamer." *Journal of the British Society for Phenomenology* 2 (1995): 116–125.

———. *Das Erbe Europas.* Frankfurt: Suhrkamp, 1989.

———. "The Future of the European Humanities." In *Hans-Georg Gadamer on Education, Poetry, and History: Applied Hermeneutics,* ed. Dieter Misgeld and Graeme Nicholson, trans. Lawrence Schmidt and Monica Reuss, 193–208. Albany: State University of New York Press, 1992.

———. *Gesammelte Werke.* 10 vols. Tübingen: Mohr Siebeck, 1995.

———. *Hans-Georg Gadamer im Gespräch.* Ed. Carsten Dutt. Heidelberg: Universitätsverlag C. Winter, 1993.

———. *Hegel's Dialectic.* Trans. P. Christopher Smith. New Haven, Conn.: Yale University Press, 1976.

———. "Heidegger's theologische Jugendschrift." In Martin Heidegger, *Phänomenologische Interpretationen zu Aristoteles,* ed. Günther Neumann, 76–86. Stuttgart: Reclam, 2003.

———. "The Limitations of the Expert." In *Hans-Georg Gadamer on Education, Poetry, and History: Applied Hermeneutics,* ed. Dieter Misgeld and Graeme Nicholson, trans.

Lawrence Schmidt and Monica Reuss, 181–192. Albany: State University of New York Press, 1992.

——. *Lob der Theorie.* Frankfurt am Main: Suhrkamp, 1983.

——. "On the Problematic Character of Aesthetic Consciousness." Trans. E. Kelly. *Graduate Faculty Philosophy Journal* 9, no. 1 (1982): 31–40.

——. *Philosophical Apprenticeships.* Trans. Robert R. Sullivan. Cambridge, Mass.: MIT Press, 1987.

——. *Philosophical Hermeneutics.* Trans. and ed. David Linge. Berkeley: University of California Press, 1976.

——. *Reason in the Age of Science.* Trans. Frederick G. Lawrence. Cambridge, Mass.: MIT Press, 1981.

——. *The Relevance of the Beautiful and Other Essays.* Trans. Nicholas Walker. New York: Cambridge University Press, 1986.

——. "Reply to David Detmer." In *The Philosophy of Hans-Georg Gadamer,* ed. Lewis Edwin Hahn, 286. Library of Living Philosophers 24. Chicago: Open Court, 1997.

——. *Truth and Method.* 2nd rev. ed. Trans. Joel Weinsheimer and Donald G. Marshall. New York: Continuum, 2000.

Gadamer, Hans-Georg, and Jürgen Habermas. *Das Erbe Hegels: Zwei Reden aus Anlaß des Hegel-Preises.* Frankfurt am Main: Suhrkamp, 1979.

Gallagher, Shaun, ed. *Hegel, History, and Interpretation.* Albany: State University of New York Press, 1997.

——. *Hermeneutics and Education.* Albany: State University of New York Press, 1992.

Galston, William A. *Kant and the Problem of History.* Chicago: University of Chicago Press, 1975.

Gander, Hans-Helmuth. "Between Strangeness and Familiarity: Towards Gadamer's Conception of Effective History." *Research in Phenomenology* 34 (2004): 121–136.

——. "Erhebung der Geschichtlichkeit des Verstehens zum hermeneutischen Prinzip." In *Hans-Georg Gadamer: Wahrheit und Methode*ed. Günter Figal, 105–125. Klassiker Auslegen 30. Berlin: Akademie Verlag, 2007.

——. "Existenzialontologie und Geschichtlichkeit." In *Martin Heidegger: Sein und Zeit,* ed. Thomas Rentsch, 227–252. Klassiker Auslegen 25. Berlin: Akademie Verlag, 2007.

——. "In den Netzen der Überlieferung: Eine hermeneutische Analyse zur geschichtlichkeit des Erkennens." In *Hermeneutische Wege: Hans-Georg Gadamer zum Hundertsten,* ed. Günter Figal, Jean Grondin, and Dennis J. Schmidt, 257–268. Tübingen: Mohr Siebeck, 2000.

Gasché, Rodolphe. *The Idea of Form: Rethinking Kant's Aesthetics.* Stanford, Calif.: Stanford University Press, 2003.

Geniusas, Saulius. "On the Oneness of the Hermeneutical Horizon(s)." *PhaenEx* 1, no. 1 (2006): 230–271.

George, Theodore. "What Is the Future of the Past? Gadamer and Hegel on Truth, Art, and the Ruptures of Tradition." *Journal of the British Society for Phenomenology* 40, no. 1 (2009): 4–20.

Gibbons, Michael T. "Hermeneutics, Political Inquiry and Practical Reason: An Evolving Challenge to Political Science." *American Political Science Review* 100, no. 4 (2006): 563–571.

Gjesdal, Kristin. "Between Enlightenment and Romanticism: Some Problems and Challenges in Gadamer's Hermeneutics." *Journal of the History of Philosophy* 46, no. 2 (2008): 285–306.

———. *Gadamer and the Legacy of German Idealism*. New York: Cambridge University Press, 2009.

———. "Reading Kant Hermeneutically: Gadamer and the *Critique of Judgment*." *Kant-Studien* 98, no. 3 (2007): 351–371.

Goethe, Johann Wolfgang. *Goethes Werke*. Stuttgart: Cotta, 1833.

Gonzalez, Francisco. "Dialectic and Dialogue in the Hermeneutics of Paul Ricoeur and H. G. Gadamer." *Continental Philosophy Review* 39 (2006): 313–345.

Gordon, Peter E. *Continental Divide: Heidegger, Cassirer, Davos*. Cambridge, Mass.: Harvard University Press, 2010.

Grondin, Jean. *Einführung in die philosophische Hermeneutik*. Darmstadt: Wissenschaftliche Buchgesellschaft, 1991.

———. *Hans-Georg Gadamer: A Biography*. New Haven, Conn.: Yale University Press, 2003.

———. "Jenseits der Wirkungsgeschichte: Gadamers sokratische Destruktion der griechischen Philosophie." *Internationale Zeitschrift für Philosophie* 1 (1992): 38–49.

———. "The Neo-Kantian Heritage in Gadamer." In *Neo-Kantianism in Contemporary Philosophy,* ed. Rudolf A. Makkreel and Sebastian Luft, 92–110. Bloomington: Indiana University Press, 2010.

———. *Von Heidegger zu Gadamer: Unterwegs zur Hermeneutik*. Darmstadt: Wissenschaftliche Buchgesellschaft, 2001.

———. "Die Wiedererweckung der Seinsfrage auf dem Weg einer phänomenologisch-hermeneutischen Destruktion." In *Martin Heidegger: Sein und Zeit*, ed. Thomas Rentsch, 1–27. Klassiker Auslegen 25. Berlin: Akademie Verlag, 2007.

Habermas, Jürgen. *Between Facts and Norms*. Trans. William Regh. Cambridge, Mass.: MIT Press, 1996.

———, ed. *Hermeneutik und Ideologiekritik*. Frankfurt am Main: Suhrkamp, 1971.

———. *On the Logic of the Social Sciences*. Trans. Ciaran Cronin. Cambridge, Mass.: MIT Press, 1988.

Hahn, Lewis Edwin, ed. *The Philosophy of Hans-Georg Gadamer*. Library of Living Philosophers 24. Chicago: Open Court, 1997.

Hance, Allen. "The Hermeneutic Significance of the *Sensus Communis*." *International Philosophical Quarterly* 37, no. 2 (1997): 133–148.

Hammermeister, Kai. "*Heimat* in Heidegger and Gadamer." *Philosophy and Literature* 24 (2000): 312–326.

Hartmann, Nicolai. "Zur Methode der Philosophiegeschichte." In *Kleinere Schriften 3,* 1–22. Berlin: de Gruyter, 1958.

Hegel, G. W. F. *Hegel: Texts and Commentary*. Trans. and ed. Walter Kaufmann. Notre Dame, Ind.: University of Notre Dame Press, 1977.

———. *Introduction to the Philosophy of History*. Trans. Leo Rauch. Indianapolis: Hackett Publishing, 1988.

———. *Die Phänomenologie des Geistes*. Frankfurt am Main: Suhrkamp, 1970. English translation: *Phenomenology of Spirit*. Trans. A. V. Miller. New York: Oxford University Press, 1977.

——. *The Philosophy of Right*. Trans. Alan White. Newburyport, Mass.: Focus Publishing, 2002.

——. *Reason in History*. Trans. Robert S. Hartman. New York: Macmillan Publishing, 1953.

——. *The Science of Logic*. Trans. George Di Giovanni. New York: Cambridge University Press, 2010.

——. *Die Vernunft in der Geschichte*. Hamburg: Felix Meiner, 1955. English translation: *Reason in History*. Trans. Robert S. Hartman. New York: Macmillan Publishing, 1953.

Heidegger, Martin. *Basic Writings*. Ed. David Farrell Krell. San Francisco: HarperCollins, 1993.

——. *Beiträge zur Philosophie (Vom Ereignis)*. G A 65. Frankfurt am Main: Klostermann, 1989. English translation: *Contributions to Philosophy: Of the Event*. Trans. Richard Rojcewicz and Daniela Vallega-Neu. Bloomington: Indiana University Press, 2012.

——. *Besinnung*, G A 66. Frankfurt am Main: Klostermann, 1997.

——. "The Concept of Time in the Science of History." Trans. Harry S. Taylor and Hans Uffelmann. *Journal of the British Society for Phenomenology* 9 (1978): 3–10.

——. *Frühe Schriften*. G A 1. Frankfurt am Main: Klostermann, 1978.

——. *Die Geschichte des Seyns*. G A 69. Frankfurt am Main: Klostermann, 1998.

——. *Die Grundprobleme der Phänomenologie*. G A 24. Frankfurt am Main: Klostermann, 1975. English translation: *Basic Problems of Phenomenology*. Trans. Albert Hofstadter. Bloomington: Indiana University Press, 1982.

——. *The Heidegger Reader*. Ed. Günter Figal and trans. Jerome Veith. Bloomington: Indiana University Press, 2009.

——. *History of the Concept of Time*. Trans. Theodore Kisiel. Bloomington: Indiana University Press, 1985.

——. *Hölderlin's Hymnen Germanien und Der Rhein*. G A 39. Frankfurt am Main: Klostermann, 1980.

——. *Holzwege*. G A 5. Frankfurt am Main: Klostermann, 1977. English translation: *Off the Beaten Track*. Trans. Julian Young and Kenneth Haynes. New York: Cambridge University Press, 2002.

——. *Identität und Differenz*. G A 11. Frankfurt am Main: Klostermann, 2006. English translation: *Identity and Difference*. Trans. Joan Stambaugh. New York: Harper & Row, 1969.

——. *Introduction to Metaphysics*. Trans. Gregory Fried and Richard Polt. New Haven, Conn.: Yale University Press, 2000.

——. *Metaphysische Anfangsgründe der Logik im Ausgang von Leibniz*. G A 26. Frankfurt am Main: Klostermann, 1978. English translation: *The Metaphysical Foundations of Logic*. Trans. Michael Heim. Indiana University Press, 1984.

——. *Nietzsche: der europäische Nihilismus*. Pfullingen: Günther Neske, 1989.

——. *Nietzsche*, vol. 3. Trans. Frank A. Capuzzi, David Farrell Krell, and Joan Staumbaugh, ed. David Farrell Krell. San Francisco: Harper San Francisco, 1987.

——. *Ontologie (Hermeneutik der Faktizität)*. G A 63. Frankfurt am Main: Klostermann, 1988. English translation: *Ontology – The Hermeneutics of Facticity*. Trans. John van Buren. Bloomington: Indiana University Press, 1999.

——. *Phänomenologie des religiösen Lebens.* GA 60. Frankfurt am Main: Klostermann, 1995. English translation: *The Phenomenology of Religious Life.* Trans. Jennifer Gosetti and Matthias Fritsch. Bloomington: Indiana University Press, 2004.

——. *Phänomenologische Interpretationen ausgewählter Abhandlungen des Aristoteles zu Ontologie und Logik.* GA 62. Frankfurt am Main: Klostermann, 2005.

——. "Preface: Letter to Fr. Richardson." In William J. Richardson, *Heidegger: Through Phenomenology to Thought,* ix–xxiii. The Hague: Martinus Nijhoff, 1963.

——. *Der Satz vom Grund.* GA 10. Frankfurt am Main: Klostermann, 1997. English translation: *The Principle of Reason.* Trans. Reginald Lilly. Indiana University Press, 1991.

——. *Sein und Zeit.* Tübingen: Niemeyer, 1953. English translations: *Being and Time.* Trans. John Macquarrie and Edward Robinson. San Francisco: Harper & Row, 1962. Also translated by Joan Stambaugh. Albany: State University of New York Press, 1996.

——. *Unterwegs zur Sprache.* GA 12. Frankfurt am Main: Klostermann, 1985. English translation: *On the Way to Language.* Trans. Peter D. Hertz. New York: Harper & Row, 1971.

——. *Wegmarken.* GA 9. Frankfurt am Main: Klostermann, 1976. English translation: *Pathmarks.* Ed. William McNeill. New York: Cambridge University Press, 1998.

——. *What Is Called Thinking?* Trans. J. Glenn Gray. New York: HarperCollins, 1968.

——. *Zur Sache des Denkens.* Tübingen: Niemeyer, 1969. English translation: *On Time and Being.* Trans. Joan Stambaugh. New York: Harper & Row, 1972.

Hekman, Susan. *Hermeneutics and the Sociology of Knowledge.* Notre Dame, Ind.: University of Notre Dame Press, 1986.

Hilmer, Brigitte, Georg Lohmann, and Tilo Wesche, eds. *Anfang und Grenzen des Sinns.* Göttingen: Velbrück Wissenschaft, 2006.

Houlgate, Stephen. *Freedom, Truth, and History: An Introduction to Hegel's Philosophy.* New York: Routledge, 1991.

——. *The Opening of Hegel's Logic: From Being to Infinity.* West Lafayette, Ind.: Purdue University Press, 2006.

——. "World History as the Progress of Consciousness: An Interpretation of Hegel's Philosophy of History." *Owl of Minerva* 22, no. 1 (1990): 69–80.

Hoy, David Couzens. *The Time of Our Lives: A Critical History of Temporality.* Cambridge, Mass.: MIT Press, 2009.

Husserl, Edmund. *The Crisis of the European Sciences and Transcendental Phenomenology.* Trans. David Carr. Evanston, Ill.: Northwestern University Press, 1970.

Hyppolite, Jean. "Anmerkungen zur Vorrede der Phänomenologie des Geistes und zum Thema: das Absolute ist Subjekt." In *Materialien zu Hegels* Phänomenologie des Geistes, ed. Hans Friedrich Fulda and Dieter Henrich, 45–53. Frankfurt am Main: Suhrkamp, 1973.

Iser, Wolfgang. *Der Akt des Lesens: Theorie Ästhetischer Wirkung.* Munich: Fink, 1976. English translation: *The Act of Reading: A Theory of Aesthetic Response.* Baltimore: Johns Hopkins University Press, 1978.

Janicaud, Dominique. "The 'Overcoming' of Metaphysics in the Hölderlin Lectures." In *Reading Heidegger: Commemorations,* ed. John Sallis, 383–391. Bloomington: Indiana University Press, 1993.

Jurist, Elliot. "Recognition and Self-Knowledge." *Hegel-Studien* 21 (1986): 143–150.

Kant, Immanuel. *Critique of Judgment.* Trans. Werner S. Pluhar. Indianapolis: Hackett, 1987.

——. *Critique of Pure Reason.* Trans. Werner S. Pluhar. Indianapolis: Hackett, 1996.

——. *Kants gesammelte Schriften.* Ed. Deutsche Akademie der Wissenschaften. Berlin: Walter de Gruyter, 1902–.

Kearney, Richard. "Between Oneself and Another: Paul Ricoeur's Diacritical Herme- neutics." In *Between Suspicion and Sympathy: Paul Ricoeur's Unstable Equilibrium,* ed. Andrzej Wiercinski, 149–161. Toronto: Hermeneutic Press, 2003.

——. *Debates in Continental Philosophy: Conversations with Contemporary Thinkers.* New York: Fordham University Press, 2004.

Kelly, George Armstrong. *Hegel's Retreat from Eleusis: Studies in Political Thought.* Princeton, N.J.: Princeton University Press, 1978.

Kerdemann, Deborah. "Exposure and Expertise: Philosophy for Teacher Education." In *Philosophy of Education 2001,* ed. Suzanne Rice, 100–103. Urbana, Ill.: Philosophy of Education Society, 2002.

Kerkhecker, Arnd. "Bedeutung der humanistischen Tradition für die Geisteswissen- schaften." In *Hans-Georg Gadamer: Wahrheit und Methode,* ed. Günter Figal, 9–27. Klassiker Auslegen 30. Berlin: Akademie Verlag, 2007.

Kisiel, Theodore. "Das Versagen von *Sein und Zeit:* 1927–1930." In *Martin Heidegger: Sein und Zeit,* ed. Thomas Rentsch, 253–279. Klassiker Auslegen 25. Berlin: Akademie Verlag, 2007.

Kisiel, Theodore, and John van Buren, eds. *Reading Heidegger from the Start: Essays in His Earliest Thought.* Albany: State University of New York, 1994.

Kögler, Hans-Herbert. *The Power of Dialogue.* Cambridge, Mass.: MIT Press, 1996.

Kojève, Alexandre. *Introduction to the Reading of Hegel: Lectures on the Phenomenology of Spirit,* trans. James H. Nichols Jr. Ithaca, N.Y.: Cornell University Press, 1969.

Koselleck, Reinhart. *Vergangene Zukunft: Zur Semantik geschichtlicher Zeiten.* Frankfurt am Main: Suhrkamp, 1979.

Krajewski, Bruce, ed. *Gadamer's Repercussions: Reconsidering Philosophical Hermeneu- tics.* Berkeley: University of California Press, 2004.

Kuehn, Manfred. *Kant: A Biography.* New York: Cambridge University Press, 2001.

——. *Scottish Common Sense in Germany, 1768–1800.* Kingston: McGill-Queen's Univer- sity Press, 1987.

Kuhn, Thomas S. *The Structure of Scientific Revolutions.* Chicago: University of Chicago Press, 1970.

Lauer, Quentin. *A Reading of Hegel's Phenomenology of Spirit.* New York: Fordham Uni- versity Press, 1993.

Lawrence, Frederick G. "Gadamer, the Hermeneutic Revolution, and Theology." In *The Cambridge Companion to Gadamer,* ed. Robert Dostal, 167–200. New York: Cam- bridge University Press, 2002.

Lebech, Flemming. "The Concept of the Subject in the Philosophical Hermeneutics of Hans- Georg Gadamer." *International Journal of Philosophical Studies* 14, no. 2 (2006): 221–236.

Llewelyn, John. *The Middle Voice of Ecological Conscience.* New York: St. Martin's, 1991.

Løvlie, Lars, Klaus Peter Mortensen, and Sven Erik Nordenbo, eds. *Educating Humanity: Bildung in Postmodernity.* Malden, Mass.: Blackwell, 2003.

Luft, Sebastian. *Subjectivity and Lifeworld in Transcendental Phenomenology.* Evanston,
Ill.: Northwestern University Press, 2011.

Lyotard, Jean-Francois. *Der Enthusiasmus: Kants Kritik der Geschichte.* Wien: Passagen,
2009.

MacIntyre, Alasdair. *After Virtue: A Study in Moral Theory.* 3rd ed. Notre Dame, Ind.:
University of Notre Dame Press, 2007.

——. "On Not Having the Last Word: Thoughts on Our Debts to Gadamer." In *Gadamer's Century,* ed. Jeff Malpas, Ulrich Arnswald, and Jens Kertscher, 157–172. Cambridge, Mass.: MIT Press, 2002.

——. *Whose Justice? Which Rationality?* Notre Dame, Ind.: University of Notre Dame
Press, 1988.

Madison, Gary Brent. "On the Importance of Getting Things Straight." *Phaenex* 1, no. 1
(2006): 257–271.

——. "The Theory of Practice/The Practice of Theory." In *The Politics of Postmodernity:
Essays in Applied Hermeneutics,* 137–162. Dordrecht: Kluwer, 2001.

Makkreel, Rudolf. "Gadamer and the Problem of How to Relate Kant and Hegel to
Hermeneutics." *Laval théologique et philosophique* 53, no. 1 (1997): 151–166.

——. *Imagination and Interpretation in Kant: The Hermeneutical Import of the Critique of
Judgment.* Chicago: University of Chicago Press, 1990.

——. "Traditional Historicism, Contemporary Interpretations of Historicity, and the
History of Philosophy." *New Literary History* 21, no. 4 (1990): 977–991.

——. "Tradition and Orientation in Hermeneutics." *Research in Phenomenology* 16
(1986): 73–85.

Makkreel, Rudolf, and Sebastian Luft, eds. *Neo-Kantianism in Contemporary Philosophy.*
Bloomington: Indiana University Press, 2010.

Maletz, Donald. "Hegel on Right as Actualized Will." *Political Theory* 17, no. 1 (1989):
33–50.

——. "History in Hegel's *Philosophy of Right.*" *Review of Politics* 42, no. 2 (1983): 209–233.

——. "An Introduction to Hegel's 'Introduction' to the *Philosophy of Right.*" *Interpretation: A Journal of Political Philosophy* 13, no. 2 (1985): 67–90.

——. "The Meaning of 'Will' in Hegel's *Philosophy of Right.*" *Interpretation: A Journal of
Political Philosophy* 13, no. 2 (1985): 195–212.

Malpas, Jeff, Ulrich Arnswald, and Jens Kertscher, eds. *Gadamer's Century: Essays in
Honor of Hans-Georg Gadamer.* Cambridge, Mass.: MIT Press, 2002.

Malpas, Jeff, and Santiago Zabala, eds. *Consequences of Hermeneutics: Fifty Years after
Gadamer's* Truth and Method. Evanston, Ill.: Northwestern University Press, 2010.

Marcuse, Herbert. *Hegel's Ontology and the Theory of Historicity,* trans. Seyla Benhabib.
Cambridge, Mass.: MIT Press, 1987.

Marino, Stefano. "Gadamer on Heidegger: Is the History of Being 'Just' Another Philosophy of History?" *Journal of the British Society for Phenomenology* 41, no. 3 (2010):
287–303.

Marsh, Julie, John Paine, and Laura Hamilton. *Making Sense of Data-Driven Decision-
Making in Education: Evidence from Recent RAND Research.* Santa Monica, Calif.:
RAND, 2006.

Marshall, Donald G. *The Force of Tradition: Response and Resistance in Literature, Reli-gion, and Cultural Studies.* New York: Rowman and Littlefield, 2005.

Martin, Wayne M. "In Defense of Bad Infinity: A Fichtean Response to Hegel's *Differen-zschrift.*" *Bulletin of the Hegel Society of Great Britain* 55/56 (2007): 168–187.

Marx, Werner. *Heidegger und die Tradition.* Hamburg: Meiner, 1980.

McDowell, John. "Gadamer and Davidson on Understanding and Relativism." In *Ga-damer's Century,* ed. Jeff Malpas, Ulrich Arnswald, and Jens Kertscher, 173–215. Cam-bridge, Mass.: MIT Press, 2002.

Meinecke, Friedrich. *Die Entstehung des Historismus.* Munich: Oldenbourg, 1936.

Meyer, Michel, ed. *Questions and Questioning.* New York: Walter de Gruyter, 1988.

Michelfelder, Diane P., and Richard E. Palmer, eds. *Dialogue and Deconstruction: The Gadamer-Derrida Encounter.* Albany: State University of New York Press, 1989.

Misgeld, Dieter, and Graeme Nicholson, eds. *Hans-Georg Gadamer on Education, Poetry, and History: Applied Hermeneutics.* Albany: State University of New York Press, 1992.

Nancy, Jean-Luc. *Hegel: The Restlessness of the Negative.* Trans. Jason Smith and Steven Miller. Minneapolis: University of Minnesota Press, 2002.

Nietzsche, Friedrich. *Sämtliche Werke: Kritische Studienausgabe.* 15 vols. Ed. Giorgio Colli and Mazzino Montinari. New York: de Gruyter, 1980.

Nussbaum, Martha C. *Not for Profit: Why Democracy Needs the Humanities.* Princeton, N.J.: Princeton University Press, 2010.

O'Brien, George Dennis. *Hegel on Reason and History: A Contemporary Interpretation.* Chicago: University of Chicago Press, 1975.

Odenstedt, Anders. "History as Conversation Versus History as Science: Gadamer and Dilthey." In *Gadamer's Hermeneutics and the Art of Conversation,* ed. Andrzej Wiercin-ski, 481–504. Piscataway, New Jersey: Transaction Publishers, 2011.

Ortega y Gasset, José. *History as System and Other Essays toward a Philosophy of History.* New York: W. W. Norton, 1961.

Ott, Hugo. *Martin Heidegger: Unterwegs zu seiner Biographie.* Frankfurt am Main: Cam-pus, 1992.

Page, Carl. "Historicist Finitude and Philosophical Hermeneutics." In *The Philosophy of Hans-Georg Gadamer,* ed. Lewis Edwin Hahn, 369–384. Chicago: Open Court, 1997.

———. *Philosophical Historicism and the Betrayal of First Philosophy.* University Park: Pennsylvania State University Press, 1995.

Palmer, Richard E. "Two Contrasting Heideggerian Elements in Gadamer's Philosophi-cal Hermeneutics." In *Consequences of Hermeneutics: Fifty Years after Gadamer's* Truth and Method, ed. Jeff Malpas and Santiago Zabala, 121–131. Evanston, Ill.: Northwest-ern University Press, 2010.

Perkins, Robert L., ed. *History and System: Hegel's Philosophy of History.* Albany: State University of New York Press, 1984.

Piercey, Robert. "Ricoeur's Acount of Tradition and the Gadamer-Habermas Debate." *Human Studies* 27 (2004): 259–280.

———. *The Uses of the Past from Heidegger to Rorty.* New York: Cambridge University Press, 2009.

Pinkard, Terry. *Hegel: A Biography.* New York: Cambridge University Press, 2000.

Pippin, Robert. "Gadamer's Hegel." In *The Cambridge Companion to Gadamer*, ed. Robert Dostal, 225–246. Cambridge: Cambridge University Press, 2002.

———. "The Unavailability of the Ordinary: Strauss on the Philosophical Fate of Modernity." In *The Persistence of Subjectivity: On the Kantian Aftermath*, 121–145. New York: Cambridge University Press, 2005.

———. "You Cannot Get There from Here: Transition Problems in Hegel's *Phenomenology of Spirit*." In *The Cambridge Companion to Hegel*, ed. Frederick Beiser, 52–85. New York: Cambridge University Press, 1993.

Rauch-Rapaport, Angelika. "Gadamer Needs Lacan and Lacan Needs Gadamer," *Journal of the British Society for Phenomenology* 34, no. 3 (2003): 309–326.

Rauch, Angelika. *The Hieroglyph of Tradition: Freud, Benjamin, Gadamer, Novalis, Kant.* Cranbury, N.J.: Associated University Presses, 2000.

Redding, Paul. *Hegel's Hermeneutics*. Ithaca, N.Y.: Cornell University Press, 1996.

Rentsch, Thomas, ed. *Martin Heidegger: Sein und Zeit.* Klassiker Auslegen 25. Berlin: Akademie Verlag, 2007.

———. "Zeitlichkeit und Alltäglichkeit." In *Martin Heidegger: Sein und Zeit,* ed. Thomas Rentsch, 199–227. Klassiker Auslegen 25. Berlin: Akademie Verlag, 2007.

Rese, Friedericke. "Erfahrung und Geschichte." In *Erfahrung und Geschichte,* ed. Thiemo Breyer and Daniel Crentz, 111–131. Berlin: De Gruyter, 2010.

———. "*Phronêsis* als Modell der Hermeneutik: Die hermeneutische Aktualität des Aristoteles." In *Hans-Georg Gadamer: Wahrheit und Methode,* ed. Günter Figal, 127–150. Klassiker Auslegen 30. Berlin: Akademie Verlag, 2007.

———. *Praxis und Logos bei Aristoteles.* Tübingen: Mohr Siebeck, 2003.

Rheinberger, Hans-Jörg. *On Historicizing Epistemology: An Essay.* Trans. David Fernbach. Stanford, Calif.: Stanford University Press, 2010.

Rickert, Heinrich. *Die Probleme der Geschichtsphilosophie.* Heidelberg: Winter, 1924.

Ricoeur, Paul. *Die erzählte Zeit.* Vol. 3 of *Zeit und Erzählung.* Munich: Fink, 2007.

———. "History and Hermeneutics." In *Philosophy of History and Action,* ed. Yirmiahu Yovel, 3–25. Boston: D. Reidel Publishing, 1978.

———. "Temporal Distance and Death in History." In *Gadamer's Century,* ed. Jeff Malpas, Ulrich Arnswald, and Jens Kertscher, 239–256. Cambridge, Mass.: MIT Press, 2002.

Riedel, Manfred. *System und Geschichte: Studien zum historischen Standort von Hegel's Philosophie.* Frankfurt am Main: Suhrkamp, 1973.

Risser, James. "The Demand of Freedom in Kant's *Critique of Judgment*." *Comparative and Continental Philosophy* 1, no. 1 (2009): 89–104.

———, ed. *Heidegger toward the Turn: Essays on the Work of the 1930s.* Albany: State University of New York Press, 1999.

———. *Hermeneutics and the Voice of the Other: Re-reading Gadamer's Philosophical Hermeneutics.* Albany: State University of New York Press, 1997.

———. "Hermeneutics of the Possible: On Finitude and Truth in Philosophical Hermeneutics." In *The Specter of Relativism: Truth, Dialogue, and Phronêsis in Philosophical Hermeneutics,* ed. Lawrence K. Schmidt, 111–128. Evanston, Ill.: Northwestern University Press, 1995.

———. "In the Shadow of Hegel: Infinite Dialogue in Gadamer's Hermeneutics." *Research in Phenomenology* 32 (2002): 86–102.

------. "Interpreting Tradition." *Journal of the British Society for Phenomenology* 34, no. 3 (2003): 297–308.

------. "The Lateness of Arrival in the Event of Understanding." *Internationales Jahrbuch für Hermeneutik* 10 (2011): 29–40.

------. "*Phronêsis* as Kairological Event," *Epoché* 7, no. 1 (2002): 107–119.

------. "Poetic Dwelling in Gadamer's Hermeneutics." *Philosophy Today* 38, no. 4 (1994): 369–379.

------. "Shared Life." *Symposium* 6, no. 2 (2002): 167–180.

Rosen, Stanley. *Hermeneutics as Politics.* 2nd ed. New Haven, Conn.: Yale University Press, 2003.

Rouse, Joseph. *Knowledge and Power: Toward a Political Philosophy of Science.* Ithaca, N.Y.: Cornell University Press, 1987.

Ruin, Hans, and Andrus Ers, eds. *Rethinking Time: Essays on History, Memory, and Representation.* Huddinge, Sweden: Södertörn, 2011.

Russon, John. *Reading Hegel's Phenomenology.* Bloomington: Indiana University Press, 2004.

Safranski, Rüdiger. *Ein Meister aus Deutschland: Heidegger und seine Zeit.* Munich: Carl Hanser, 1994. English translation: *Martin Heidegger: Between Good and Evil.* Trans. Ewald Osers. Cambridge, Mass.: Harvard University Press, 1999.

Sallis, John. *Delimitations: Phenomenology and the End of Metaphysics.* 2nd expanded ed. Bloomington: Indiana University Press, 1995.

Schaeffer, John D. *Sensus Communis: Vico, Rhetoric, and the Limits of Relativism.* Durham, N.C.: Duke University Press, 1990.

Schäfer, Alfred, and Michael Wimmer, eds. *Tradition und Kontingenz.* Münster: Waxmann, 2004.

Scheibler, Ingrid. *Gadamer: Between Heidegger and Habermas.* New York: Rowman and Littlefield, 2000.

Schiller, Friedrich. *On the Aesthetic Education of Man in a Series of Letters.* Trans. Reginald Snell. New York: Ungar, 1974.

Schlink, Bernhard. "The Presence of the Past." Accessed 8 September 2013. http://worldofideas.wbur.org/2009/02/15/the-presence-of-the-past.

Schmidt, Dennis J. "Aesthetics and Subjectivity." In *Hans-Georg Gadamer: Wahrheit und Methode,* ed. Günter Figal, 29–43. Klassiker Auslegen 30. Berlin: Akademie Verlag, 2007.

------. "Einige Betrachtungen zur Sprache und Freiheit." In *Dimensionen des Hermeneutischen,* ed. Günter Figal and Hans-Helmuth Gander, 59–72. Frankfurt am Main: Klostermann, 2005.

------. "On the Idiom of Truth and the Movement of Life: Some Remarks on the Task of Hermeneutics." *Internationales Jahrbuch für Hermeneutik* 10 (2011): 41–53.

------. "On the Incalculable: Language and Freedom from a Hermeneutic Point of View." *Research in Phenomenology* 34, no. 1 (2004): 31–44.

------. *The Ubiquity of the Finite: Hegel, Heidegger, and the Entitlements of Philosophy.* Cambridge, Mass.: MIT Press, 1988.

Schmidt, Lawrence K., ed. *The Specter of Relativism: Truth, Dialogue, and Phronêsis in Philosophical Hermeneutics.* Evanston, Ill.: Northwestern University Press, 1995.

Schnepf, Robert. "Der hermeneutische Vorrang der Frage: Die Logik der Fragen und das Problem der Ontologie." In *Gadamer Verstehen/Understanding Gadamer,* ed. Mirko Wischke and Michael Hofer, 302–323. Darmstadt: Wissenschaftliche Buchgesellschaft, 2003.

Schuchman, Paul. "Aristotle's *Phronêsis* and Gadamer's Hermeneutics." *Philosophy Today* 23, no. 1 (1979): 41–50.

Schwartz, Barry. *Practical Wisdom: The Right Way to Do the Right Thing.* New York: Riverhead, 2010.

Scott, Charles E. *The Language of Difference.* Atlantic Highlands, N.J.: Humanities Press, 1987.

———. "The Question of Ethics in Heidegger's Account of Authenticity." In *Heidegger Toward the Turn: Essays on the Work of the 1930s,* ed. James Risser, 211–224. Albany: State University of New York Press, 1999.

Sheehan, Thomas, and Corinne Painter. "Choosing One's Fate: A Re-reading of *Sein und Zeit* §74." *Research in Phenomenology* 28 (1999): 63–82.

Shell, Susan Meld. *Kant and the Limits of Autonomy.* Cambridge, Mass.: Harvard University Press, 2009.

Shirley, Dennis. "American Perspectives on German Educational Theory and Research: A Closer Look at Both the American Educational Context and the German Didaktik Tradition." In *Allgemeine Didaktik und Lehr-Lernforschung: Kontroversen und Entwicklungsperspektiven einer Wissenschaft von Unterricht,* ed. Karl-Heinz Arnold, Sigrid Blömeke, Rudolf Messner, and Jörg Schlömerkemper, 195–209. Bad Heilbrunn: Klinkhardt, 2009.

Singer, Alan. "Aesthetic Community: Recognition as an Other Sense of *Sensus Communis*." *Boundary 2* 24, no. 1 (1997): 205–236.

Smith, Christopher P. *Hermeneutics and Finitude: Toward a Theory of Ethical Understanding.* New York: Fordham University Press, 1991.

———. "*Phronêsis,* the Individual, and the Community: Divergent Appropriations of Aristotle's Ethical Discernment in Heidegger's and Gadamer's Hermeneutics." In *Gadamer Verstehen/Understanding Gadamer,* ed. Mirko Wischke, 169–185. Darmstadt: Wissenschaftliche Buchgesellschaft, 2003.

Staiti, Andrea. *Geistigkeit, Leben und geschichtliche Welt in der Transzendentalphänomenologie Husserls.* Würzburg: Ergon, 2010.

Steinmann, Michael. "The Negativity of Hermeneutics and the Culture of Understanding." Paper presented at the 49th annual meeting of the Society for Phenomenological and Existential Philosophy, Montreal, November 4–6, 2010.

———. *Die Offenheit des Sinns. Untersuchungen zu Sprache und Logik bei Martin Heidegger.* Tübingen: Mohr Siebeck, 2008.

Strauss, Leo. "Political Philosophy and History." In *What Is Political Philosophy?,* 56–77. Chicago: University of Chicago Press, 1988.

Strauss, Leo, and H.-G. Gadamer. "Correspondence Concerning *Wahrheit und Methode:* Leo Strauss and Hans-Georg Gadamer." *Independent Journal of Philosophy* 2 (1978): 5–12.

Svenaeus, Fredrik. "Hermeneutics of Medicine in the Wake of Gadamer: The Issue of Phronêsis." *Theoretical Medicine* 24 (2003): 407–431.

Taylor, Charles. "Gadamer on the Human Sciences." In *The Cambridge Companion to Gadamer*, ed. Robert Dostal, 126–142. New York: Cambridge University Press, 2002.

Teichert, Dieter. *Verstehen und Wirkungsgeschichte*. Bonn: Bouvier Verlag, 2000.

Thaning, Morten Sørensen. "Freiheit und Verantwortung bei Heidegger und Gadamer." In *Frei sein, frei handeln: Freiheit zwischen theoretischer und praktischer Philosophie*, ed. Diego D'Angelo, Sylvaine Gourdain, Tobias Keiling, and Nikola Mirkovic, 29–57. Freiburg: Alber, 2013.

Thompson, Iain. "Ontotheology? Understanding Heidegger's *Destruktion* of Metaphysics." In *Heidegger Reexamined*, ed. Hubert Dreyfus and Mark Wrathall, 2:107–128. New York: Routledge, 2002.

Valgenti, Robert T. "The Tradition of Tradition in Philosophical Hermeneutics." In *Consequences of Hermeneutics: Fifty Years after Gadamer's* Truth and Method, ed. Jeff Malpas and Santiago Zabala, 66–80. Evanston, Ill.: Northwestern University Press, 2010.

Vallega, Alejandro. "'Beyng-Historical Thinking' in Heidegger's *Contributions to Philosophy*." In *Companion to Heidegger's* Contributions to Philosophy, ed. Charles E. Scott, Susan M. Schoenbohm, Daniela Vallega-Neu, and Alejandro Vallega, 48–65. Bloomington: Indiana University Press, 2001.

Van Buren, John. *Young Heidegger: Rumor of the Hidden King*. Bloomington: Indiana University Press, 1994.

Van Erp, Herman. "The End of History and Hegel's Conception of Modernity." *Ideas y Valores* 107 (1998): 3–16.

Vattimo, Gianni. *The End of Modernity*. Baltimore: Johns Hopkins University Press, 1988.

Veith, Jerome. "Concerned with Oneself as One Person: Self-Knowledge in *Phronêsis*." *Epoché* 18, no. 1 (2013): 17–27.

———. "*Destruktion* and Repetition: Freedom and Historical Belonging in Heidegger." In *Heideggers Marburger Zeit: Themen, Argumente, Konstellationen*, ed. Tobias Keiling, 305–318. Frankfurt am Main: Klostermann, 2013.

———. "Dichten, Denken, Sagen: Wirkungen des Kunstwerkaufsatzes im späteren Sprachdenken Heideggers." In *Heideggers 'Ursprung des Kunstwerks': Ein kooperativer Kommentar*, ed. David Espinet and Tobias Keiling, 234–240. Frankfurt am Main: Vittorio Klostermann, 2011.

———. "Waves and Horizons: Literary Response in the Space of Questionability." *International Yearbook for Hermeneutics* 13 (2014): 144–159.

Velkley, Rickard L. *Freedom and the End of Reason: On the Moral Foundation of Kant's Critical Philosophy*. Chicago: University of Chicago Press, 1989.

———. "Gadamer and Kant: The Critique of Modern Aesthetic Consciousness in Truth and Method." *Interpretation* 9, nos. 2–3 (1980–81): 353–364.

Verene, Donald Phillip. *The Art of Humane Education*. Ithaca, N.Y.: Cornell University Press, 2002.

Warnke, Georgia. *Gadamer: Hermeneutics, Tradition, and Reason*. Stanford, Calif.: Stanford University Press, 1987.

———. "Legitimate Prejudices." *Laval theologique et philosophique* 53, no. 1 (1997): 89–102.

Watson, Stephen H. *Tradition(s): Refiguring Community and Virtue in Classical German Thought*. Bloomington: Indiana University Press, 1997.

——. *Tradition(s) II: Hermeneutics, Ethics, and the Dispensation of the Good*. Blooming-ton: Indiana University Press, 2001.

Wentzer, Thomas Schwarz. "Das Diskrimen der Frage." In *Hermeneutische Wege: Hans-Georg Gadamer zum Hundertsten,* ed. Günter Figal, Jean Grondin, and Dennis J. Schmidt, 219–240. Tübingen: Mohr Siebeck, 2000.

——. "Toward a Phenomenology of Questioning: Gadamer on Questions and Questioning." In *Gadamer's Hermeneutics and the Art of Conversation,* ed. Andrzej Wiercinski, 243–266. Piscataway, N.J.: Transaction Publishers, 2011.

Westphal, Merold. *Hegel, Freedom, and Modernity*. Albany: State University of New York Press, 1992.

——. *History and Truth in Hegel's Phenomenology*. Bloomington: Indiana University Press, 1998.

Whan, Michael. "On the Nature of Practice." *British Journal of Social Work* 16 (1986): 243–250.

Winfield, Richard Dien. "The Theory and Practice of the History of Freedom: On the Right of History in Hegel's *Philosophy of Right*." In *History and System: Hegel's Philosophy of History,* ed. Robert L. Perkins, 123–144. Albany: State University of New York Press, 1984.

Wright, Kathleen. *Festivals of Interpretation: Essays on Hans-Georg Gadamer's Work*. Albany: State University of New York Press, 1990.

Young, Julian. *Heidegger's Philosophy of Art*. Cambridge: Cambridge University Press, 2001.

Index

JEROME VEITH is an instructor of philosophy at Seattle University. He is the translator of the *Heidegger Reader* (IUP, 2009) and Günter Figal's *Aesthetics as Phenomenology: The Appearance of Things* (IUP, 2015).